3rd Workshop on Narrative Understanding (WNU 2021)

Online
11 June 2021

ISBN: 978-1-7138-3033-7

Printed from e-media with permission by:

Curran Associates, Inc.
57 Morehouse Lane
Red Hook, NY 12571

Some format issues inherent in the e-media version may also appear in this print version.

Printed with permission by Curran Associates, Inc. (2021)

For permission requests, please contact the Association for Computational Linguistics at the address below.

Association for Computational Linguistics
209 N. Eighth Street
Stroudsburg, Pennsylvania 18360

Phone: 1-570-476-8006
Fax: 1-570-476-0860

acl@aclweb.org

Additional copies of this publication are available from:

Curran Associates, Inc.
57 Morehouse Lane
Red Hook, NY 12571 USA
Phone: 845-758-0400
Fax: 845-758-2633
Email: curran@proceedings.com
Web: www.proceedings.com

NAACL HLT 2021

Workshop on Narrative Understanding (WNU)

Proceedings of the Third Workshop

June 11, 2021

Introduction

Welcome to the 3rd Workshop on Narrative Understanding!

This is the 3rd iteration of the workshop, which brings together an **interdisciplinary** group of researchers from AI, ML, NLP, Computer Vision and other related fields, as well as scholars from the humanities to discuss **methods to improve automatic narrative understanding capabilities**.

We are happy to present 10 papers on this topic (along with 3 non-archival papers to be presented only at the workshop). These papers take on the complex challenges presented by diverse texts in areas of film, dialogue and literature as they look to improve methods for event extraction, gender and representation bias, controllable generation, quality assessment, and other tasks related to the workshop theme. We would like to thank everyone who submitted their work to this workshop and the program committee for their helpful feedback.

We would also like to thank our invited speakers for their participation in this workshop: David Bamman, Nate Chambers, Nasrin Mostafazadeh, Nanyun Peng, Laure Thompson, and Prashant Pandey.

Elizabeth, Faeze, Lara, Mohit, Nader and Snigdha

Organizers:

Nader Akoury, University of Massachusetts Amherst
Faeze Brahman, University of California, Santa Cruz
Snigdha Chaturvedi, University of North Carolina, Chapel Hill
Elizabeth Clark, University of Washington
Mohit Iyyer, University of Massachusetts Amherst
Lara J. Martin, Georgia Institute of Technology

Program Committee:

Apoorv Agarwal, Text IQ
Antoine Bosselut, Stanford University
Jan Buys, University of Cape Town
Somnath Basu Roy Chowdhury, Microsoft, India
Saadia Gabriel, University of Washington
Seraphina Goldfarb-Tarrant, University of Edinburgh
Andrew Gordon, University of Southern California
Ari Holtzman, University of Washington
Adam Jatowt, Kyoto University
Yangfeng Ji, University of Virginia
Evgeny Kim, University of Stuttgart, Germany
Roman Klinger, University of Stuttgart, Germany
Rik Koncel-Kedziorski, University of Washington
Faisal Ladhak, Columbia University
Ashutosh Modi, Indian Institute of Technology, Kanpur, India
Pedram Hosseini, George Washington University
Mark Riedl, Georgia Tech
Melissa Roemmele, SDL Research
Mrinmaya Sachan, ETH Zurich
Maarten Sap, University of Washington
Joao Sedoc, NYU
Shashank Srivastava, UNC Chapel Hill
Katherine Thai, UMass Amherst
Shufan Wang, UMass Amherst
Chao Zhao, UNC Chapel Hill
Guanhua Zhang, Tencent AI, China

Invited Speakers:

David Bamman, University of California, Berkeley
Nate Chambers, US Naval Academy
Nasrin Mostafazadeh, Verneek
Nanyun Peng, University of California, Los Angeles
Laure Thompson, University of Massachusetts, Amherst
Prashant Pandey, Screenwriter, Bollywood

Table of Contents

Workshop Program

Friday, June 11, 2021

8:45–9:00 Opening Remarks

9:00–10:30 Invited Talks

10:30–11:30 Poster Session 1

11:30–13:00 Lunch

13:00–14:00 Invited Talks

14:00–15:00 Panel Discussion

15:00–16:00 Poster Session 2

Invited Speakers and Panelists

David Bamman

Nate Chambers

Nasrin Mostafazadeh

Prashant Pandey

Nanyun Peng

Friday, June 11, 2021 (continued)

Laure Thompson

Papers (Archival)

Hierarchical Encoders for Modeling and Interpreting Screenplays
Gayatri Bhat, Avneesh Saluja, Melody Dye and Jan Florjanczyk

FanfictionNLP: A Text Processing Pipeline for Fanfiction
Michael Yoder, Sopan Khosla, Qinlan Shen, Aakanksha Naik, Huiming Jin, Hariharan Muralidharan and Carolyn Rosé

Learning Similarity between Movie Characters and Its Potential Implications on Understanding Human Experiences
Zhilin Wang, Weizhe Lin and Xiaodong Wu

Document-level Event Extraction with Efficient End-to-end Learning of Cross-event Dependencies
Kung-Hsiang Huang and Nanyun Peng

Gender and Representation Bias in GPT-3 Generated Stories
Li Lucy and David Bamman

Transformer-based Screenplay Summarization Using Augmented Learning Representation with Dialogue Information
Myungji Lee, Hongseok Kwon, Jaehun Shin, WonKee Lee, Baikjin Jung and Jong-Hyeok Lee

Plug-and-Blend: A Framework for Controllable Story Generation with Blended Control Codes
Zhiyu Lin and Mark Riedl

Automatic Story Generation: Challenges and Attempts
Amal Alabdulkarim, Siyan Li and Xiangyu Peng

Fabula Entropy Indexing: Objective Measures of Story Coherence
Louis Castricato, Spencer Frazier, Jonathan Balloch and Mark Riedl

Towards a Model-Theoretic View of Narratives
Louis Castricato, Stella Biderman, David Thue and Rogelio Cardona-Rivera

Papers (Non-Archival)

Telling Stories through Multi-User Dialogue by Modeling Character Relations
Wai Man Si, Prithviraj Ammanabrolu and Mark Riedl

Inferring the Reader: Guiding Automated Story Generation with Commonsense Reasoning
Xiangyu Peng, Siyan Li, Sarah Wiegreffe and Mark Riedl

Tell Me A Story Like I'm Five: Story Generation via Question Answering
Louis Castricato, Spencer Frazier, Jonathan Balloch, Nitya Tarakad and Mark Riedl

Hierarchical Encoders for Modeling and Interpreting Screenplays

Gayatri Bhat* Bloomberg New York, NY, USA gbhat7@bloomberg.net

Avneesh Saluja **Melody Dye** **Jan Florjanczyk** Netflix Los Angeles, CA, USA {asaluja,mdye,jflorjanczyk}@netflix.com

Abstract

While natural language understanding of long-form documents remains an open challenge, such documents often contain structural information that can inform the design of models encoding them. Movie scripts are an example of such richly structured text – scripts are segmented into scenes, which decompose into dialogue and descriptive components. In this work, we propose a neural architecture to encode this structure, which performs robustly on two multi-label tag classification tasks without using handcrafted features. We add a layer of insight by augmenting the encoder with an unsupervised 'interpretability' module, which can be used to extract and visualize narrative trajectories. Though this work specifically tackles screenplays, we discuss how the underlying approach can be generalized to a range of structured documents.

1 Introduction

As natural language understanding of sentences and short documents continues to improve, interest in tackling longer-form documents such as academic papers (Ren et al., 2014; Bhagavatula et al., 2018), novels (Iyyer et al., 2016) and screenplays (Gorinski and Lapata, 2018) has been growing. Analyses of such documents can take place at multiple levels, e.g. identifying both document-level labels (such as genre) and narrative trajectories (how do levels of humor and romance vary over the course of a romantic comedy?). However, one key challenge for these tasks is the low signal-to-noise ratio in lengthy texts (as indicated by the performance of such models on curated datasets like NarrativeQA (Kočiský et al., 2018)), which makes it difficult to apply end-to-end (E2E) neural network solutions that have recently achieved state-of-the-art on other tasks (Barrault et al., 2019; Williams et al., 2018; Wang et al., 2019).

Instead, models either rely on a) a *pipeline* that provides a battery of syntactic and semantic information from which to craft features (e.g., the BookNLP pipeline (Bamman et al., 2014) for literary text, graph-based features (Gorinski and Lapata, 2015) for movie scripts, or outputs from a discourse parser (Ji and Smith, 2017) for text categorization) and/or b) the *linguistic intuitions* of the model designer to select features relevant to the task at hand (e.g., rather than ingest the entire text, Bhagavatula et al. (2018) only consider certain sections like the title and abstract of an academic publication). While there is much to recommend these approaches, E2E neural modeling offers several key advantages: it obviates the need for auxiliary feature-generating models, minimizes the risk of error propagation, and offers improved generalization across large-scale corpora. This work explores how the inherent structure of a document class can be leveraged to facilitate an E2E approach. We focus on screenplays, investigating whether we can effectively extract key information by first segmenting them into scenes, and further exploiting the structural regularities within each scene.

With an average of >20k tokens per script in our evaluation corpus, extracting salient aspects is far from trivial. Through a series of carefully controlled experiments, we show that a structure-aware approach significantly improves document classification by effectively collating sparsely distributed information. Further, this method produces both document- and scene-level embeddings, which can be used downstream to visualize narrative trajectories of interest (e.g., the prominence of various themes across a script). The overarching strategy of this work is to incorporate structural priors as biases into the neural *architecture* itself (e.g., Socher et al. (2013), Strubell et al. (2018), *inter alia*), whereby, as Henderson (2020) observe, "locality in the model structure can reflect locality in the linguistic structure" to boost

*Work done during an internship at Netflix

Proceedings of the 3rd Workshop on Narrative Understanding, pages 1–12
June 11, 2021.

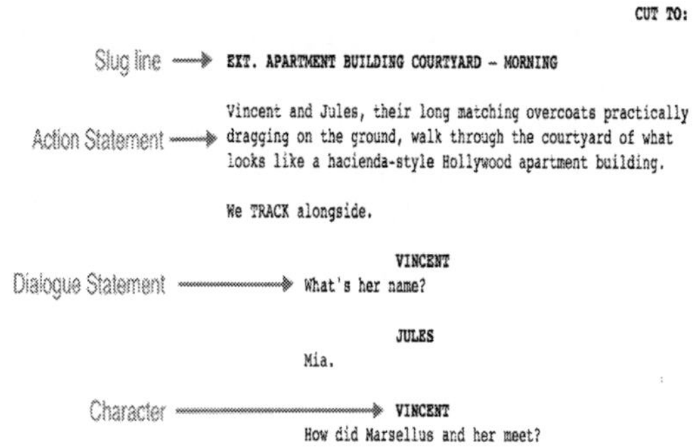

Figure 1: A portion of the screenplay for *Pulp Fiction*, annotated with the common scene components.

accuracy over feature-engineering approaches. The methods we propose can readily generalize to any long-form text with an exploitable internal structure, including novels (chapters), theatrical plays (scenes), chat logs (turn-taking), online games (levels/rounds/gameplay events), and academic texts (sections and subsections).

We begin by detailing how a script can be formally decomposed first into scenes and further into granular elements with distinct discourse functions, in §2. We then propose an encoder based on hierarchical attention (Yang et al., 2016) that effectively leverages this structure in §3. In §5.3, the predictive performance of the hierarchical encoder is validated on two multi-label tag prediction tasks, one of which rigorously establishes the utility of modeling structure at multiple granularities (i.e. at the level of line, scene, and script). Notably, while the resulting scene-encoded representation is useful for prediction tasks, it is not amenable to easy interpretation or examination. To shed light on the encoded document representations, in §4, we propose an unsupervised interpretability module that can be attached to an encoder of any complexity. §5.5 outlines our application of this module to the scene encoder, and the resulting visualizations of the screenplay, which illustrate how plot elements vary over the course of the narrative arc. §6 draws connections to related work, before concluding.

2 Script Structure

Movie and television scripts (or screenplays) are traditionally segmented into *scenes*, with a rough rule of thumb being that each scene lasts about a minute on-screen. A scene is not necessarily a distinct narrative unit (which is most often a sequence of several consecutive scenes), but is constituted by a piece of continuous action at a single location.

Title	Line	Scene	Type	Character	Text
Pulp Fiction	204	4	Scene		EXT. APART..
Pulp Fiction	205	4	Action		Vincent and Jules.
Pulp Fiction	206	4	Action		We TRACK...
Pulp Fiction	207	4	Dial.	VINCENT	What's her name?
Pulp Fiction	208	4	Dial.	JULES	Mia.
Pulp Fiction	209	4	Dial.	VINCENT	How did...

Table 1: Post-processed version of Fig.1.

Fig. 1 contains a segment of a scene from the screenplay for the *Pulp Fiction*, a 1994 American film. These segments tend to follow a standard format. Each scene starts with a scene heading or 'slug line' that briefly describes the scene setting. A sequence of statements follow, and screenwriters typically use formatting to distinguish between dialogue and action statements (Argentini, 1998). A dialogue identifies the character who utters it either on- or off-screen (the latter is often indicated with '(V.O.)' for voice-over). Parentheticals might be used to include special instructions regarding dialogue delivery. Action statements are all non-dialogue constituents of the screenplay "often used by the screenwriter to describe character actions, camera movement, appearance, and other details" (Pavel et al., 2015). In this work, we consider action and dialogue statements, as well as character identities for each dialogue segment, ignoring slug lines and parentheticals.

3 Hierarchical Scene Encoders

The large size of a movie script makes it computationally infeasible for recurrent encoders to ingest these screenplays as single blocks of text. Instead, we propose a hierarchical encoder that mirrors the structure of a screenplay (§2) – a sequence of scenes, each of which is an interwoven sequence of action and dialogue statements. The encoder is three-tiered, as illustrated in Fig. 2, and processes the text of a script as follows.

3.1 Model Architecture

First, an **action-statement encoder** transforms the sequence of words in an action statement (represented by their pretrained word embeddings) into an action statement embedding. Next, an **action-scene encoder** transforms the chronological sequence of action statement embeddings within a scene into an action scene embedding. Analogously, a **dialogue-statement encoder** and a **dialogue-scene encoder** generate dialogue statement embeddings and aggregate them into dialogue scene embeddings. To incorporate character information, characters are represented as embeddings (randomly initialized and updated during model training), and an average of embeddings of all characters with at least one dialogue in the scene is computed.[1] Finally, the action, dialogue and averaged character embeddings for a scene are concatenated into a single scene embedding. Scene-level predictions can be obtained by feeding scene embeddings into a subsequent neural module, e.g. a feedforward layer for supervised tagging. Alternatively, a final **script encoder** can be used to transform the sequence of scene embeddings into a script embedding representing the entire screenplay.

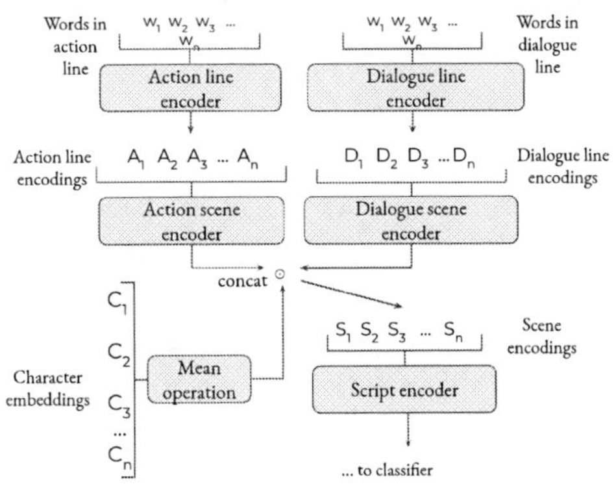

Figure 2: The architecture of our script encoder, largely following the structure in Fig. 1.

A key assumption underlying the model is that action and dialogue statements – as instances of written narrative and spoken language respectively – are distinct categories of text that must be processed separately. We evaluate this assumption in §5.3.

3.2 Encoders

The proposed model incorporates strong inductive biases regarding the overall structure of input documents. In addition, since the aforementioned encoders §3.1 are underspecified, we evaluate three instantiations of the encoder components:

1. **Sequential (GRU):** A bidirectional GRU (Bahdanau et al., 2015) encodes input sequences (of words, statements or scenes). Given a sequence of input embeddings $\mathbf{e}_1, \ldots, \mathbf{e}_T$, we obtain GRU outputs $\mathbf{c}_1, \ldots, \mathbf{c}_T$, and use $\mathbf{c}_T$ as the recurrent encoder's final output.

2. **Sequential with Attention (GRU + Attn):** Attention (Bahdanau et al., 2015) is used to combine $\mathbf{c}_1, \ldots, \mathbf{c}_T$. This allows more or less informative inputs to be filtered accordingly. We calculate attention weights using a parametrized vector $\mathbf{p}$ of the same dimensionality as the GRU outputs (Sukhbaatar et al., 2015; Yang et al., 2016):

$$\alpha_i = \frac{\mathbf{p}^T \mathbf{c}_i}{\Sigma_{j=1}^{T} \mathbf{p}^T \mathbf{c}_j} \tag{1}$$

   These weights are used to compute the final encoder output:

$$\mathbf{c} = \Sigma_{j=1}^{T} \alpha_i \mathbf{c}_i \tag{2}$$

3. **Bag-of-Embeddings with Attention (BoE + Attn):** These encoders disregard sequential information to compute an attention-weighted average of the encoder's inputs:

$$\alpha_i = \frac{\mathbf{p}^T \mathbf{e}_i}{\Sigma_{j=1}^{T} \mathbf{p}^T \mathbf{e}_j} \tag{3}$$

$$\mathbf{c} = \Sigma_{j=1}^{T} \alpha_i \mathbf{e}_i \tag{4}$$

   In contrast, a bag-of-embeddings (BoE) encoder computes a simple average of its inputs. While defining a far more constrained function space than recurrent encoders, BoE and BoE + Attn representations have the advantage of remaining in the input word embedding space. We leverage this property in §4 where we develop an interpretability layer on top of the encoder outputs.

3.3 Loss for Tag Classification

The final script embedding is passed into a feedforward classifier (FFNN). As both supervised learning tasks in our evaluation are multi-label classification problems, we use a variant of a simple multi-label one-versus-rest loss, where correlations among tags are ignored. The tag sets have high cardinalities and the fractions of positive samples are inconsistent across tags (see Appendix Tables 3 & 4); this motivates the use of a reweighted loss function:

$$\begin{aligned} L(y, z) = \tfrac{1}{NL} \Sigma_{i=1}^{N} \Sigma_{j=1}^{L} [y_{ij} \log \sigma(z_{ij}) \\ + \lambda_j (1 - y_{ij})(1 - \log \sigma(z_{ij}))] \end{aligned} \tag{5}$$

where N is the number of samples, L is the number of tag labels, $y \in \{0, 1\}$ is the target label, z is the

[1] We only take into account characters at the *scene* level, i.e. we do not associate characters with each dialogue statement, leaving this addition to future work.

output of the FFNN, σ is the sigmoid function, and λ_j is the ratio of positive to negative samples (precomputed over the entire training set, since the development set is too small to tune this parameter) for the jth tag label. With this loss function, we account for label imbalance without tuning separate thresholds for each tag on the validation set.

4 Interpreting Scene Embeddings

As the complexity of learning methods used to encode sentences and documents has increased, so has the need to understand the properties of the encoded representations. Probing methods (Linzen et al., 2016; Conneau et al., 2018) gauge the information captured in an embedding by evaluating its performance on downstream classification tasks, either with manually collected annotations (Shi et al., 2016) or self-supervised proxies (Adi et al., 2016). In our case, it is laborious and expensive to collect such annotations at the scene level (requiring domain experts), and the proxy evaluation tasks proposed in literature do not probe the narrative properties we wish to surface.

Instead, we take inspiration from Iyyer et al. (2016) to learn an unsupervised **scene descriptor model** that can be trained without relying on such annotations. Using a dictionary learning technique (Olshausen and Field, 1997), the model learns to represent each scene embedding as a weighted mixture of various topics estimated over the entire corpus. It thus acts as an 'interpretability layer' that can be applied over the scene encoder. This model is similar in spirit to dynamic topic models (Blei and Lafferty, 2006), with the added advantage of producing topics that are both more coherent and more interpretable than those generated by LDA (He et al., 2017; Mitcheltree et al., 2018).

4.1 Scene Descriptor Model

The model has three main components: a **scene encoder** whose outputs we wish to interpret, a set of topics or **descriptors** that are the 'basis elements' used to describe an interpretable scene, and a **predictor** that predicts weights over descriptors for a given scene embedding. The scene encoder uses the text of a given scene s_t to produce a corresponding scene embedding $\mathbf{v}_t$. This encoder can take any form – from an extractor that derives a hand-crafted feature set from the scene text, as in Gorinski and Lapata (2018), to the scene encoder in §3.

To probe the contents of scene embedding $\mathbf{v}_t$, we compute a descriptor-based representation $\mathbf{w}_t \in \mathbb{R}^d$ in terms of a descriptor matrix $\mathbf{R} \in \mathbb{R}^{k \times d}$ that stores k topics or descriptors:

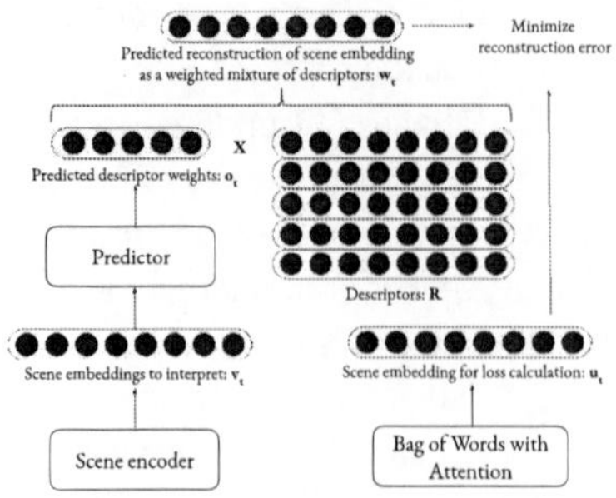

Figure 3: A pictorial representation of the descriptor model.

$$\mathbf{o}_t = \text{softmax}(f(\mathbf{v}_t)) \quad (6)$$
$$\mathbf{w}_t = \mathbf{R}^T \mathbf{o}_t$$

where $\mathbf{o}_t \in \mathbb{R}^k$ is the weight (probability) vector over k descriptors and $f(\mathbf{v}_t)$ is a predictor (illustrated by the leftmost pipeline in Fig. 3) which converts $\mathbf{v}_t$ into $\mathbf{o}_t$. Two variants are $f = \text{FFNN}(\mathbf{v}_t)$ and $f = \text{FFNN}([\mathbf{v}_t; \mathbf{o}_{t-1}])$ (concatenation); we use the former in §5.5. Furthermore, we can incorporate additional recurrence into the model by modifying Eq. 6 to add the previous state:

$$\mathbf{o}_t = (1 - \alpha) \cdot \text{softmax}(\text{FFNN}([\mathbf{v}_t; \mathbf{o}_{t-1}])) + \alpha \cdot \mathbf{o}_{t-1} \quad (7)$$

Descriptors are initialized either randomly (Glorot and Bengio, 2010) or with the centroids of a k-means clustering of the input word embeddings. For the predictor, f is a two-layer FFNN with ReLU activations and a softmax layer that transforms $\mathbf{v}_t$ (from the scene encoder) into a 100-dimensional intermediate state and then into $\mathbf{o}_t$.

4.2 Reconstruction Task

We wish to minimize the reconstruction error between two scene representations: (1) the descriptor-based embedding $\mathbf{w}_t$ which depends on the scene embedding $\mathbf{v}_t$, and (2) an attention-weighted bag-of-words embedding for s_t. This encourages the computed descriptor weights to be indicative of the scene's actual content (the portions of its text that indicate attributes of interest such as genre, plot, and mood). We use a `BoE+Attn` scene encoder (§3.2) pretrained on the tag classification task (bottom right of Fig. 3), which yields a vector $\mathbf{u}_t \in \mathbb{R}^d$ for scene s_t. The scene descriptor model is then trained using a hinge loss objective (Weston et al., 2011) to minimize the reconstruction error between $\mathbf{w_t}$ and $\mathbf{u}_t$, with an additional orthogonality constraint on $\mathbf{R}$ to encourage semantically distinct descriptors:

$$L = \Sigma_{j=1}^{n} \max(0, 1 - \mathbf{w}_t^T \mathbf{u}_t + \mathbf{w}_t^T \mathbf{u}_j) + \lambda \|\mathbf{R}\mathbf{R}^T - \mathbf{I}\|_2 \quad (8)$$

where $\mathbf{u}_1 \dots \mathbf{u}_n$ are n negative samples selected from other scenes in the same screenplay.

We use a `BoE+Attn` scene encoder as a "target" $\mathbf{u}_t$ to force $\mathbf{w}_t$ (and therefore the rows in $\mathbf{R}$) in the same space as the input word embeddings. Thus, a given descriptor can be semantically interpreted by querying its nearest neighbors in the word embedding space. The predicted descriptor weights for a scene s_t are obtained by running a forward pass through the model.

5 Evaluation

We evaluate the proposed script encoder and its variants through two supervised multilabel tag prediction tasks, and a qualitative analysis via the unsupervised extraction of descriptor trajectories.

5.1 Datasets

We base our evaluation on the ScriptBase-J corpus released by Gorinski and Lapata (2018) to directly compare our approach with the multilabel encoder proposed in Gorinski and Lapata (2018) and to provide an open-source evaluation standard.[2] In this corpus, each movie is associated with a set of expert-curated tags that range across 6 tag attributes: mood, plot, genre, attitude, place, and flag; in addition, we also evaluate on an internal dataset of labels assigned to the same movies by in-house domain experts, across 3 tag attributes: genre, plot, and mood. The two taxonomies are distinct. (See Appendix Table 3).

Script Preprocessing

As in Pavel et al. (2015), we leverage the standard screenplay format (Argentini, 1998) to extract structured representations of scripts (formatting cues included capitalization and tab-spacing; see Fig. 1 and Table 1 for an example). Filtering erroneously processed scripts removes 6% of the corpus, resulting in a total of 857 scripts. We hold out 20% (172) scripts for evaluation and use the rest for training. The average number of tokens per script is around 23k; additional statistics are shown in Appendix Table 1.

To keep within GPU memory limits, we split extremely long scenes to retain no more than 60 action and 60 dialogue lines per scene. The vocabulary is composed of words with at least 5 occurrences across the script corpus. The number of scripts per tag value ranges from high (e.g. for some Genre tags) to low (for most Plot and Mood tags) in both datasets (see Appendix Table 4), which along with high tag cardinality for each attribute motivates the use of the reweighted loss in Eq. 5.

5.2 Experimental Setup

All inputs to the hierarchical scene encoder are 100-dimensional GloVe embeddings (Pennington et al., 2014).[3] Our sequential models are bi-GRUs with a single 50-dimensional hidden layer in each direction, resulting in 100-dimensional outputs. The attention parameter $\mathbf{p}$ is 100-dimensional; BoE models naturally output 100-dimensional representations, and character embeddings are 10-dimensional. The script encoder's output is passed through a linear layer with sigmoid activation and binarized by thresholding at 0.5.

One simplification we use is to utilize the same encoder *type* for all encoders described in §3.1. However, particular encoder types might suit different tiers of the architecture: e.g. scene embeddings could be aggregated in a permutation-invariant manner, since narratives are interwoven and scenes may not be truly sequential.

We implement the script encoder on top of AllenNLP (Gardner et al., 2017) and PyTorch (Paszke et al., 2019), and all experiments are conducted on an AWS `p2.8xlarge` machine. We use the Adam optimizer with an initial learning rate of 0.005, clip gradients at a maximum norm of 5, and use no dropout. The model is trained for up to 20 epochs to maximize average precision score, with early stopping if the validation metric does not improve for 5 consecutive epochs.

5.3 Tag Prediction Experiments

ScriptBase-J also comes with loglines, or short, 1-2 sentence human-crafted summaries of the movie's plot and mood (see Appendix Table 2). A model

[2] https://github.com/EdinburghNLP/scriptbase

[3] Using richer contextual word representations will improve performance, but is orthogonal to the purpose of this work.

trained on these summaries can be expected to provide a reasonable baseline for tag prediction, since logline curators are likely to highlight information relevant to this task. The `Loglines` model is a bi-GRU with inputs of size 100 (GloVe embeddings) and hidden units of size 50 in each direction, whose output feeds into a linear classifier.[4]

Model	**Genre**	**Plot**	**Mood**
Loglines	49.9 (0.8)	12.7 (0.9)	17.5 (0.2)
Comparing encoder variations:			
BoE	49.0 (1.1)	8.3 (0.6)	12.9 (0.7)
BoE + Attn	51.9 (2.3)	11.3 (0.4)	16.3 (0.6)
GRU	57.9 (1.9)	13.0 (1.3)	19.1 (1.0)
GRU + Attn	60.5 (2.0)	**15.2** (0.4)	**22.9** (1.4)
Variants on GRU + Attn for action & dialog:			
+ Chars	**62.5** (0.7)	11.7 (0.3)	18.2 (0.3)
- Action	60.5 (2.9)	13.5 (1.4)	20.0 (1.2)
- Dialogue	60.5 (0.6)	13.4 (1.7)	19.1 (1.4)
2-tier	61.3 (2.3)	13.7 (1.7)	20.6 (1.2)
HAN	61.5 (0.6)	14.2 (1.7)	20.7 (1.4)

Table 2: Investigation of the effects of different architectural (BoE +/- Attn, GRU +/- Attn) and structural choices on a tag prediction task, using an internally tagged dataset: F-1 scores with sample standard deviation in parentheses. Across the 3 tag attributes we find that modeling sentential and scene-level structure helps, and attention helps extract representations more salient to the task at hand.

Table 2 contains results for the tag prediction task on our internally-tagged dataset. First, a set of models trained using action and dialogue inputs are used to evaluate the architectural choices in §3.1. We find that modeling recurrence at sentential and scene levels and selecting relevant words/scenes with attention are prominent factors in the robust improvement over the `Loglines` baseline (see the first five rows in Table 2).

Next, we assess the effect that various structural elements of a screenplay have on classification performance. Notably, the difficulty of the prediction task is directly related to the number of labels per tag attribute: higher-cardinality tag attributes with correlated tag values (like plot and mood) are far more difficult to predict than lower-cardinality tags with more discriminable values (like genre). We find that adding character information to the best-performing GRU + Attn model (`+Char`) improves prediction of genre, while using both dialogue and action statements improves performance on plot and mood when compared to using only one or the other. We also evaluate (1) a `2-tier` variant of the `GRU+Attn` model without action/dialogue-statement encoders (i.e., all action statements are concatenated into a single sequence of words and passed into the action-scene encoder, and similarly with dialogue) and (2) a variant similar to Yang et al. (2016) (`HAN`) that does not distinguish between action and dialogue (i.e., all statements in a scene are encoded using a single statement encoder and statement embeddings are passed to a scene encoder, the output of which is passed into the script encoder). Both models perform slightly better than `GRU+Attn` on genre, but worse on plot and mood, indicating that incorporating hierarchy and distinguishing between dialogue and action statements helps on the more difficult prediction tasks.

Tag	**G&L**	**HSE**
Attitude	72.6	70.1
Flag	52.5	52.6
Genre	55.1	42.5
Mood	45.5	51.2
Place	57.7	29.1
Plot	34.6	34.5

Table 3: F-1 scores on ScriptBase-J provided tag set, comparing Gorinski and Lapata (2018)'s approach to ours.

For the results in Table 3, we compared the `GRU+Attn` configuration in Table 2 (`HSE`) with an implementation of Gorinski and Lapata (2018) (`G&L`) that was run on the previous train-test split. `G&L` contains a number of handcrafted lexical, graph-based, and interactive features that were designed for optimal performance on screenplay analysis. In contrast, `HSE` directly encodes standard screenplay structure into a neural network architecture, and is an alternative, arguably more lightweight way of building a domain-specific textual representation. Our results are comparable, with the exception of 'place', which can often be identified deterministically from scene headings.

5.4 Similarity-based F-1

Results in Tables 2 and 3 check for an exact match between predicted and true tag values to report standard multi-label F-1 scores (one-vs-rest classification evaluation, micro-averaged over tag attributes). However, the characteristics of our tag taxonomies suggest that this measure may not be ideal, since human-crafted tag sets include dozens of highly correlated, overlapping values, and the dataset includes instances of missing tags. A standard scoring procedure may underestimate model

[4]We tried both with and without attention and found the variant without attention to give slightly better results.

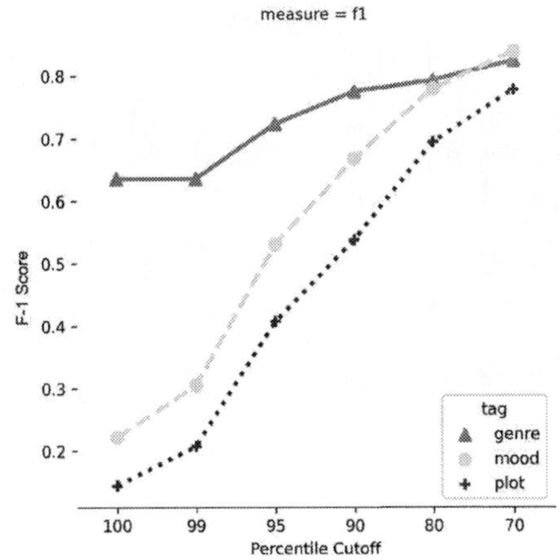

Figure 4: F1 score of various tag attributes as a function of the similarity threshold percentile.

performance when, e.g., a prediction of 'Crime' is equally penalized for a target labels of 'Heist' and 'Romance' (see Appendix Table 5).

We use a similarity-based scoring procedure (see Maynard et al. (2006) for related approaches) to assess the impact of such effects. In particular, we calculate cosine similarities between tag embeddings trained on a similar task (see Appendix for details) and evaluate a prediction based the percentile of its similarity to the actual label. Such a measure takes into account the latent relationships among tags via *similarity thresholding*, wherein a prediction is counted as correct if it is sufficiently similar to the target. The percentile cutoff can be varied to estimate model performance as a function of the threshold percentile.

In Fig. 4 we re-evaluate the `GRU + Attn` model outputs (row 5 in Table 2) with this evaluation metric to examine how our results might vary if we adopted a similarity-based scoring procedure. When the similarity percentile cutoff equals 100, the result is identical to the standard F-1 score. Even decreasing the cutoff to the 90th percentile shows striking improvements for high-cardinality attributes (180% for `mood` and 250% for `plot`). Notably, using a similarity-based scoring procedure for complex tag taxonomies may yield results that more accurately reflect human perception of the model's performance (Maynard et al., 2006).

5.5 Qualitative Scene-level Analysis

To extract narrative trajectories with the scene descriptor model, we analyze the scene encoder from the `GRU+Attn` model, which performs best on the Plot and Mood tag attributes and does reasonably well on Genre. Similarly to Iyyer et al. (2016), we limit the input vocabulary for the `BoE+Attn` encoders that yield target vectors $\mathbf{u}_t$ to words occurring in at least 50 movies (7.3% of the training set), while also filtering the 500 most frequent words in the corpus. We set the number of descriptors k to 25 to allow for a wide range of topics while keeping manual examination feasible.

Further modeling choices are evaluated using the semantic coherence metric (Mimno et al., 2011), which assesses the quality of word clusters induced by topic modeling algorithms. These choices include: the presence of recurrence in the predictor (i.e. toggling between Eqns. 6 and 7, with $\alpha = 0.5$) and the value of hyperparameter λ. While the k-means initialized descriptors score slightly higher on semantic coherence, they remain close to the initial centroids and do not reflect the corpus as well as the randomly initialized version, which is the initialization we eventually used. We also find that incorporating recurrence and $\lambda = 10$ (tuned using simple grid search) result in the highest coherence.

The outputs of the scene descriptor model are shown in Table 4 and Figure 5. Table 4 presents five example descriptors, each identified by the representative words closest to them in the word embedding space (topic names are manually annotated). Figure 5 presents the narrative trajectories of a subset of descriptors for three screenplays: Pretty Woman, Pulp Fiction, and Pearl Harbor, using a *streamgraph* (Byron and Wattenberg, 2008). The descriptor weight $\mathbf{o}_t$ (Eq. 6) as a function of scene number/order is rescaled and smoothed, with the width of a color band indicating the weight value. A critical event for each screenplay is indicated by a letter on each trajectory. A qualitative analysis of such events indicates general alignment between scripts and their topic trajectories, and the potential applicability of this method to identifying significant moments in long-form documents.

Topic	Words
Violence	fires blazes explosions grenade blasts
Residential	loft terrace courtyard foyer apartments
Military	leadership army victorious commanding elected
Vehicles	suv automobile wagon sedan cars
Geography	sand slope winds sloping cliffs

Table 4: Examples of retrieved descriptors. Trajectories for "Violence", "Military", and "Residential" are shown in Fig. 5.

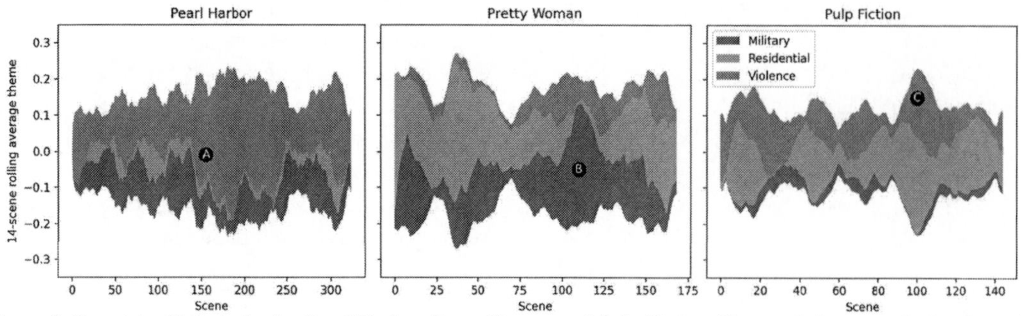

Figure 5: Descriptor Trajectories for *Pearl Harbor*, *Pretty Woman*, and *Pulp Fiction*. The y-axis is a smoothed and rescaled descriptor weight, i.e. $\mathbf{o}_t$ in Eq. 6. Events: (A) Attack on Pearl Harbor begins (B) Rising tension at the equestrian club and (C) Confrontation at the pawn shop. Word clusters corresponding to each descriptor are in Table 4.

6 Related Work

Computational narrative analysis of large texts has been explored in a range of contexts (Mani, 2012) over the past few decades (Lehnert, 1981). Recent work has analyzed narrative from plot (Chambers and Jurafsky, 2008; Goyal et al., 2010) and character (Elsner, 2012; Bamman et al., 2014) perspectives. While movie narratives have received attention (Bamman et al., 2013; Chaturvedi et al., 2018; Kar et al., 2018), the computational analysis of entire screenplays is not as common.

Notably, Gorinski and Lapata (2015) introduced a summarization method for scripts, extracting graph-based features that summarize the key scene sequences. Gorinski and Lapata (2018) built on top of this work, crafting additional features for a specially-designed multilabel encoder, while also emphasizing the difficulty of the tag prediction task. Our work suggests an orthogonal approach using automatically learned scene representations instead of feature-engineered inputs. We also consider the possibility that at least some of the task difficulty owes not to the length or richness of the text, but rather to the complexity of the tag taxonomy. The pattern of results we obtain from a similarity-based scoring measure offers a brighter picture of model performance, and suggests that the standard multilabel F1 measure may not be appropriate for such complex tag sets (Maynard et al., 2006).

Nevertheless, dealing with long-form text remains a significant challenge. One possible solution is to infer richer representations of latent structure using a structured attention mechanism (Liu and Lapata, 2018), which might highlight key dependencies between scenes in a script. Another method could be to define auxiliary tasks as in Jiang and Bansal (2018) to encourage better selection. Lastly, sparse versions of the softmax function (Martins and Astudillo, 2016) could be used to address the sparse distribution of salient information across a screenplay.

7 Conclusion

In this work, we propose and evaluate various neural network architectures for learning fixed-dimensional representations of full-length film scripts. We hypothesize that a network design mimicking the documents' internal structure will boost performance. Experiments on two tag prediction tasks support this hypothesis, confirming the benefits of using hierarchical attention-based models and of incorporating distinctions between various scene components directly into the model. In order to explore the information contained within scene-level embeddings, we present an unsupervised technique for bootstrapping scene "descriptors" and visualizing their trajectories over the course of the screenplay. For future work, we plan to investigate richer ways of representing character identities, which could allow character embeddings to be compared across movies and linked to character archetypes. A persona-based characterization of the screenplay would provide a complementary view to the current plot-based analysis.

Scripts and screenplays are an underutilized and underanalyzed data source in modern NLP - indeed, most work on narratology in NLP concentrates on short stories and book/movie summaries. This paper shows that capitalizing on their rich internal structure largely obviates the need for feature-engineering, or other more complicated architectures, a lesson that may prove instructive in other areas of discourse processing. Our hope is that these results encourage more people to work on this fascinating domain.

Acknowledgments

The authors would like to thank the anonymous reviewers for their valuable comments and feedback, and Ashish Rastogi for his support and guidance.

References

Yossi Adi, Einat Kermany, Yonatan Belinkov, Ofer Lavi, and Yoav Goldberg. 2016. Fine-grained analysis of sentence embeddings using auxiliary prediction tasks. *Proceedings of ICLR.*

Paul Argentini. 1998. *Elements of Style for Screenwriters*. Lone Eagle Publishing.

Dzmitry Bahdanau, Kyunghyun Cho, and Yoshua Bengio. 2015. Neural machine translation by jointly learning to align and translate. In *Proceedings of ICLR.*

David Bamman, Brendan O'Connor, and Noah A. Smith. 2013. Learning latent personas of film characters. In *Proceedings of ACL.*

David Bamman, Ted Underwood, and Noah A. Smith. 2014. A bayesian mixed effects model of literary character. In *Proceedings of ACL.*

Loïc Barrault, Ondřej Bojar, Marta R. Costa-jussà, Christian Federmann, Mark Fishel, Yvette Graham, Barry Haddow, Matthias Huck, Philipp Koehn, Shervin Malmasi, Christof Monz, Mathias Müller, Santanu Pal, Matt Post, and Marcos Zampieri. 2019. Findings of the 2019 conference on machine translation (wmt19). In *Proceedings of WMT.*

Chandra Bhagavatula, Sergey Feldman, Russell Power, and Waleed Ammar. 2018. Content-based citation recommendation. In *Proceedings NAACL.*

David M. Blei and John D. Lafferty. 2006. Dynamic topic models. In *Proceedings of ICML.*

L Byron and M. Wattenberg. 2008. Stacked graphs – geometry aesthetics. *IEEE Transactions on Visualization and Computer Graphics.*

Nathanael Chambers and Dan Jurafsky. 2008. Unsupervised learning of narrative event chains. In *Proceedings of ACL.*

Snigdha Chaturvedi, Shashank Srivastava, and Dan Roth. 2018. Where have I heard this story before? identifying narrative similarity in movie remakes. In *Proceedings of NAACL.*

Alexis Conneau, German Kruszewski, Guillaume Lample, Loïc Barrault, and Marco Baroni. 2018. What you can cram into a single vector: Probing sentence embeddings for linguistic properties. *Proceedings of ACL.*

Micha Elsner. 2012. Character-based kernels for novelistic plot structure. In *Proceedings of EACL.*

Matt Gardner, Joel Grus, Mark Neumann, Oyvind Tafjord, Pradeep Dasigi, Nelson F. Liu, Matthew Peters, Michael Schmitz, and Luke S. Zettlemoyer. 2017. Allennlp: A deep semantic natural language processing platform.

Xavier Glorot and Yoshua Bengio. 2010. Understanding the difficulty of training deep feedforward neural networks. In *Proceedings of AIStats.*

Philip John Gorinski and Mirella Lapata. 2015. Movie script summarization as graph-based scene extraction. In *Proceedings of NAACL.*

Philip John Gorinski and Mirella Lapata. 2018. What's this movie about? a joint neural network architecture for movie content analysis. In *Proceedings of NAACL.*

Amit Goyal, Ellen Riloff, and Hal Daumé, III. 2010. Automatically producing plot unit representations for narrative text. In *Proceedings of EMNLP.*

Ruidan He, Wee Sun Lee, Hwee Tou Ng, and Daniel Dahlmeier. 2017. An unsupervised neural attention model for aspect extraction. In *Proceedings of ACL.*

James Henderson. 2020. The unstoppable rise of computational linguistics in deep learning. In *Proceedings of ACL.*

Mohit Iyyer, Anupam Guha, Snigdha Chaturvedi, Jordan Boyd-Graber, and Hal Daumé III. 2016. Feuding families and former Friends: Unsupervised learning for dynamic fictional relationships. In *Proceedings of NAACL.*

Yangfeng Ji and Noah A. Smith. 2017. Neural discourse structure for text categorization. In *Proceedings of ACL.*

Yichen Jiang and Mohit Bansal. 2018. Closed-book training to improve summarization encoder memory. In *Proceedings of EMNLP.*

Sudipta Kar, Suraj Maharjan, and Thamar Solorio. 2018. Folksonomication: Predicting tags for movies from plot synopses using emotion flow encoded neural network. In *Proceddings of COLING.*

Tomáš Kočiský, Jonathan Schwarz, Phil Blunsom, Chris Dyer, Karl Moritz Hermann, Gábor Melis, and Edward Grefenstette. 2018. The NarrativeQA reading comprehension challenge. *Transactions of the ACL.*

Wendy G. Lehnert. 1981. Plot units and narrative summarization. *Cognitive Science.*

Tal Linzen, Emmanuel Dupoux, and Yoav Goldberg. 2016. Assessing the ability of LSTMs to learn syntax-sensitive dependencies. *Transactions of the ACL.*

Yang Liu and Mirella Lapata. 2018. Learning structured text representations. *Transactions of the Association for Computational Linguistics.*

Inderjeet Mani. 2012. *Synthesis Lectures on Human Language Technologies: Computational Modeling of Narrative*. Morgan Claypool.

Andre Martins and Ramon Astudillo. 2016. From softmax to sparsemax: A sparse model of attention and multi-label classification. In *Proceedings of ICML*.

Diana Maynard, Wim Peters, and Yaoyong Li. 2006. Metrics for evaluation of ontology-based information extraction. In *CEUR Workshop Proceedings*.

David Mimno, Hanna M Wallach, Edmund Talley, Miriam Leenders, and Andrew McCallum. 2011. Optimizing semantic coherence in topic models. In *Proceedings of EMNLP*.

Christopher Mitcheltree, Skyler Wharton, and Avneesh Saluja. 2018. Using aspect extraction approaches to generate review summaries and user profiles. In *Proceedings of NAACL*.

Bruno A Olshausen and David J Field. 1997. Sparse coding with an overcomplete basis set: A strategy employed by v1? *Vision Research*.

Adam Paszke, Sam Gross, Francisco Massa, Adam Lerer, James Bradbury, Gregory Chanan, Trevor Killeen, Zeming Lin, Natalia Gimelshein, Luca Antiga, Alban Desmaison, Andreas Kopf, Edward Yang, Zachary DeVito, Martin Raison, Alykhan Tejani, Sasank Chilamkurthy, Benoit Steiner, Lu Fang, Junjie Bai, and Soumith Chintala. 2019. Pytorch: An imperative style, high-performance deep learning library. In *Proceedings of NeurIPS*.

Amy Pavel, Dan B. Goldman, Björn Hartmann, and Maneesh Agrawala. 2015. Sceneskim: Searching and browsing movies using synchronized captions, scripts and plot summaries. In *Proceedings of UIST*.

Jeffrey Pennington, Richard Socher, and Christopher D. Manning. 2014. Glove: Global vectors for word representation. In *Proceedings of EMNLP*.

Xiang Ren, Jialu Liu, Xiao Yu, Urvashi Khandelwal, Quanquan Gu, Lidan Wang, and Jiawei Han. 2014. Cluscite: Effective citation recommendation by information network-based clustering. In *Proceedings of KDD*.

Xing Shi, Inkit Padhi, and Kevin Knight. 2016. Does string-based neural mt learn source syntax? In *Proceedings of EMNLP*.

Richard Socher, Alex Perelygin, Jean Wu, Jason Chuang, Christopher D. Manning, Andrew Ng, and Christopher Potts. 2013. Recursive deep models for semantic compositionality over a sentiment treebank. In *Proceedings of EMNLP*.

Emma Strubell, Patrick Verga, Daniel Andor, David Weiss, and Andrew McCallum. 2018. Linguistically-informed self-attention for semantic role labeling. In *Proceedings of EMNLP*.

Sainbayar Sukhbaatar, arthur szlam, Jason Weston, and Rob Fergus. 2015. End-to-end memory networks. In *Proceedings of NeurIPS*.

Alex Wang, Amanpreet Singh, Julian Michael, Felix Hill, Omer Levy, and Samuel R. Bowman. 2019. GLUE: A multi-task benchmark and analysis platform for natural language understanding. In *Proceedings of ICLR*.

Jason Weston, Samy Bengio, and Nicolas Usunier. 2011. Wsabie: Scaling up to large vocabulary image annotation. In *Proceedings of IJCAI*.

Adina Williams, Nikita Nangia, and Samuel Bowman. 2018. A broad-coverage challenge corpus for sentence understanding through inference. In *Proceedings of NAACL*.

Zichao Yang, Diyi Yang, Chris Dyer, Xiaodong He, Alex Smola, and Eduard Hovy. 2016. Hierarchical attention networks for document classification. In *Proceedings of NAACL*.

A Appendix

A.1 Additional Dataset Statistics

In this section, we present additional statistics on the evaluation sets used in this work.

Min	10th %	90th %	Max
4025	16,240	29,376	52,059

Table 5: Statistics on the number of tokens per script in the Scriptbase-J corpus. We use the same script corpus with two different tag sets – the Jinni tags provided with ScriptBase and a tag set designed by internal annotators.

Tag	Value
Genre	Crime, Independent
Mood	Clever, Witty, Stylized
Attitude	Semi Serious, Realistic
Plot	Tough Heroes, Violence Spree, On the Run
Place	California, Los Angeles, Urban
Flag	Drugs/Alcohol, Profanity, Violent Content
Logline	"The lives of two mob hit men, a boxer, a gangster's wife, and a pair of diner bandits intertwine in four tales of violence and redemption."

Table 6: Examples of Scriptbase-J tag attributes, tag values, and a logline, for the film "Pulp Fiction".

Tag	Internal	Scriptbase-J
Genre	9	31
Mood	65	18
Attitude	-	8
Plot	82	101
Place	-	24
Flag	-	6

Table 7: The number of distinct tag values for each tag attribute across the two datasets. Cardinalities for Scriptbase-J tag attributes are identical to Gorinski and Lapata (2018) except for the removal of one mood tag value when filtering for erroneously preprocessed scripts.

Tag	Avg. #tags/script	Min #scripts/tag	Max #scripts/tag
Genre	1.74	17	347
Mood	3.29	15	200
Plot	2.50	15	73

Table 8: Statistics for the three tag attributes applied in our internally-tagged dataset: average number of tags per script, and the minimum/maximum number of movies associated with any single value.

A.2 Tag Similarity Scoring

To estimate tag-tag similarity percentiles, we calculate the distance between tag embeddings learned via an auxiliary model trained on a related supervised learning task. In our case, the related task is to predict the audience segment of a movie, given a tag set. The general approach is easily replicable via any model that projects tags into a well-defined similarity space (e.g., knowledge-graph embeddings (?) or tag-based autoencoders).

Tag	Target	Similar	Unrelated
Genre	Period	Historical	Fantasy
Mood	Witty	Humorous	Bleak
Plot	Hitman	Deadly	Love/Romance

Table 9: Examples of closely related and unrelated tag values in the Scriptbase-J tag set.

Given a tag embedding space, the similarity percentile of a pair of tag values is estimated as follows. For a given tag attribute, the pairwise cosine distance between tag embeddings is computed for all tag-tag value pairs. For a given pair, its similarity percentile is then calculated with reference to the overall distribution for that attribute.

Similarity thresholding simplifies the tag prediction task by significantly reducing the *perplexity* of the tag set, while only marginally reducing its *cardinality*. Cardinality can be estimated via permutations. If n is the cardinality of the tag set, the number of permutations p of different tag pairs $(k = 2)$ is:

$$p(n, k) = \frac{n!}{(n-k)!} \tag{9}$$

which simplifies to $n^2 - n - p = 0$.

Likewise, the entropy of a list of n distinct tag values of varying probabilities is given by:

$$H(X) = H(\text{tag}_1, ..., \text{tag}_n) = -\sum_{i=1}^{n} \text{tag}_i \log_2 \text{tag}_i \tag{10}$$

The perplexity over tags is then simply $2^{H(X)}$.

Tag	Perplexity	Cardinality
Genre	42%	16%
Mood	77%	16%
Plot	79%	16%

Table 10: The percent decrease in perplexity and cardinality, respectively, as the similarity threshold decreases from 100th percentile similarity (baseline) to 70th percentile.

As the similarity threshold decreases, the number of tags treated as equivalent correspondingly increases. Mapping these "equivalents" to a shared label in our list of tag values allows us to calculate updated values for tag (1) perplexity and (2) cardinality. As illustrated by Table 10, rather than leading to large reductions in the overall cardinality of the tag set, similarity thresholding mainly serves to decrease perplexity by eliminating redundant/highly similar alternatives. Thus, thresholding at once significantly decreases the complexity of the prediction task, while yielding a potentially more representative picture of model performance.

FanfictionNLP: A Text Processing Pipeline for Fanfiction

Michael Miller Yoder*, Sopan Khosla*, Qinlan Shen, Aakanksha Naik, Huiming Jin, Hariharan Muralidharan, Carolyn P. Rosé
Language Technologies Institute
Carnegie Mellon University
Pittsburgh, PA, USA
{yoder,sopank,qinlans,anaik,huimingj,hmuralid,cprose}@cs.cmu.edu

Abstract

Fanfiction presents an opportunity as a data source for research in NLP, education, and social science. However, answering specific research questions with this data is difficult, since fanfiction contains more diverse writing styles than formal fiction. We present a text processing pipeline for fanfiction, with a focus on identifying text associated with characters. The pipeline includes modules for character identification and coreference, as well as the attribution of quotes and narration to those characters. Additionally, the pipeline contains a novel approach to character coreference that uses knowledge from quote attribution to resolve pronouns within quotes. For each module, we evaluate the effectiveness of various approaches on 10 annotated fanfiction stories. This pipeline outperforms tools developed for formal fiction on the tasks of character coreference and quote attribution.

1 Introduction

A growing number of natural language processing tools and approaches have been developed for fiction (Agarwal et al., 2013; Bamman et al., 2014; Iyyer et al., 2016; Sims et al., 2019). These tools generally focus on published literary works, such as collections of novels. We present an NLP pipeline for processing fanfiction, amateur writing from fans of TV shows, movies, books, games, and comics.

Fanfiction writers creatively change and expand on plots, settings, and characters from original media, an example of "participatory culture" (Jenkins, 1992; Tosenberger, 2008). The community of fanfiction readers and writers, now largely online, has been studied for its mentorship and support for writers (Evans et al., 2017) and for the broad representation of LGBTQ+ characters and relationships in fan-written stories (Lothian et al., 2007; Dym et al., 2019). Fanfiction presents an opportunity as a data source for research in a variety of fields, from those studying learning in online communities to social science analysis of how community norms develop in an LGBTQ-friendly environment. For NLP researchers, fanfiction provides a large source of literary text with metadata, and has already been used in applications such as authorship attribution (Kestemont et al., 2018) and character relationship classification (Kim and Klinger, 2019).

There is an vast amount of fanfiction in online archives. As of March 2021, over 7 million stories were hosted on just one fanfiction website, Archive of Our Own, and there exist other online archives of similar or even larger sizes (Yin et al., 2017). We present a pipeline that enables structured insight into this vast amount of text by identifying sets of characters in fanfiction stories and attributing narration and quotes to these characters.

Knowing who the characters are and what they do and say is essential for understanding story structure (Bruce, 1981; Wall, 1984). Such processing is also useful for researchers in the humanities and social sciences investigating identification with characters and the representation of characters of diverse genders, sexualities, and ethnicities (Green et al., 2004; Kasunic and Kaufman, 2018; Felski, 2020). The presented pipeline, which extracts text related to characters in fanfiction, can assist researchers building NLP tools for literary domains, as well those analyzing characterization in fields such as digital humanities. For example, the pipeline could be used to explore how characters are voiced and described differently when cast in queer versus straight relationships.

The presented pipeline contains three main modules: character coreference resolution, quote attribution, and extraction of "assertions", narration that relates to particular characters. We incorporate new and existing methods into the pipeline that perform well on an annotated set of 10 fanfiction stories. This includes a novel method using

* Denotes equal contribution.

Proceedings of the 3rd Workshop on Narrative Understanding, pages 13–23
June 11, 2021. ©2021 Association for Computational Linguistics

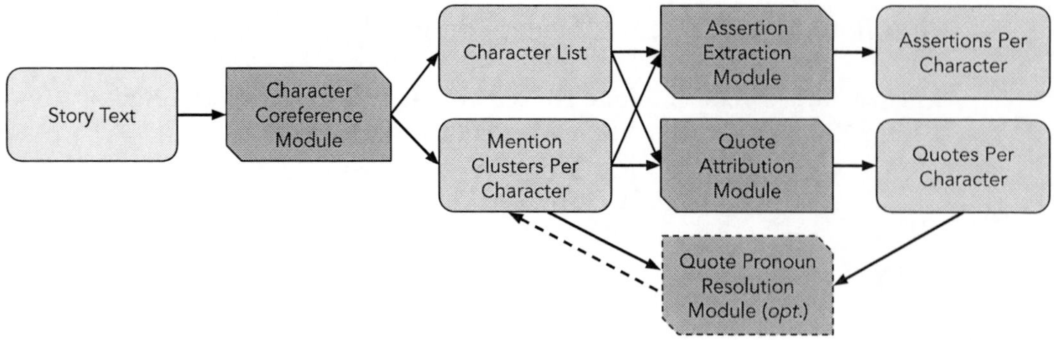

Figure 1: Fanfiction NLP pipeline overview. From the text of a fanfiction story, the pipeline assigns character mentions to character clusters (character coreference). It then attributes assertions and quotes to each character, optionally using the quote attribution output to improve coreference resolution within quotes (see Section 3.3).

quote attribution information to resolve first- and second-person pronouns within quotes.

Fanfiction is written by amateur writers of all ages and education levels worldwide, so it contains much more variety in style and genre than formal fiction. It is not immediately clear that techniques for coreference resolution or quote attribution that perform well on news data or formal fiction will be effective in the informal domain of fanfiction. We demonstrate that this pipeline outperforms existing tools designed for formal fiction on the tasks of character coreference resolution and quote attribution (Bamman et al., 2014).

Contributions. We contribute a fanfiction processing pipeline that outperforms prior work designed for formal fiction. The pipeline includes novel interleaving of coreference and quote attribution to improve the resolution of first- and second-person pronouns within quotes in narrative text. We also introduce an evaluation dataset of 10 fanfiction stories with annotations for character coreference, as well as for quote detection and attribution.

2 Fanfiction and NLP

Data from fanfiction has been used in NLP research for a variety of tasks, including authorship attribution (Kestemont et al., 2018), action prediction (Vilares and Gómez-Rodríguez, 2019), fine-grained entity typing (Chu et al., 2020), and tracing the sources of derivative texts (Shen et al., 2018). Computational work focusing on characterization in fanfiction includes the work of Milli and Bamman (2016), who found that fanfiction writers are more likely to emphasize female and secondary characters. Using data from WattPad, a platform that includes fanfiction along with original fiction, Fast et al. (2016) find that portrayals of gendered characters generally align with mainstream stereotypes.

We are not aware of any text processing system for fanfiction specifically, though BookNLP (Bamman et al., 2014) is commonly used as an NLP system for formal fiction. We evaluate our pipeline's approaches to character coreference resolution and quote attribution against BookNLP, as well as against other task-specific approaches, on an evaluation dataset of fanfiction.

3 Fanfiction Processing Pipeline

We introduce a publicly available pipeline for processing fanfiction.[1] This pipeline is a command-line tool developed in Python. From the text of a fanfiction story, the pipeline extracts a list of characters, each mention of a character, as well as what each character does and says (Figure 1). More specifically, the pipeline first performs character coreference resolution, extracting character mentions and attributing them to character clusters with a single standardized character name (Section 3.1). After coreference, the pipeline outputs quotes uttered by each character using a sieve-based approach from Muzny et al. (2017) (Section 3.2). These quote attribution results are optionally used to aid the resolution of first- and second-person pronouns within quotes to improve coreference output (Section 3.3). In parallel with quote attribution, the pipeline extracts "assertions", topically coherent segments of text that mention a character (Section 3.4).

[1]The pipeline is available at `https://github.com/michaelmilleryoder/fanfiction-nlp`.

3.1 Character Coreference Module

The story text is first passed through the coreference resolution module, which extracts mentions of characters and attributes them to character clusters. These mentions include alternative forms of names, pronouns, and anaphoric references such as "the bartender". Each cluster is then given a single standardized character name.

Coreference Resolution. We use SpanBERT-base (Joshi et al., 2020), a neural method with state-of-the-art performance on formal text, for coreference resolution. This model uses SpanBERT-base embeddings to create mention representations and employs Lee et al. (2017)'s approach to calculate the coreferent pairs. SpanBERT-base is originally trained on OntoNotes (Pradhan et al., 2012). However, we further fine-tune SpanBERT-base on LitBank (Bamman et al., 2020), a dataset with coreference annotations for works of literature in English, a domain more similar to fanfiction. The model takes the raw story text as input, identifies spans of text that mention characters, and outputs clusters of mentions that refer to the same character.

Character Standardization. We then assign representative character names for each coreference cluster. These names are simply the most frequent capitalized name variant, excluding pronouns and address terms, such as *sir*. If there are no capitalized terms in the cluster or if there are only pronouns and address terms, the most frequent mention is chosen as the name.

Post-processing. SpanBERT-base resolves all entity mentions. In order to focus solely on characters, we post-process the cluster outputs. We remove plural pronouns (*we*, *they*, *us*, *our*, etc.) and noun phrases, demonstrative pronouns (*that*, *this*), as well as *it* mentions. We also remove clusters whose standardized representative names are not named entities and have head words that are not descendants of *person* in WordNet (Miller, 1995). Thus clusters with standardized names such as "the father" are kept (since they are descendants of *person* in WordNet), yet clusters with names such as "his workshop" are removed.

For each character cluster, a standardized name and list of the mentions remaining after post-processing is produced, along with pointers to the position of each mention in the text. This coreference information is then used as input to quote attribution and assertion extraction modules.

3.2 Quote Attribution Module

To extract quotes, we simply extract any spans between quotation marks, a common approach in literary texts (O'Keefe et al., 2012). For the wide variety of fanfiction, we recognize a broader set of quotation marks than are recognized in BookNLP's approach for formal fiction.

The pipeline attributes quotes to characters with the deterministic approach of Muzny et al. (2017), which uses sieves such as looking for character mentions that are the head words of known speech verbs. We use a standalone re-implementation of this approach by Sims and Bamman (2020) that allows using the pipeline's character coreference as input. Muzny et al. (2017)'s approach assigns quotes to character mentions and then to character clusters. We simply assign quotes to the names of these selected character clusters.

3.3 Quote Pronoun Resolution Module

Recent advances in coreference resolution, such as the SpanBERT-base system incorporated in the pipeline, leverage contextualized word embeddings to compute mention representations and to cluster these mentions from pairwise or higher-order comparisons. They also concatenate features such as the distance between the compared mentions to their representations. However, these approaches to not capture the change in point of view caused by quotes within narratives, so they suffer when resolving first- and second-person pronouns within quotes. To alleviate this issue, we introduce an optional step in the pipeline that uses the output from quote attribution to inform the resolution of first- and second-person pronouns within quotes.

Prior work (Almeida et al., 2014) proposed a joint model for entity-level quotation attribution and coreference resolution, exploiting correlations between the two tasks. However, in this work, we propose an interleaved setup that is modular and allows the user of the pipeline to use independent off-the-shelf pre-trained models of their choice for both coreference resolution and quote attribution.

More specifically, once the quote attribution module predicts the position of each quote (q_i) and its associated speaker (s_i), the first-person pronouns within the quote (e.g. *I*, *my*, *mine*, *me*) are resolved to the speaker of that quote, s_i. For second-person pronouns (e.g. *you*, *your*, *yours*), we assume that they point to the addressee of the quote (a_i), which is resolved to be the speaker of the nearest

Fandom	Primary media type(s)
Marvel	Comics, movies
Supernatural	TV show
Harry Potter	Books, movies
DCU	Comics, movies
Sherlock Holmes	Books, TV show
Teen Wolf	TV show
Star Wars	Movies
Doctor Who	TV show
The Lord of the Rings	Books, movies
Dragon Age	Video game

Table 1: The most popular 10 fandoms on Archive of Our Own by number of works, as of September 2018. We annotate 1 story from each fandom to form our test set.

quote before the current quote ($a_i = s_{i-j}$ such that $s_{i-j} \neq s_i$). We only consider the previous 5 quotes to find a_i.

Since there are no sieves for quote attribution that consider pronouns within quotes, the improved coreference within quotes from this optional step does not affect quote attribution. Thus, this "cycle" of character coreference, then quote attribution, then improved character coreference, need only be run once. However, the improved coreference resolution could impact which assertions are associated with characters.

3.4 Assertion Extraction Module

After coreference, the pipeline also extracts what we describe as "assertions", topically coherent segments of text that mention a character. The motivation for this is to identify longer spans of exposition and narrative that relate to characters for building embedding representations for these characters. Parsing these assertions would also facilitate the extraction of descriptive features such as verbs for which characters are subjects and adjectives used to describe characters.

To identify such spans of texts that relate to characters, we first segment the text with a topic segmentation approach called TextTiling (Hearst, 1997). We then assign segments (with quotes removed) to characters if they contain at least one mention of the character within the span. If multiple characters are mentioned, the span is included in extracted assertions for each of the characters.

Evaluation Dataset	
# stories	10
# words	22,283
# character mentions	2,808
# quotes	876

Table 2: Fanfiction evaluation dataset statistics

4 Fanfiction Evaluation Dataset

To evaluate our pipeline, we annotate a dataset of 10 publicly available fanfiction stories for all mentions of characters and quotes attributed to these characters, which is similar in size to the test set used in LitBank (Bamman et al., 2020). We select these stories from Archive of Our Own[2], a large fanfiction archive that is maintained and operated by a fan-centered non-profit organization, the Organization for Transformative Works (Fiesler et al., 2016). To capture a representative range of fanfiction, we choose one story from each of the 10 most popular *fandoms* on Archive of Our Own when we collected data in 2018 (Table 1). *Fandoms* are fan communities organized around a particular original media source. For each fandom, we randomly sampled a story in English that has fewer than 5000 words and does not contain explicit sexual or violent content.

Two of the authors annotated the 10 stories for each of the tasks of character coreference and quote attribution. All annotators were graduate students working in NLP. Statistics on this evaluation dataset and the annotations can be found in Table 2.

These stories illustrate the expanded set of challenges and variety in fanfiction. In one story, all of the characters meet clones of themselves as male if they are female, or female if they are male. This is a variation on the practice of "genderswapping" characters in fanfiction (McClellan, 2014). Coreference systems can struggle to keep up with characters with the same name but different genders. Another story in our test set is a genre of fanfiction called "songfic", which intersperses song lyrics into the narrative. These song lyrics often contain pronouns such as *I* and *you* that do not refer to any character.

For quote attribution, challenges in the test set include a variation of quotation marks, sometimes used inconsistently. There is also great variation in the number of indirect quotes without clear quota-

[2] `http://archiveofourown.org/`

tives such as "she said". This can be a source of ambiguity in published fiction as well, but we find a large variety of styles in fanfiction. One fanfiction story in our evaluation dataset, for example, contains many implicit quotes in conversations among three or more characters, which can be difficult for quote attribution.

Annotation details and inter-annotator agreement for this evaluation dataset are described below. An overview of inter-annotator agreement is provided in Table 3.

4.1 Character Coreference Annotation

To annotate character mentions in our evaluation dataset, annotators (two of the authors) were instructed to identify and group all mentions of singular characters, including pronouns, generic phrases that refer to characters such as "the boy", and address terms. Possessive pronouns were also annotated, with nested mentions for phrases such as `<char1><char2>his</char2> sister</char1>`. Determiners and prepositional phrases attached to nouns were annotated, since they can specify characters and contribute to characterization. For an example, `<char1>an old friend of <char2>my</char2> parents</char1>`. Note that "parents" is not annotated in this example since it does not refer to a singular character. Appositives were annotated, while relative clauses ("the woman who sat on the left") and phrases after copulas ("he was a terrible lawyer") were not annotated, as we found them to act more as descriptions of characters than mentions.

After extracting character mentions, annotators grouped these mentions into character clusters that refer to the same character in the story. Note that since we focus on characters, we do not annotate other non-person entities usually included in coreference annotations. Full annotation guidelines are available online[3].

To create a unified set of gold annotations, we resolved disagreements between annotators in a second round of annotation. The final test set of 10 annotated stories contains 2,808 annotated character mentions.

In Table 3, we first provide inter-annotator agreement on extracting the same spans of text as character mentions by comparing BIO labeling at the token level. Tokens that begin a mention are labeled B, tokens that are inside or end a mention are labeled I, and all other tokens are labeled O.

[3]https://github.com/michaelmilleryoder/fanfiction-nlp/annotation_guidelines.md

	Character Coreference	Quote Attribution
Extraction (BIO)	0.95	0.97
Attribution (all)	0.84	0.89
Attribution (agreed)	0.95	0.98

Table 3: Inter-annotator agreement (Cohen's κ) between two annotators for each task, averaged across 10 fics. Extraction (BIO) is agreement on extracting the same spans of text (not attributing them to characters) with token-level BIO annotation. Attribution (all) refers to attribution of spans to characters where missed spans receive a NULL character attribution. Attribution (agreed) refers to attribution of spans that both annotators marked.

Which mentions are identified affects the agreement of attributing those mentions to characters. For this reason, we provide two attribution agreement scores. First, we calculate agreement on mentions annotated by either annotator, with a NULL character annotation if any annotator did not annotate a mention (Attribution (all) in Table 3). We also calculate agreement only for character mentions annotated by both annotators (Attribution (agreed) in Table 3). Character attribution was labeled as matching if there was significant overlap between primary character names chosen for each cluster by annotators; there were no disagreements on this.

For all these categories, inter-annotator agreement was 0.84 Cohen's κ or above, "near perfect", for character coreference (Table 3).

4.2 Quote Attribution Annotation

Two of the authors annotated all quotes that were said aloud or written by a singular character, and attributed them to a list of characters determined from the character coreference annotations. Annotation was designed to focus on characters' voices as displayed in the stories. Thus characters' thoughts were not annotated as quotes, nor were imagined or hypothetical utterances. We also chose not to annotate indirectly reported quotes, such as "the friend said I was very strange" since this could be influenced more by the character or narrator reporting the quote than the original character who spoke it. However, we did annotate direct quotes that are reported by other characters.

Inter-annotator agreement on quote attribution

was 0.89 Cohen's κ on the set of all quotes annotated by any annotator (see Table 3). Attribution agreement on the set of quote spans identified by both annotators was very high, 0.98 κ. Token-level BIO agreement for marking spans as quotes was 0.97 κ. The final test set of 10 stories contains 876 annotated quotes.

5 Pipeline Evaluation

We evaluate the pipeline against BookNLP, as well as other state-of-the-art approaches for coreference resolution and quote attribution.

5.1 Character Coreference Evaluation

We evaluate the performance of the character coreference module on our 10 annotated fanfiction stories using the CoNLL metric (Pradhan et al., 2012; the average of MUC, B^3, and CEAFE) and LEA metric (Moosavi and Strube, 2016).

We compare our approach against different state-of-the-art approaches used for coreference resolution in the past. Along with BookNLP's approach, we consider the Stanford CoreNLP deterministic coreference model (CoreNLP (dcoref); Raghunathan et al., 2010; Recasens et al., 2013; Lee et al., 2011) and the CoreNLP statistical model (CoreNLP (coref); Clark and Manning, 2015) as traditional baselines. As a neural baseline, we evaluate the more recently proposed BERT-base model (Joshi et al., 2019), which replaces the original GloVe embeddings (Pennington et al., 2014) with BERT (Devlin et al., 2019) in Lee et al. (2017)'s coreference resolution approach.

Micro-averaged results across the 10 annotated stories are shown in Table 4. The FanfictionNLP approach is SpanBERT-base fine-tuned on LitBank, with the post-hoc removal of non-person and plural mentions and clusters (as described in Section 3.1). Note that these results are without the quote pronoun resolution module described in Section 3.3. Traditional approaches like BookNLP and CoreNLP (dcoref, coref) perform significantly worse than the neural models, especially on recall. Neural models that are further fine-tuned on LitBank (OL) outperform the ones that are only trained on OntoNotes (O). This suggests that further training the model on literary text data does indeed improve its performance on fanfiction narrative. Furthermore, the SpanBERT-base approaches outperform their BERT-base counterparts with an absolute improvement of 4-5 CoNLL F1 percentage points and 6 LEA F1 percentage points. Post-hoc removal of non-person and plural entities improves CoNLL precision on characters by more than 12 percentage points over SpanBERT-base OL.

	CoNLL (Avg.)			LEA
	P	R	F1	F1
BookNLP	67.7	27.4	38.5	28.7
CoreNLP (dcoref)	26.9	49.5	29.6	21.9
CoreNLP (coref)	39.8	47.0	40.5	36.7
BERT-base O	45.8	53.2	49.2	50.9
BERT-base OL	55.0	62.3	58.4	63.1
SpanBERT-base OL	60.3	**71.1**	64.8	69.4
FanfictionNLP	**72.6**	70.1	**71.4**	**73.5**

Table 4: Character coreference performance on CoNLL and LEA metrics. **O**: Model is trained on OntoNotes. **L**: Model is also fine-tuned on LitBank corpus. **FanfictionNLP** is the SpanBERT-base OL model with post-hoc removal of non-person entities. Note that none of the approaches had access to our fanfiction data. These results are without the quote pronoun resolultion module described in Section 3.3.

5.2 Quote Attribution Evaluation

Using our expanded set of quotation marks, we reach 96% recall and 95% precision of extracted quote spans, micro-averaged over the 10 test stories, compared with 25% recall and 55% precision for BookNLP.

For attributing these extracted quotes to characters, we report average F1, precision, and recall under different coreference inputs (Table 5). To determine correct quote attributions, the canonical name for the character cluster attributed by systems to each quote is compared with the gold attribution name for that quote. A match is assigned if a) an assigned name has only one word, which matches any word in the gold cluster name (such as *Tony* and *Tony Stark*), or b) if more than half of the words in the name match between the two character names, excluding titles such as *Ms.* and *Dr.* Name-matching is manually checked to ensure no system is penalized for selecting the wrong name within a correct character cluster. Any quote that a system fails to extract is considered a mis-attribution (an attribution to a NULL character).

As baselines, we consider BookNLP and the approach of He et al. (2013), who train a RankSVM model supervised on annotations from the novel

	With system coreference			*With gold coreference*			*With gold quote extraction*		
	P	R	F1	P	R	F1	P	R	F1
BookNLP	54.6	25.4	34.7	66.8	38.9	49.2	65.0	49.7	56.3
He et al. (2013)	54.0	53.3	53.6	56.5	55.7	56.1	56.7	56.0	56.3
Muzny et al. (2017) **(FanfictionNLP)**	**68.7**	**67.0**	**67.8**	**73.5**	**75.4**	**74.4**	**77.5**	**77.5**	**77.5**

Table 5: Quote attribution evaluation scores. Scores are reported using the respective system's coreference (*system coreference*), with gold character coreference supplied (*gold coreference*) and with gold character and gold quote spans supplied (*gold quote extraction*). Attribution is calculated by a character name match to the gold cluster name. If a quote span is not extracted by a system, it is counted as a mis-attribution. Micro-averages across the 10-story test set are reported. We include Muzny et al. (2017)'s approach in the FanfictionNLP pipeline.

Pride and Prejudice.

The quality of character coreference affects quote attribution. If an entire character is not identified, there is no chance for the system to attribute a quote to that character. If a system attributes a quote to the nearest character mention and that mention is not attributed to the correct character cluster, the quote attribution will likely be incorrect. For this reason, we evaluate quote attribution with different coreference settings. *System coreference* in Table 5 refers to quote attribution performance when using the respective system's coreference. That is, BookNLP's coreference was evaluated with BookNLP's quote attribution and FanfictionNLP's coreference with FanfictionNLP's quote attribution. We test He et al. (2013)'s approach with the same coreference input as FanfictionNLP. Evaluations are also reported with gold character coreference, as well as with gold character coreference and with gold quote extractions, to measure attribution without the effects of differences in quote extraction accuracy.

The deterministic approach of Muzny et al. (2017), incorporated in the pipeline, outperforms both BookNLP and He et al. (2013)'s RankSVM classifier in this informal narrative domain.

5.3 Quote Pronoun Resolution Module Evaluation

We test our approach for resolving pronouns within quotes (Section 3.3) on character coreference on the fanfiction evaluation set. We show results using gold quote attribution as an upper bound of the prospective improvement, and using quote attributions predicted by Muzny et al. (2017)'s approach adopted in the fanfiction pipeline. As shown in Table 6, post-hoc resolution of first-person (*I*) and second-person (*you*) pronouns with perfect quote annotation information (Gold QuA) substantially improves the overall performance of coreference resolution across both CoNLL and LEA F1 scores (by 1.6 and 3.5 percentage points respectively).

	CoNLL			**LEA**
	P	R	F1	F1
FanfictionNLP	72.6	70.1	71.4	73.5
+ I (Muzny QuA)	72.9	70.2	71.6	74.4
+ I + You (Muzny QuA)	73.1	70.2	**71.7**	**74.5**
+ I (Gold QuA)	73.9	71.2	72.5	76.0
+ I + You (Gold QuA)	74.6	71.6	**73.1**	**77.2**

Table 6: Quote Pronoun Resolution evaluation scores. Coreference resolution scores on the 10 fanfiction evaluation stories are reported. Improvements gained from changing the attribution of *I* and *you* within quotes are shown, with both the Muzny et al. (2017) quotation attribution system used in the FanfictionNLP pipeline, as well as the upper bound of improvement with gold quote annotation predictions.

Similarly, coreference resolution using information from a state-of-the-art quote attribution system (Muzny et al., 2017) also results in statistically significant, although smaller, improvements across both metrics (by 0.3 percentage points and 0.8 percentage points respectively) on the 10 fanfiction stories. These results suggest that our approach is able to leverage the quote attribution outputs (speaker information) to resolve the first and second-person pronouns within quotations. It does so by assuming that the text within a quote is from the point of view of the speaker of the quote, as attributed by the quote attribution system.

Table 7 shows the qualitative results on three consecutive quotes from one of the stories in our fanfiction dataset. For the first two quotations, FanfictionNLP incorrectly resolves *your/you* to the char-

Quote	Speaker (Muzny QuA / *Gold QuA*)	Addressee (Muzny QuA / *Gold QuA*)	FanFictionNLP	FanFictionNLP + I + You (Muzny QuA / *Gold QuA*)
"Alright , give me [**your**] phone . These questions are lame ."	Caitlin / *Caitlin*	Cisco / *Cisco*	**your** = Caitlin	**your** = [Cisco / *Cisco*]
"Would [**you**] rather give up showering for a month or the Internet for a month ?"	Caitlin / *Caitlin*	Cisco / *Cisco*	**you** = Caitlin	**you** = [Cisco / *Cisco*]
"[**You**] know what , do n't reply to that one , [**I**] do n't want to know ."	Cisco / *Caitlin*	Caitlin / *Cisco*	**I** = Cisco **You** = Cisco	**I** = [Cisco / *Caitlin*] **You** = [Caitlyn / *Cisco*]

Table 7: Coreference Resolution of first- and second-person pronouns in three consecutive quotes from one of the fanfiction stories in our dataset. Results show the impact of the Quote Attribution predictions on the performance of the algorithm described in Section 3.3.

acter *Caitlin*. However, FanfictionNLP + I + You correctly maps the mentions to *Cisco*. In the third example, we find that FanfictionNLP + I + You (Muzny QuA) does not perform correct resolution as the speaker output by the quote attribution module is incorrect. This shows the dependence of this algorithm on quality quote attribution predictions.

5.4 Assertion Extraction Qualitative Evaluation

There is no counterpart to the pipeline's assertion extraction in BookNLP or other systems. Qualitatively, the spans identified by TextTiling include text that relates to characterization beyond simply selecting sentences that mention characters, and with more precision than selecting whole paragraphs that mention characters.

For example, our approach captured sentences that described how characters were interpreting their environment. In one fanfiction story in our test set, a character "could see stars and planets, constellations and black holes. Everything was distant, yet reachable." Such sentences do not contain character mentions, but certainly contribute to character development and contain useful associations made with characters.

These assertions also capture narration that mentions interactions between characters, but which may not mention any one character individually. In another fanfiction story in which two wizards are dueling, extracted assertions for each character includes, "Their wands out, pointed at each other, each shaking with rage." These associations are important to characterization, but fall outside sentences that contain individual character mentions.

6 Ethics

Though most online fanfiction is publicly available, researchers must consider how users themselves view the reach of their content (Fiesler and Proferes, 2018). Anonymity and privacy are core values of fanfiction communities; this is especially important since many participants identify as LGBTQ+ (Fiesler et al., 2016; Dym et al., 2019). We informed Archive of Our Own, with our contact information, when scraping fanfiction and modified fanfiction examples given in this paper for privacy. We urge researchers who may use the fanfiction pipeline we present to consider how their work engages with fanfiction readers and writers, and to honor the creativity and privacy of the community and individuals behind this "data".

7 Conclusion

We present a text processing pipeline for the domain of fanfiction, stories that are written by fans and inspired by original media. Large archives of fanfiction are available online and present opportunities for researchers interested in community writing practices, narrative structure, fan culture, and online communities. The presented text processing pipeline allows researchers to extract and cluster mentions of characters from fanfiction stories, along with what each character does (assertions) and says (quotes).

We assemble state-of-the-art NLP approaches for each module of this processing pipeline and evaluate them on an annotated test set, outperforming a pipeline developed for formal fiction on character coreference and quote attribution. We also present improvements in character coreference with a post-processing step that uses information from quote attribution to resolve first- and second-person pronouns within quotes. Our hope is that this pipeline will be a step toward enabling structured analysis of the text of fanfiction stories, which contain more variety than published, formal fiction. The pipeline could also be applied to other formal or informal narratives outside of fanfiction, though we have not evaluated it in other domains.

Acknowledgements

This work was supported in part by NSF grant DRL 1949110. We acknowledge Shefali Garg, Ethan Xuanyue Yang, and Luke Breitfeller for work on an earlier version of this pipeline, and Matthew Sims and David Bamman for their quote attribution re-implementation. We also thank the fanfiction writers on Archive of Our Own whose creative work allowed the creation and evaluation of this pipeline.

References

Apoorv Agarwal, Anup Kotalwar, and Owen Rambow. 2013. Automatic Extraction of Social Networks from Literary Text: A Case Study on Alice in Wonderland. In *International Joint Conference on Natural Language Processing*, October, pages 1202–1208.

Mariana SC Almeida, Miguel B Almeida, and André FT Martins. 2014. A joint model for quotation attribution and coreference resolution. In *Proceedings of the 14th Conference of the European Chapter of the Association for Computational Linguistics*, pages 39–48.

David Bamman, Olivia Lewke, and Anya Mansoor. 2020. An Annotated Dataset of Coreference in English Literature. In *Proceedings of the 12th Language Resources and Evaluation Conference*, pages 44–54.

David Bamman, Ted Underwood, and Noah A. Smith. 2014. A Bayesian Mixed Effects Model of Literary Character. *Proceedings of the 52nd Annual Meeting of the Association for Computational Linguistics (ACL 2014)*, pages 370–379.

Bertram Bruce. 1981. A social interaction model of reading. *Discourse Processes*, 4(4):273–311.

Cuong Xuan Chu, Simon Razniewski, and Gerhard Weikum. 2020. EntyFi: Entity typing in fictional texts. *WSDM 2020 - Proceedings of the 13th International Conference on Web Search and Data Mining*, pages 124–132.

Kevin Clark and Christopher D Manning. 2015. Entity-centric coreference resolution with model stacking. In *Proceedings of the 53rd Annual Meeting of the Association for Computational Linguistics and the 7th International Joint Conference on Natural Language Processing (Volume 1: Long Papers)*, pages 1405–1415.

Jacob Devlin, Ming-Wei Chang, Kenton Lee, and Kristina Toutanova. 2019. Bert: Pre-training of deep bidirectional transformers for language understanding. In *Proceedings of the Conference of the North American Chapter of the Association for Computational Linguistics: Human Language Technologies (NAACL-HLT)*, pages 4171–4186.

Brianna Dym, Jed R. Brubaker, Casey Fiesler, and Bryan Semaan. 2019. "Coming Out Okay": Community Narratives for LGBTQ Identity Recovery Work. *Proceedings of the ACM on Human-Computer Interaction*, 3(CSCW):1–28.

Sarah Evans, Katie Davis, Abigail Evans, Julie Ann Campbell, David P Randall, Kodlee Yin, and Cecilia Aragon. 2017. More Than Peer Production: Fanfiction Communities as Sites of Distributed Mentoring. *Proceedings of the 2017 ACM Conference on Computer Supported Cooperative Work and Social Computing*, pages 259–272.

Ethan Fast, Tina Vachovsky, and Michael S Bernstein. 2016. Shirtless and dangerous: Quantifying linguistic signals of gender bias in an online fiction writing community. In *Proceedings of the 10th International Conference on Web and Social Media (ICWSM)*, pages 112–120.

Rita Felski. 2020. *Hooked: Art and Attachment*. University of Chicago Press.

Casey Fiesler, Shannon Morrison, and Amy S. Bruckman. 2016. An Archive of Their Own. *Proceedings of the 2016 CHI Conference on Human Factors in Computing Systems - CHI '16*, pages 2574–2585.

Casey Fiesler and Nicholas Proferes. 2018. "Participant" Perceptions of Twitter Research Ethics. *Social Media and Society*, 4(1).

Melanie C. Green, Timothy C. Brock, and Geoff F. Kaufman. 2004. Understanding media enjoyment: The role of transportation into narrative worlds. *Communication Theory*, 14(4):311–327.

Hua He, Denilson Barbosa, and Grzegorz Kondrak. 2013. Identification of speakers in novels. In *Proceedings of the 51st Annual Meeting of the Association for Computational Linguistics (Volume 1: Long Papers)*, pages 1312–1320.

Marti A. Hearst. 1997. TextTiling: Segmenting text into multi-paragraph subtopic passages. *Computational Linguistics*, 23(1):33–64.

Mohit Iyyer, Anupam Guha, Snigdha Chaturvedi, Jordan Boyd-Graber, and Hal Daumé III. 2016. Feuding families and former friends: Unsupervised learning for dynamic fictional relationships. In *Proceedings of the Conference of the North American Chapter of the Association for Computational Linguis-*

tics: Human Language Technologies (NAACL-HLT), pages 1534–1544.

Henry Jenkins. 1992. *Textual Poachers: Television Fans and Participatory Culture*. Routledge.

Mandar Joshi, Danqi Chen, Yinhan Liu, Daniel S. Weld, Luke Zettlemoyer, and Omer Levy. 2020. SpanBERT: Improving pre-training by representing and predicting spans. *Transactions of the Association for Computational Linguistics*, 8:64–77.

Mandar Joshi, Omer Levy, Luke Zettlemoyer, and Daniel Weld. 2019. BERT for coreference resolution: Baselines and analysis. In *Proceedings of the 2019 Conference on Empirical Methods in Natural Language Processing and the 9th International Joint Conference on Natural Language Processing (EMNLP-IJCNLP)*, pages 5803–5808, Hong Kong, China. Association for Computational Linguistics.

Anna Kasunic and Geoff Kaufman. 2018. Learning to Listen: Critically Considering the Role of AI in Human Storytelling and Character Creation. In *Proceedings ofthe First Workshop on Storytelling*, pages 1–13.

Mike Kestemont, Michael Tschuggnall, Efstathios Stamatatos, Walter Daelemans, Günther Specht, Benno Stein, and Martin Potthast. 2018. Overview of the author identification task at PAN-2018: Cross-domain authorship attribution and style change detection. *CEUR Workshop Proceedings*, 2125.

Evgeny Kim and Roman Klinger. 2019. Frowning Frodo, Wincing Leia, and a Seriously Great Friendship: Learning to Classify Emotional Relationships of Fictional Characters. In *Proceedings of the Conference of the North American Chapter of the Association for Computational Linguistics: Human Language Technologies (NAACL-HLT)*, pages 647–653.

Heeyoung Lee, Yves Peirsman, Angel Chang, Nathanael Chambers, Mihai Surdeanu, and Dan Jurafsky. 2011. Stanford's multi-pass sieve coreference resolution system at the conll-2011 shared task. In *Proceedings of the 15th Conference on Computational Natural Language Learning: Shared Task*, pages 28–34.

Kenton Lee, Luheng He, Mike Lewis, and Luke Zettlemoyer. 2017. End-to-end neural coreference resolution. In *Proceedings of the 2017 Conference on Empirical Methods in Natural Language Processing*, pages 188–197.

Alexis Lothian, Kristina Busse, and Robin Anne Reid. 2007. Yearning void and infinite potential: Online slash fandom as queer female space. *English Language Notes*, 45(2).

Ann McClellan. 2014. Redefining genderswap fan fiction: A Sherlock case study. *Transformative Works & Cultures*, 17.

George A Miller. 1995. WordNet: a lexical database for English. *Communications of the ACM*, 38(11):39–41.

Smitha Milli and David Bamman. 2016. Beyond Canonical Texts : A Computational Analysis of Fanfiction. *Proceedings of the 2016 Conference on Empirical Methods in Natural Language Processing (EMNLP-16)*, pages 2048–2053.

Nafise Sadat Moosavi and Michael Strube. 2016. Which coreference evaluation metric do you trust? a proposal for a link-based entity aware metric. In *Proceedings of the 54th Annual Meeting of the Association for Computational Linguistics (Volume 1: Long Papers)*, pages 632–642, Berlin, Germany. Association for Computational Linguistics.

Felix Muzny, Michael Fang, Angel X. Chang, and Dan Jurafsky. 2017. A two-stage sieve approach for quote attribution. In *Proceedings of the 15th Conference of the European Chapter of the Association for Computational Linguistics (EACL 2017)*, volume 1, pages 460–470.

Tim O'Keefe, Silvia Pareti, James R. Curran, Irena Koprinska, and Matthew Honnibal. 2012. A sequence labelling approach to quote attribution. *Proceedings of the 2012 Joint Conference on Empirical Methods in Natural Language Processing and Computational Natural Language Learning*, (July):790–799.

Jeffrey Pennington, Richard Socher, and Christopher D Manning. 2014. Glove: Global vectors for word representation. In *Proceedings of the 2014 Conference on Empirical Methods in Natural Language Processing (EMNLP)*, pages 1532–1543.

Sameer Pradhan, Alessandro Moschitti, Nianwen Xue, Olga Uryupina, and Yuchen Zhang. 2012. Conll-2012 shared task: Modeling multilingual unrestricted coreference in ontonotes. In *Proceedings of the 2012 Joint Conference on Empirical Methods in Natural Language Processing and Computational Natural Language Learning*, page 1–40, USA.

Karthik Raghunathan, Heeyoung Lee, Sudarshan Rangarajan, Nathanael Chambers, Mihai Surdeanu, Dan Jurafsky, and Christopher D Manning. 2010. A multi-pass sieve for coreference resolution. In *Proceedings of the 2010 Conference on Empirical Methods in Natural Language Processing*, pages 492–501.

Marta Recasens, Marie-Catherine de Marneffe, and Christopher Potts. 2013. The life and death of discourse entities: Identifying singleton mentions. In *Proceedings of the 2013 Conference of the North American Chapter of the Association for Computational Linguistics: Human Language Technologies*, pages 627–633.

Bingyu Shen, Christopher W. Forstall, Anderson De Rezende Rocha, and Walter J. Scheirer. 2018. Practical text phylogeny for real-world settings. *IEEE Access*, 6:41002–41012.

Matthew Sims and David Bamman. 2020. Measuring information propagation in literary social networks. In *Proceedings of the 2020 Conference on Empirical Methods in Natural Language Processing (EMNLP)*, pages 642–652, Online. Association for Computational Linguistics.

Matthew Sims, Jong Ho Park, and David Bamman. 2019. Literary event detection. In *Proceedings of the 57th Annual Meeting of the Association for Computational Linguistics*, pages 3623–3634, Florence, Italy. Association for Computational Linguistics.

Catherine Tosenberger. 2008. Homosexuality at the Online Hogwarts: Harry Potter Slash Fanfiction. *Children's Literature*, 36(1):185–207.

David Vilares and Carlos Gómez-Rodríguez. 2019. Harry Potter and the action prediction challenge from natural language. *NAACL HLT 2019 - 2019 Conference of the North American Chapter of the Association for Computational Linguistics: Human Language Technologies - Proceedings of the Conference*, 1:2124–2130.

Anthony Wall. 1984. Characters in Bakhtin's Theory. *Studies in 20th Century Literature*, 9(1):2334–4415.

Kodlee Yin, Cecilia Aragon, Sarah Evans, and Katie Davis. 2017. Where no one has gone before: A meta-dataset of the world's largest fanfiction repository. In *Proceedings of the Conference on Human Factors in Computing Systems*, pages 6106–6110.

Learning Similarity between Movie Characters and Its Potential Implications on Understanding Human Experiences

Zhilin Wang[1] **Weizhe Lin**[2] **Xiaodong Wu**[2]
[1]University of Washington, United States
[2]University of Cambridge, United Kingdom
zhilinw@uw.edu, {wl356, xw338}@cam.ac.uk

Abstract

While many different aspects of human experiences have been studied by the NLP community, none has captured its full richness. We propose a new task[1] to capture this richness based on an unlikely setting: movie characters. We sought to capture theme-level similarities between movie characters that were community-curated into 20,000 themes. By introducing a two-step approach that balances performance and efficiency, we managed to achieve 9-27% improvement over recent paragraph-embedding based methods. Finally, we demonstrate how the thematic information learnt from movie characters can potentially be used to understand themes in the experience of people, as indicated on Reddit posts.

1 Introduction

What makes a person similar to another? While there is no definitive answer, some aspects that have been investigated in the NLP community are personality(Gjurković and Šnajder, 2018; Conway and O'Connor, 2016), demographics(Nguyen et al., 2016) as well as personal beliefs and intents (Sap et al., 2019). While each of these aspects is valuable on its own, they also seem somewhat lacking to sketch a complete picture of a person. Researchers who recognise such limitations seek to ameliorate them by jointly modelling multiple aspects at the same time (Benton et al., 2017). Yet, we intuitively know that as humans, we are more than the sum of the multiple aspects that constitutes our individuality. Our human experiences are marked by so many different aspects that interact in ways that we can not anticipate. What then can we do to better capture the degree of similarity between different people?

Finding similar movie characters can be an interesting first step to understanding humans better. Many characters are inspired by and related to true stories of people so understanding how to identify similarities between character descriptions might ultimately help us to better understand similarities in human characteristics and experiences. One way of defining what makes movie character descriptions similar is when community-based contributors on All The Tropes[2] classify them into the same theme (also known as a trope), with an example from the trope "Driven by Envy" shown in Table 1. Other themes (tropes) include "Parental Neglect", "Fallen Hero", and "A Friend in Need".

Such community-based curation allows All The Tropes to reap the same advantages as Wikipedia and open-sourced software: a large catalog can be created with high internal-consistency given the in-built self-correction mechanisms. This approach allowed us to collect a dataset of >100 thousand characters labelled with >20,000 themes without requiring any annotation cost. Based on this dataset, we propose a model that can be used to identify similar movie characters precisely yet efficiently. While movie characters may not be the perfect reflection of human experience, we ultimately show that they are good enough proxies when collecting a dataset of similar scale with real people would be extremely expensive.

Our key contributions are as follows:

1. We conduct a pioneering study on identifying similar movie character descriptions using weakly supervised learning, with potential implications on understanding similarities in human characteristics and experiences.

2. We propose a two-step generalizable approach that can be used to identify similar movie characters precisely yet efficiently and demonstrate that our approach performs at least 9-27% better than methods employing recent paragraph embedding-based approaches.

[1]Code and data available at https://github.com/Zhilin123/similar_movie_characters

[2]https://allthetropes.org

Proceedings of the 3rd Workshop on Narrative Understanding, pages 24–35
June 11, 2021.

Superman's 1990s enemy Conduit.
Conduit hates Superman because he knows if Superman wasn't around he would be humanity's greatest hero instead ...

Loki
Loki's constant scheming against Thor in his efforts to one-up him gave Odin and the rest of Asgard more and more reasons to hate Loki ...

Table 1: Character descriptions from the trope "Driven by Envy"

3. We show that our model, which is trained on identifying similar movie characters, can be related to themes in human experience found in Reddit posts.

2 Related Work

2.1 Analysis of characters in film and fiction

Characters in movies and novels have been computationally analyzed by many researchers. Bamman et al. (2013, 2014) attempted to cluster various characters into prototypes based on topic modelling techniques (Blei et al., 2003). On the other hand, Frermann and Szarvas (2017) and Iyyer et al. (2016) sought to cluster fictional characters alongside the relationships between them using recurrent neural networks and matrix factorization. While preceded by prior literature, our work is novel in framing character analysis as a supervised learning problem rather than an unsupervised learning problem.

Specifically, we formulate it as a similarity learning task between characters. Tapping on fan-curated movie-character labels (ie tropes) can provide valuable information concerning character similarity, which previous literature did not use. A perceptible effect of this change in task formulation is that our formulation allows movie characters to be finely distinguished amongst $>$ 20000 themes versus $<$ 200 in prior literature. Such differences in task formulation can contribute a fresh perspective into this research area and inspire subsequent research.

Furthermore, the corpus we use differs significantly from those used in existing research. We use highly concise character descriptions of around 200 words whereas existing research mostly uses movie/book-length character mentions. Concise character descriptions can exemplify specific traits/experiences of characters. This allows the differences between characters to be more discriminative compared to a longer description, which might include more points of commonality (going to school/work, eating and having a polite conversation). This means that such concise descriptions can eventually prove more helpful in understanding characteristics and experiences of humans.

2.2 Congruence between themes in real-life experiences and movie tropes

Mostly researched in the field of psychology, real-life experiences are often analyzed through asking individuals to document and reflect upon their experiences. Trained analysts then seek to classify such writing into predefined categories.

Demorest et al. (1999) interpreted an individual's experience in the form of three key stages: an individual's wish, the response from the other and the response from the self in light of the response from the other. Each stage consists of around ten predefined categories such as wanting to be autonomous (Stage 1), being denied of that autonomy (Stage 2) and developing an enmity against the other (Stage 3). Thorne and McLean (2001) organized their analysis in terms of central themes. These central themes include experiences of interpersonal turmoil, having a sense of achievement and surviving a potentially life-threatening event/illness.

Both studies above code individuals' personal experiences into categories/themes that greatly resemble movie tropes. Because of this congruence, it is very likely that identifying similarity between characters in the same trope can inform about similarity between people in real-life. A common drawback of Demorest et al. (1999) and Thorne and McLean (2001) lie in their relatively small sample size (less than 200 people classified into tens of themes/categories). Comparatively, our study uses $>$ 100,000 characters fine-grainedly labelled by fans into $>$20,000 tropes. As a result, this study has the potential of supporting a better understanding of tropes, which we have shown to be structurally similar to themes in real-life experiences.

2.3 Candidate selection in information retrieval

Many information retrieval pipelines involve first identifying likely candidates and then post-processing these candidates to determine which among them are most suitable. The most widely-used class of approaches for this purpose is known as Shingling and Locally Sensitive Hashing (Leskovec et al., 2020; Rodier and Carter, 2020). Such approaches first represent documents as Bag-of-Ngrams before hashing such representation into shorter integer-vector signatures. These signatures contain information on n-gram overlap between documents and hence encode lexical features that characterize similar documents. However, such approaches are unable to identify documents that are similar based on abstract semantic features rather than superficial lexical similarities.

Recent progress in language modelling has enabled the semantic meaning of short paragraphs to be encoded beyond lexical features (Peters et al., 2018; Devlin et al., 2019; Howard and Ruder, 2018; Raffel et al., 2019). This has reaped substantial gains in text similarity tasks including entailment tasks (Bowman et al., 2015; Williams et al., 2018), duplicate questions tasks (Sharma et al., 2019; Nakov et al., 2017) and others (Cer et al., 2017; Dolan and Brockett, 2005). Yet, such progress has yet to enable better candidate selection based on semantic similarities. As a result, relatively naive approaches such as exhaustive pairwise comparisons and distance-based measures continue to be the dominant approach in identifying similar documents encoded into dense contextualized embeddings (Reimers and Gurevych, 2019). To improve this gap in knowledge, this study proposes and validates a candidate selection method that is compatible with recent progress in text representation.

3 Task formulation

There is a set of unique character descriptions from the All The Tropes ($Character_0$, $Character_1$ ... $Character_n$), each associated with a non-unique trope (theme) ($Trope_0$, $Trope_0$ ... $Trope_p$). Given this set, find the k (where k = 1, 5 or 10) most similar character(s) to each character without making explicit use of the trope association of each character. In doing so, the goal is to have a maximal proportion of most similar character(s) which share the same tropes.

4 Methods

In this section, we first discuss how we prepare the dataset and trained a BERT Next Sentence Prediction (NSP) model to identify similar characters. Based on this model, we present a 2-step **Select** and **Refine** approach, which can be utilized to find the most similar characters quickly yet effectively.

4.1 Dataset

Character descriptions from All The Tropes[3] were used. We downloaded all character descriptions that had more than 100 words because character descriptions that are too short are unlikely to provide sufficient textual information for comparing similarity with other character descriptions. We then filtered our data to retain only tropes that contain more than one character descriptions. Character descriptions were then randomly split into training and evaluation sets (evaluation set = 20%). Inspired by BERT NSP dataset construction Devlin et al. (2019), we generated all possible combination-pairs of character descriptions that are classified under each trope (i.e. an unordered set) and gave the text-pair a label of `IsSimilar`, For each `IsSimilar` pair in the training set, we took the first item, randomly selected a character description that is not in the same trope as the first item and gave the new pair a label of `NotSimilar`.

Descriptive statistics are available in Table 2.

4.2 Training BERT Next Sentence Prediction model

We trained a BERT Next Sentence Prediction model (English-base-uncased)[4] with the pre-trained weights used as an initialization. As this model was trained to perform pair-wise character comparison instead of next sentence prediction, we thereafter name it as Character Comparison Model (CCM).

All hyper-parameters used to train the model were default[5] except adjusting the maximum sequence length to 512 tokens (to adapt to the paragraph-length text), batch-size per GPU to 8 and epoch number to 2, as recommended by Devlin et al. (2019). Among the training set, 1% was separated as a validation set during the training process. We also used the default pre-trained BERT English-base-uncased tokenizer because only a small proportion of words ($< 0.5\%$) in the training corpus were out-of-vocabulary, of which most were names. As a result, training took 3 days on 4 Nvidia Tesla P100 GPUs.

[3]https://allthetropes.org

[4]12-layer, 768-hidden, 12-heads, 110M parameters with only Next Sentence Prediction loss, accessed from https://github.com/huggingface/transformers

[5]https://github.com/huggingface/transformers/

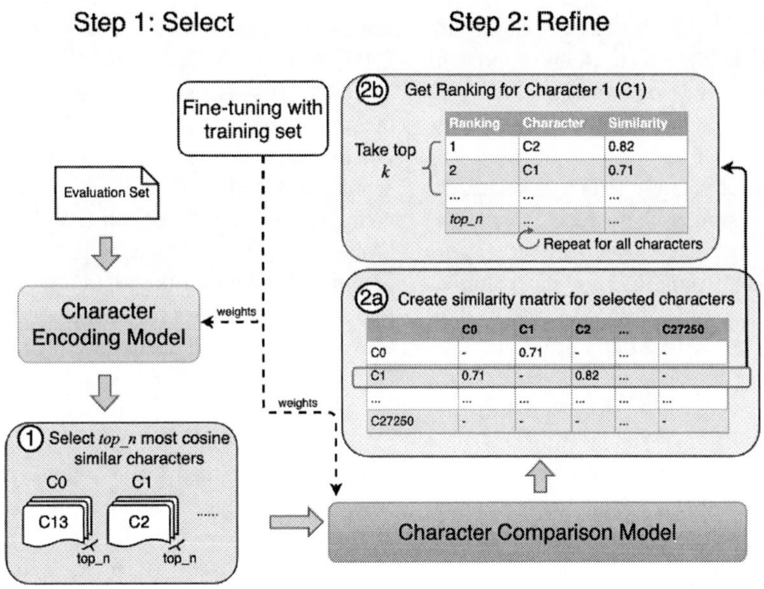

Figure 1: Workflow of finding most similar characters: BERT NSP model is first trained on the training set (Section 4.2) top_n characters are then selected using cosine similarity based on the Character Embedding Model or using a Siamese-BERT model, which has been omitted from the illustration for clarity (Section 4.3.1). This selection is then refined using the Character Comparison Model to create a similarity matrix, which can then be sorted to identified most similar characters. (Section 4.3.2)

	Training Set	Evaluation Set
Characters	109000	27250
Words per character	172 (σ = 101)	172 (σ = 102)
Tropes	13160	8669
Characters per trope	5.39 (σ = 9.66)	1.33 (σ = 2.64)
Character-pairs	2375298 (50% `IsSimilar`)	72705 (only `IsSimilar`)

Table 2: Descriptive statistics of dataset

4.3 Select and Refine

To address the key limitation of utilizing exhaustive pairwise comparison in practice - its impractically long computation time ($\approx$ 10 thousand GPU-hours on Nvidia Tesla P100), we propose a two-step Select and Refine approach. The Select step first identifies a small set of likely candidates in a coarse but computationally efficient manner. Then, the Refine step re-ranks these candidates using a precise but computationally expensive model. In doing so, it combines their strengths to precisely identify similar characters while being computationally efficient. While the Select and Refine approach is designed for identifying similar characters, this novel approach can also be directly used in other tasks involving semantic similarities between a pair of texts.

4.3.1 Select

Characters that are likely to be similar to each character are first selected using a variant of our `CCM` model - named the Character Encoding Model (thereafter `CEM`). This model differs from the `CCM` model in that it does not utilize the final classifier layer. Therefore it can process a character description individually (instead of in pairs) to output an embedding that represents the character. The shared weights with `CCM` means that it encodes semantic information in a a similar way. This makes it likely that the most cosine similar character descriptions based on their character embedding are likely to have high (but not necessarily the highest) character-pair similarity.

Beyond the `CEM`, any model capable of efficiently generating candidates for similar character description texts in O(n) time can also be used for this Select step, allowing immense flexibility in the application of the Select and Refine approach. To demonstrate this, we also test a Siamese-BERT model for the Select step, with the details of its preparation in Section 5.2.

In this step, we effectively reduced the search space for the most similar characters. We choose top_n candidates characters which are most similar to each character, forming top_n most similar character-pairs. top_n is a hyper-parameter that can range from 1 to 500. Strictly speaking, this step requires $O(n^2)$ comparisons to find the top_n most similar character-pairs. However, each cosine similarity calculation is significantly less computationally demanding compared to each BERT NSP operation (note that `CCM` is trained from an NSP model). This also applies to the Siamese-BERT model because character embeddings can be cached, meaning that only a single classification layer operation needs to be repeated $O(n^2)$ times. This means that computational runtime is dominated by $O(n)$ BERT NSP operations in the subsequent Refine step, given the huge constant factor for BERT NSP operations. Overall, this step took 0.25 GPU-hours.

4.3.2 Refine

The initial selection of candidates for most similar characters to each character will then be refined using the `CCM` model. This step is more computationally demanding (0.25 * top_n GPU-hours) but can more effectively determine the extent to which characters are similar. Character Comparison Model (`CCM`) will then only be used on the top_n most similar candidate character-pairs, reducing the number of operations for each character from the total number of characters (n_{chars}) to only top_n. As a consequence, the runtime complexity of the overall operation is reduced from $O(n^2_{chars})$ to $O(top\_n \cdot n_{chars}) == O(n_{chars})$, given top_n is a constant.

5 Evaluation

In this section, we first present evaluation metrics and then present the preparation of baseline models including state-of-the-art paragraph-level embedding models. Finally, we analyze the performance of our models relative to baseline models.

5.1 Evaluation metrics

Recall @ k considers the proportion of all ground-truth pairs found within the k (1, 5 or 10) most similar characters to each character (Manning et al., 2008). Normalized Discounted Cumulative Gain @ k (**nDCG @ k**) is a precision metric that considers the proportion of predicted k most similar characters to each character that are in the ground-truth character-pairs. It also takes into account the order amongst top k predicted most similar characters (Wang et al., 2013). Mean reciprocal rank (**MRR**) identifies the rank of the first correctly predicted most similar character for each character and averages the reciprocal of their ranks. (Voorhees, 2000). Higher is better for all metrics.

5.2 Baseline Models

Baseline measurements were obtained for Google Universal Sentence Encoder-large (Cer et al., 2018), BERT-base (Devlin et al., 2019) and Siamese-BERT-base[6] (Reimers and Gurevych, 2019).

Google Universal Sentence Encoder-large model[7] (**USE**) on Tensorflow Hub was used to obtain a 512-dimensional vector representation of each character description. Bag of Words (**BoW**) was implemented by lowercasing all words and counting the number of times each word occurred in each character description. **BERT** embedding of 768 dimensions were obtained by average-pooling all the word embedding of tokens in the second-to-last layer, as recommended by (Xiao, 2018). The English-base-uncased version[8] was used. For each type of embedding, the most similar characters were obtained by finding other characters whose embeddings are most cosine similar.

Siamese-BERT was obtained based on training a Siamese model architecture connected to a BERT base model on the training set in Section 4.1. We follow the optimal model configuration for sentence-pair classification tasks described in Reimers and Gurevych (2019), which involves taking the mean of all tokens embeddings in the final layer. With the mean embedding for each character description, an absolute difference between them was taken. The mean embedding for character A, mean embedding for character B and their absolute difference was then entered into a feedforward neural network, which makes the prediction. Siamese-BERT was chosen as a baseline due to its outstanding performance in sentence-pair classifi-

[6] 12-layer, 768-hidden, 12-heads and 110M parameters

[7] https://tfhub.dev/google/universal-sentence-encoder-large/3

[8] 12-layer, 768-hidden, 12-heads and 110M parameters

cation tasks such as Semantic Textual Similarity (Cer et al., 2017) and Natural Language Inference (Bowman et al., 2015; Williams et al., 2018). For this baseline, the characters most similar to a character are those with the highest likelihood of being predicted `IsSimilar` with the character.

5.3 Suitability of Siamese-BERT and CEM for Step 1: Select

While the prohibitively high computational demands of exhaustive pairwise comparison ($\approx$ 10 thousand GPU-hours) prevents a full-scale evaluation of the adequateness of Siamese-BERT and `CEM` for Step 1:Select, we conducted a small-scale experiment on 100 randomly chosen characters from the test set. First, an exhaustive pairwise comparison was conducted between these randomly chosen characters and all characters in the test set. From this, 100 characters with the highest `CCM` similarity value with each of the randomly chosen characters were identified. Next, various methods in Table 3 were attempted to identify 500 characters with the highest cosine similarity with the randomly chosen characters. Finally, the proportion of overlap between `CCM` and each method was calculated. Results demonstrate that Siamese-BERT and `CEM` have the greatest overlap and hence, the use of Siamese-BERT and `CEM` can select for the most number of highly similar characters to be refined by the `CCM`.

	`CCM` overlap (%)
Siamese-BERT	**36.15**
`CEM`	24.21
BERT	16.90
USE	16.27
BoW	7.41

Table 3: Proportion of 100 characters with high `CCM` similarity value that overlaps with each method for Step 1: Select

5.4 Selecting hyper-parameter top_n for Step 2: Refine

Based on Figure 2, the ideal *top_n* for the Select and Refine model with Siamese-BERT varies between 7 and 25 depending on the metric that is optimised for. In general, a lower value for *top_n* is preferred when optimizing for Recall@k and nDCG@k with smaller values of k. The metrics reported in Table 4 consist of the optimal value for each metric at various *top_n*.

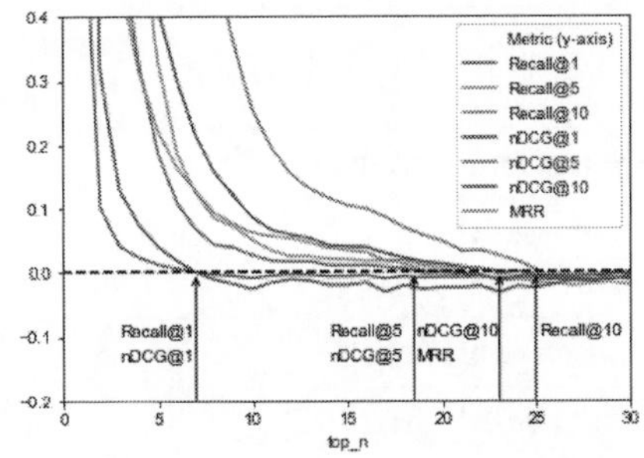

Figure 2: Percent change in metrics with each additional *top_n* for Select and Refine model with Siamese-BERT. Average smoothing applied over a range of 10 to improve clarity. Points annotated where each metric is at 0.

On the other hand, there is no ideal value for *top_n* when using the Select and Refine model with `CEM`. Instead, the metrics continue to improve over large values of *top_n*, albeit at a gradually reduced rate. However, due to practical considerations relating to GPU computation time, we terminated our search at *top_n* = 500 and report metrics for that value of *top_n*.

Together, this means that the Select and Refine model using Siamese-BERT achieves peak performance with significant less computational resources compared to the one using `CEM` (2-6 GPU-hours vs. 125 GPU-hours).

5.5 Comparing Select and Refine models with baseline models

As shown in Table 4, the highest value for all metrics lies below 40% suggesting that identifying similar characters is a novel and challenging task. This is because there are only very few correct answers (characters from the same trope) out of 27,000 possible characters. The poor performance of the Bag-of-Words baseline also demonstrates that abstract semantic similarity between characters is significantly different from their superficial lexical similarity. In face of such challenges, the Select and Refine model using Siamese-BERT performed 9-27 % better on all metrics than the best performing paragraph-embedding-based baseline. This suggests the importance of refining initial selection of candidates instead of using them directly, even when the baseline model has relatively good performance.

Comparing the Select and Refine models, Siamese-BERT performed much better than `CEM`

	Recall @ k (in %)			nDCG @ k (in %)			MRR
	k = 1	k = 5	k = 10	k = 1	k = 5	k = 10	(in %)
Select and Refine models							
Siamese-BERT	**6.921**	**23.53**	**36.14**	**21.82**	**19.13**	**19.71**	26.56
CEM	6.184	20.74	31.02	19.50	17.02	17.26	**28.50**
Baseline models							
Siamese-BERT	5.437	19.53	30.65	17.14	15.51	16.15	25.99
CEM	2.802	8.852	13.26	8.832	7.119	7.126	14.61
BERT	1.238	3.636	5.514	3.904	3.035	3.109	7.182
USE	1.277	4.427	6.956	4.025	3.599	3.866	7.810
BoW	0.4632	1.344	1.987	1.46	1.087	1.052	2.824

Table 4: Performance of Select and Refine models compared to baseline models. Higher is better for all metrics.

while having a significantly low top_n, which means that less computational resources is required. The superior performance and efficiency of Siamese-BERT means that it is more suitable for Step 1: Select. This is likely caused by the higher performance of Siamese-BERT as a baseline model. While it was surprising that using Siamese-BERT outperformed CEM, which directly shares weights with the CCM, such an observation also shows the relatively low coupling between the Select and Refine steps. This means that the Select and Refine approach that we propose can continue to be relevant when model architectures that are more optimized for each step are introduced in the future.

The significantly higher performance of Select and Refine models can be attributed to the ability of underlying BERT NSP architecture in our CCM to consider complex word relationships across the two character descriptions. A manual examination of correct pairs captured only by Select and Refine models but not baseline models revealed that these pairs often contain words relating to multiple common aspects. As an example, one character description contains “magic, enchanter” and “training, candidate, learn” while the other character in the ground-truth pair contains “spell, wonder, sphere” and “researched, school”. Compressing these word-level aspects into a fixed-length vector would cause some important semantic information - such as the inter-relatedness between aspects - to be lost (Conneau et al., 2018). As a result, capturing similarities between these pairs prove to be difficult in baseline models, leading to sub-optimal ranking of the most similar characters.

6 Implications for understanding themes in real-life experiences

6.1 Relating movie characters to Reddit posts

To demonstrate the potential applications of this study in understanding human experiences, we designed a task that can show how the model can be used with zero-shot transfer learning. Specifically, we used our model to identify the movie-characters that are most fitting to a description of people's life experiences. To do this, we collected 50 posts describing people's real-life experiences from a forum r/OffMyChest on Reddit[9], on which people share their life experiences with strangers online.

Then, we used our models to identify 10 movie characters (from our test set) that are most befitting to each post. For each of these 10 movie characters suggested by model, three graduate students independently rated whether the character matches the concepts, ideas and themes expressed in each post, while blind to information on which model the characters were generated by. Because the extent of similarity between a movie character and a Reddit post can be ambiguous, a binary annotation was chosen over a Likert scale for clarity of annotation. Annotators were instructed to annotate "similar" when they can **specify** at least one area of overlap between the concepts, ideas and themes of a Reddit post and a movie character. Examples of some characters that are indicated as "similar" to two posts are shown in Appendix A. Annotators agree on 94.2% of labels (Cohen's $\kappa = 0.934$). Where the annotators disagree, the majority opinion out of three is taken. From these annotations,

[9] https://www.reddit.com/r/offmychest/

	Precision @ k (in %)		
	k = 1	k = 5	k = 10
Select and Refine models			
Siamese-BERT	**98.0** (14.0)	**92.4** (14.4)	**87.0** (8.79)
CEM	82.0 (39.6)	77.6 (17.9)	70.2 (8.94)
Baseline models			
Siamese-BERT	76.0 (42.8)	73.2 (14.9)	70.8 (8.31)
CEM	48.0 (38.4)	33.2 (20.5)	27.2 (11.3)
BERT	40.0 (48.9)	21.2 (12.7)	12.8 (5.98)
USE	32.0 (46.6)	15.6 (13.3)	9.2 (7.23)
BoW	16.0 (36.6)	7.2 (9.17)	4.4 (4.9)

Table 5: Precision @ k (std. dev.) for movie characters identified by each model.

Precision @ k is calculated, considering the proportion of all characters identified within the k (1, 5 or 10) that are labelled as "similar" (Manning et al., 2008).

In Table 5, the performance of our Select and Refine models reflects a similar extent of improvement compared to our main learning task. This shows that the model that was trained to disambiguate movie character similarity can also determine the extent of similarity between movie characters and people's life experiences. Beyond the relative performance gains, the Select and Refine model on this task also demonstrates an excellent absolute performance of precision @ 1 = 98.00%. This means that our model can be used on this task without any fine-tuning.

Illustrating the difference in performance of the various models in Table 6, the better performing models on this task are generally better at capturing thematic similarities in terms of the abstract sense of recollection and memory, which are thematically more related to the Reddit post. Our Select and Refine model (with Siamese-BERT) is particularly effective at capturing both a sense of recollection as well as a sense of reverence towards a respected figure (historical figure and father respectively). In contrary, the poorer performing models contain phrase-level semantic overlap (USE: picture with facial recognition; BoW: killed and passed away; eyes and recognize) but fail to capture thematic resemblance. This suggests our learning of similarities between movie characters of the same trope can effectively transfer onto thematic similarities between written human experiences and movie characters.

6.2 Future directions

We are excited about the diversity of research directions that this study can complement. One possible area is social media analysis (Zirikly et al., 2019; Amir et al., 2019; Hauser et al., 2019). Researchers can make use of movie characters with known experiences (e.g. mental health, personal circumstances or individual interests) to identify similar experiences in social media when collecting large amounts of text labelled with such experiences directly is difficult.

Another area would be personalizing dialogue agents (Tigunova et al., 2020; Zhang et al., 2018). In the context of limited personality-related training data, movie characters with personality that are similar to a desired dialogue agent can be found. Using this, a dialogue agent can be trained with movie subtitle language data (involving the identified movie character). Thereby, the augmented linguistic data enables the dialogue agent to have a well-defined, distinct and consistent personality.

A final area that can benefit from this study is media recommendations (Rafailidis et al., 2017). Users might be suggested media content based on the extent to which movie characters resonate with their own/friends' experiences. Additionally, with social environments being formed in games (particularly social simulation games such as Animal Crossing, The Sims and Pokemon) as well as in virtual reality (Chu et al., 2020), participants can even assume the identity of movie characters that they are similar to, so as to have an interesting and immersive experience.

Reddit post	My father passed away when I was 6 so I didn't really remember much of him but the fact that I didn't recognize his picture saddens me.
Select and Refine	
Siamese-BERT	**Sisko in Star Trek: Deep Space Nine (Past Tense)** When he encountered an entry about the historical figure, passed comment about how closely Sisko resembled a picture of him (the picture, of course, being that of Sisko.)
`CEM`	**Roxas in Kingdom Hearts: Chain of Memories** His memories are wiped by Ansem the Wise and placed in a simulated world with a completely new identity
Baseline	
Siamese-BERT	**Audrina, My Sweet Audrina by V.C Andrews** is a girl living in the constant shadow of her elder sister who had died nine years before she was born
`CEM`	**Macsen Wledig in The Mabinogion** An amazing memory was an important necessity to the job, but remembering many long stories was much more important than getting one right after days of wandering around madly muttering
BERT	**Kira in Push** is made to think that her entire relationship with Nick was a false memory that she gave him and she's been pushing his thoughts the entire time they were together.
USE	**EyeRobot in Fallout: New Vegas** can recognize your face and voice with advanced facial and auditory recognition technology
BoW	**Magneto** took Ron the Death Eater Up to Eleven to show him as he "truly" was in Morrison's eyes, and ended with him (intended as) Killed Off for Real

Table 6: Most similar character predicted by each model to a post from Reddit r/OffMyChest. Excerpts of Reddit post mildly paraphrased to protect anonymity.

7 Conclusion

We introduce a pioneering study on identifying similar movie characters through weakly supervised learning. Based on this task, we introduce a novel Select-and-Refine approach that allows us to match characters belonging to a common theme, which simultaneously optimize for efficiency and performance. Using this trained model, we demonstrate the potential applications of this study in identifying movie characters that are similar to human experiences as presented in Reddit posts, without any fine-tuning. This represents an early step into understanding the complexity and richness of our human experience, which is not only interesting in itself but can also complement research in social media analysis, personalizing dialogue agents and media recommendations/interactions.

Acknowledgements

We would like to thank the anonymous reviewers for their helpful feedback.

References

Silvio Amir, Mark Dredze, and John W. Ayers. 2019. Mental health surveillance over social media with digital cohorts. In *Proceedings of the Sixth Workshop on Computational Linguistics and Clinical Psychology*, pages 114–120, Minneapolis, Minnesota. Association for Computational Linguistics.

David Bamman, Brendan O'Connor, and Noah A Smith. 2013. Learning latent personas of film characters. In *Proceedings of the 51st Annual Meeting of the Association for Computational Linguistics (Volume 1: Long Papers)*, pages 352–361.

David Bamman, Ted Underwood, and Noah A Smith. 2014. A bayesian mixed effects model of literary character. In *Proceedings of the 52nd Annual Meeting of the Association for Computational Linguistics (Volume 1: Long Papers)*, pages 370–379.

Adrian Benton, Margaret Mitchell, and Dirk Hovy. 2017. Multitask learning for mental health conditions with limited social media data. In *Proceedings of the 15th Conference of the European Chapter of the Association for Computational Linguistics: Volume 1, Long Papers*, pages 152–162, Valencia, Spain. Association for Computational Linguistics.

David M. Blei, Andrew Y. Ng, and Michael I. Jordan. 2003. Latent dirichlet allocation. *J. Mach. Learn. Res.*, 3:993–1022.

Samuel R. Bowman, Gabor Angeli, Christopher Potts, and Christopher D. Manning. 2015. A large annotated corpus for learning natural language inference. In *Proceedings of the 2015 Conference on Empirical Methods in Natural Language Processing (EMNLP)*. Association for Computational Linguistics.

Daniel Cer, Mona Diab, Eneko Agirre, Iñigo Lopez-Gazpio, and Lucia Specia. 2017. SemEval-2017 task 1: Semantic textual similarity multilingual and crosslingual focused evaluation. In *Proceedings of the 11th International Workshop on Semantic Evaluation (SemEval-2017)*, pages 1–14, Vancouver, Canada. Association for Computational Linguistics.

Daniel Cer, Yinfei Yang, Sheng-yi Kong, Nan Hua, Nicole Limtiaco, Rhomni St John, Noah Constant, Mario Guajardo-Cespedes, Steve Yuan, Chris Tar, et al. 2018. Universal sentence encoder for english. In *Proceedings of the 2018 Conference on Empirical Methods in Natural Language Processing: System Demonstrations*, pages 169–174.

Hang Chu, Shugao Ma, Fernando De la Torre, Sanja Fidler, and Yaser Sheikh. 2020. Expressive telepresence via modular codec avatars. In *Computer Vision – ECCV 2020*, pages 330–345, Cham. Springer International Publishing.

Alexis Conneau, German Kruszewski, Guillaume Lample, Loïc Barrault, and Marco Baroni. 2018. What you can cram into a single $&!#* vector: Probing sentence embeddings for linguistic properties. In *Proceedings of the 56th Annual Meeting of the Association for Computational Linguistics (Volume 1: Long Papers)*, pages 2126–2136, Melbourne, Australia. Association for Computational Linguistics.

Mike Conway and Daniel O'Connor. 2016. Social media, big data, and mental health: current advances and ethical implications. *Current Opinion in Psychology*, 9:77 – 82. Social media and applications to health behavior.

Amy Demorest, Paul Crits-Christoph, Mary Hatch, and Lester Luborsky. 1999. A comparison of interpersonal scripts in clinically depressed versus nondepressed individuals. *Journal of Research in Personality*, 33(3):265–280.

Jacob Devlin, Ming-Wei Chang, Kenton Lee, and Kristina Toutanova. 2019. BERT: Pre-training of deep bidirectional transformers for language understanding. In *Proceedings of the 2019 Conference of the North American Chapter of the Association for Computational Linguistics: Human Language Technologies, Volume 1 (Long and Short Papers)*, pages 4171–4186, Minneapolis, Minnesota. Association for Computational Linguistics.

William B. Dolan and Chris Brockett. 2005. Automatically constructing a corpus of sentential paraphrases. In *Proceedings of the Third International Workshop on Paraphrasing (IWP2005)*.

Lea Frermann and György Szarvas. 2017. Inducing semantic micro-clusters from deep multi-view representations of novels. In *Proceedings of the 2017 Conference on Empirical Methods in Natural Language Processing*, pages 1873–1883.

Matej Gjurković and Jan Šnajder. 2018. Reddit: A gold mine for personality prediction. In *Proceedings of the Second Workshop on Computational Modeling of People's Opinions, Personality, and Emotions in Social Media*, pages 87–97, New Orleans, Louisiana, USA. Association for Computational Linguistics.

Michael Hauser, Evangelos Sariyanidi, Birkan Tunc, Casey Zampella, Edward Brodkin, Robert Schultz, and Julia Parish-Morris. 2019. Using natural conversations to classify autism with limited data: Age matters. In *Proceedings of the Sixth Workshop on Computational Linguistics and Clinical Psychology*, pages 45–54, Minneapolis, Minnesota. Association for Computational Linguistics.

Jeremy Howard and Sebastian Ruder. 2018. Universal language model fine-tuning for text classification. *arXiv preprint arXiv:1801.06146*.

Mohit Iyyer, Anupam Guha, Snigdha Chaturvedi, Jordan Boyd-Graber, and Hal Daumé III. 2016. Feuding families and former friends: Unsupervised learning for dynamic fictional relationships. In *Proceedings of the 2016 Conference of the North American Chapter of the Association for Computational Linguistics: Human Language Technologies*, pages 1534–1544.

Jure Leskovec, Anand Rajaraman, and Jeffrey David Ullman. 2020. *Finding Similar Items*, 3 edition, page 78–137. Cambridge University Press.

Christopher D. Manning, Prabhakar Raghavan, and Hinrich Schütze. 2008. *Introduction to Information Retrieval*. Cambridge University Press, Cambridge, UK.

Preslav Nakov, Doris Hoogeveen, Lluís Màrquez, Alessandro Moschitti, Hamdy Mubarak, Timothy Baldwin, and Karin Verspoor. 2017. SemEval-2017 task 3: Community question answering. In *Proceedings of the 11th International Workshop on Semantic Evaluation (SemEval-2017)*, pages 27–48, Vancouver, Canada. Association for Computational Linguistics.

Dong Nguyen, A. Seza Doğruöz, Carolyn P. Rosé, and Franciska de Jong. 2016. Computational sociolinguistics: A survey. *Computational Linguistics*, 42(3):537–593.

Matthew E Peters, Mark Neumann, Mohit Iyyer, Matt Gardner, Christopher Clark, Kenton Lee, and Luke Zettlemoyer. 2018. Deep contextualized word representations. *arXiv preprint arXiv:1802.05365*.

D. Rafailidis, P. Kefalas, and Y. Manolopoulos. 2017. Preference dynamics with multimodal user-item interactions in social media recommendation. *Expert Systems with Applications*, 74:11 – 18.

Colin Raffel, Noam Shazeer, Adam Roberts, Katherine Lee, Sharan Narang, Michael Matena, Yanqi Zhou, Wei Li, and Peter J. Liu. 2019. Exploring the limits of transfer learning with a unified text-to-text transformer. *ArXiv*, abs/1910.10683.

Nils Reimers and Iryna Gurevych. 2019. Sentence-BERT: Sentence embeddings using Siamese BERT-networks. In *Proceedings of the 2019 Conference on Empirical Methods in Natural Language Processing and the 9th International Joint Conference on Natural Language Processing (EMNLP-IJCNLP)*, pages 3982–3992, Hong Kong, China. Association for Computational Linguistics.

Simon Rodier and Dave Carter. 2020. Online near-duplicate detection of news articles. In *Proceedings of The 12th Language Resources and Evaluation Conference*, pages 1242–1249, Marseille, France. European Language Resources Association.

Maarten Sap, Ronan Le Bras, Emily Allaway, Chandra Bhagavatula, Nicholas Lourie, Hannah Rashkin, Brendan Roof, Noah A. Smith, and Yejin Choi. 2019. Atomic: An atlas of machine commonsense for if-then reasoning. *Proceedings of the AAAI Conference on Artificial Intelligence*, 33(01):3027–3035.

Lakshay Sharma, Laura Graesser, Nikita Nangia, and Utku Evci. 2019. Natural language understanding with the quora question pairs dataset. *CoRR*, abs/1907.01041.

Avril Thorne and Kate C. McLean. 2001. *Manual for Coding Events in Self-Defining Memories*. Unpublished Manuscript.

Anna Tigunova, Andrew Yates, Paramita Mirza, and Gerhard Weikum. 2020. CHARM: Inferring personal attributes from conversations. In *Proceedings of the 2020 Conference on Empirical Methods in Natural Language Processing (EMNLP)*, pages 5391–5404, Online. Association for Computational Linguistics.

Ellen M Voorhees. 2000. The trec-8 question answering track report. Technical report.

Yining Wang, Liwei Wang, Yuanzhi Li, Di He, and Tie-Yan Liu. 2013. A theoretical analysis of ndcg type ranking measures. In *COLT*.

Adina Williams, Nikita Nangia, and Samuel Bowman. 2018. A broad-coverage challenge corpus for sentence understanding through inference. In *Proceedings of the 2018 Conference of the North American Chapter of the Association for Computational Linguistics: Human Language Technologies, Volume 1 (Long Papers)*, pages 1112–1122. Association for Computational Linguistics.

Han Xiao. 2018. bert-as-service. `https://github.com/hanxiao/bert-as-service`.

Saizheng Zhang, Emily Dinan, Jack Urbanek, Arthur Szlam, Douwe Kiela, and Jason Weston. 2018. Personalizing dialogue agents: I have a dog, do you have pets too? In *Proceedings of the 56th Annual Meeting of the Association for Computational Linguistics (Volume 1: Long Papers)*, pages 2204–2213, Melbourne, Australia. Association for Computational Linguistics.

Ayah Zirikly, Philip Resnik, Özlem Uzuner, and Kristy Hollingshead. 2019. CLPsych 2019 shared task: Predicting the degree of suicide risk in Reddit posts. In *Proceedings of the Sixth Workshop on Computational Linguistics and Clinical Psychology*, pages 24–33, Minneapolis, Minnesota. Association for Computational Linguistics.

A Appendix A

Reddit post	My father passed away when I was 6 so I didn't really remember much of him but the fact that I didn't recognize his picture saddens me.
Movie characters	1. **Sisko in Star Trek: Deep Space Nine (Past Tense)** When he encountered an entry about the historical figure, passed comment about how closely Sisko resembled a picture of him (the picture, of course, being that of Sisko.) 2. **Arator the Redeemer in World of Warcraft** As Arator never knew his father, he asks several of the veteran members of Alliance Expedition about Turalyon for information and leads on Turalyon's current location. Several people then gave their opinion on how great a guy Turalyon was, but sadly, he has been MIA for 15 years. 3. **Kira in Push** The reality of a photo taken at Coney Island is the key evidence that causes her to realize that this was a fake memory. 4. **Todd Aldridge in Mindwarp** Todd shows up back in town; to him, there was a bright light one night, and he returned several months later with no knowledge of the intervening period. 5. **Parker Girls in Stranger in Paradise** However, when the operation collapsed after the death of Darcy Parker many Parker Girls were trapped in their cover identities, unable to extricate themselves from the lives they had established.
Reddit post	The black ladies I work with make me feel the most loved I've felt in years. I've had a horrible past 10 years. Childhood trauma and depression, addiction, abuse etc
Movie characters	1. **Shinjiro Aragaki in Persona 3** First of all, he's an orphan. During those two years, he began taking drugs to help control his Persona. Said drugs are slowly killing him. He has his own Social Link with the female protagonist where it becomes painfully clear that he really is a nice guy, and he slowly falls in love with her. 2. **Mami in Breath of Fire IV** Country Mouse finds King in the Mountain God-Emperor that The Empire (that aforementioned God-Emperor founded) is trying very, very hard to kill. Country Mouse Mami nurses God-Emperor Fou-lu back to health. Mami and Fou-lu end up falling in love. 3. **Emi in Katawa Shoujo** The loss of her legs was traumatic, but she learned to cope with that well. The loss of her dad she did not cope with at all. Part of getting her happy ending is to help her deal with her loss. 4. **Harry in Harry Potter** Harry reaches out, has friends, and even in the moments when the school turns against him, he still has a full blown group of True Companions to help him, thus making him well adjusted and pretty close to normal. 5. **Commander Shepard in the Mass Effect series** If the right dialogue is chosen, s/he's cynical and bitter with major emotional scars from his/her past experiences. It becomes pretty clear how emotionally burned out s/he really is.

Table 7: Excepts from Posts from Reddit r/OffMyChest to five similar movie characters. Excerpts of Reddit posts mildly paraphrased to protect anonymity.

Document-level Event Extraction with Efficient End-to-end Learning of Cross-event Dependencies

Kung-Hsiang Huang[1] **Nanyun Peng**[1,2]
[1] Information Sciences Institute, University of Southern California
[2] Computer Science Department, University of California, Los Angeles
kunghsia@usc.edu, violetpeng@cs.ucla.edu

Abstract

Fully understanding narratives often requires identifying events in the context of whole documents and modeling the event relations. However, document-level event extraction is a challenging task as it requires the extraction of event and entity coreference, and capturing arguments that span across different sentences. Existing works on event extraction usually confine on extracting events from single sentences, which fail to capture the relationships between the event mentions at the scale of a document, as well as the event arguments that appear in a different sentence than the event trigger. In this paper, we propose an end-to-end model leveraging Deep Value Networks (DVN), a structured prediction algorithm, to efficiently capture cross-event dependencies for document-level event extraction. Experimental results show that our approach achieves comparable performance to CRF-based models on ACE05, while enjoys significantly higher computational efficiency.

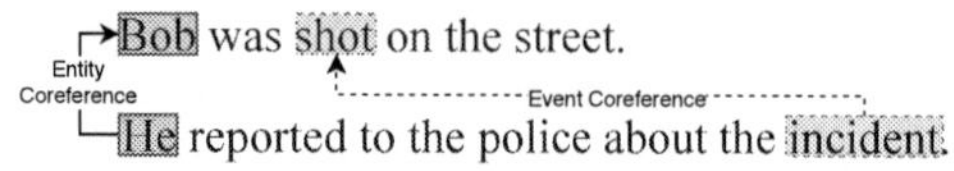

(a) Coreference Example.

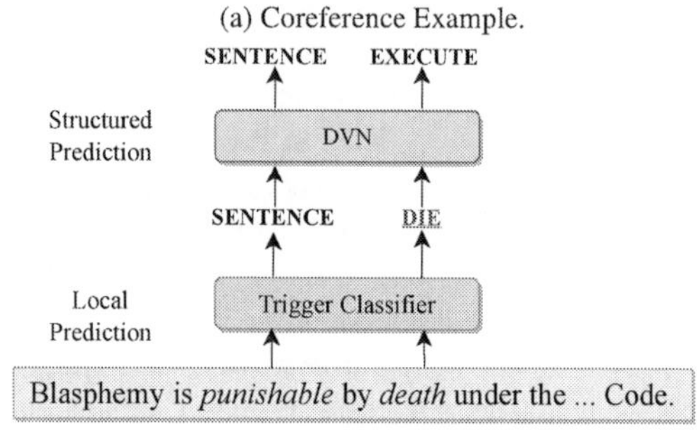

(b) Cross-event Dependencies Example.

Figure 1: (a) demonstrates why coreference resolution is essential for event extraction. In the second sentence, without entity coreference, an event extraction system cannot identify which real-world entity does *He* refer to. Similarly, *incidence* and *shot* will be incorrectly linked to two different real-world events without event coreference. (b) shows the importance of cross-event dependencies. The local trigger classifier falsely classifies *death* as type DIE. Instead, it is an EXECUTE event as a person's life is taken away by an authority. A structured prediction model that learns cross-event interactions can potentially infer the correct event type for *death* given the previous SENTENCE event is often carried out by authorities.

1 Introduction

Narratives are account of a series of related events or experiences (Urdang, 1968). Extracting events in literature can help machines better understand the underlying narratives. A robust event extraction system is therefore crucial for fully understanding narratives.

Event extraction aims to identify events composed of a trigger of pre-defined types and the corresponding arguments from plain text (Grishman et al., 2005). To gain full information about the extracted events, entity coreference and event coreference are important, as demonstrated in Figure 1a. These two tasks require document-level modeling. The majority of the previous event extraction works focus on sentence level (Li and Ji, 2014; Huang et al., 2020; Lin et al., 2020). Some later works leverage document-level features, but still extract events at the scope of sentence (Yang and Mitchell, 2016; Zhao et al., 2018b; Wadden et al., 2019). More recently, Du and Cardie (2020) and Du et al. (2020) treat document-level event extraction as a template-filling task. Li et al. (2020a) performs event mention extraction and the two coreference tasks independently using a pipeline approach. However, none of the previous works learn entity and event coreference jointly with event mention extraction. We hypothesize that joint learning event mention extraction, event coreference, and entity coreference can result in richer representations and better performance.

Proceedings of the 3rd Workshop on Narrative Understanding, pages 36–47
June 11, 2021.

Moreover, learning cross-event dependencies is crucial for event extraction. Figure 1b shows a real example from the ACE05 dataset on how learning dependencies among event mentions can help correct errors made by local trigger classifiers. However, efficiency is a challenge when modeling such dependencies at the scale of document. While some works attempted to capture such dependencies with conditional random field or other structured prediction algorithms on hand-crafted features (Li et al., 2013; Lin et al., 2020), these approaches subject to scalablility issue and require certain level of human efforts. In this work, we study end-to-end learning methods of an efficient energy-based structured prediction algorithm, Deep Value Networks (DVN), for document-level event extraction.

The contribution of this work is two-fold. First, we propose a document-level event extraction model, DEED (**D**ocument-level **E**vent **E**xtraction with **D**VN). DEED utilizes DVN for capturing cross-event dependencies while simultaneously handling event mention extraction, event coreference, and entity coreference. Using gradient ascent to produce structured trigger prediction, DEED enjoys a significant advantage on efficienty for capturing inter-event dependencies. Second, to accommodate evaluation at the document level, we propose two evaluation metrics for document-level event extraction. Experimental results show that the proposed approach achieve comparable performance with much better training and inference efficiency than strong baselines on the ACE05 dataset.

2 Related Works

In this section, we summarize existing works on document-level information extraction and event extraction, and the application of structured prediction to event extraction tasks.

Document-level Information Extraction Information extraction (IE) is mostly studied at the scope of sentence by early works. (Ju et al., 2018; Qin et al., 2018; Stanovsky et al., 2018). Recently, there has been increasing interest in extracting information at the document-level. Jia et al. (2019) proposed a multiscale mechanism that aggregates mention-level representations into entity-level representations for document-level N-ary relation extraction. Jain et al. (2020) presented a dataset for salient entity identification and document-level N-ary relation extraction in scientific domain. Li et al. (2020b) utilized a sequence labeling model with feature extractors at different level for document-level relation extraction in biomedical domain. Hu et al. (2020) leveraged contextual information of multi-token entities for document-level named entity recognition. A few studies which tackled document-level event extraction will be reviewed in Section 2.

Document-level Event Extraction Similar to other IE tasks, most event extraction methods make predictions within sentences. Initial attempts on event extraction relied on hand-crafted features and a pipeline architecture (Ahn, 2006; Gupta and Ji, 2009; Li et al., 2013). Later studies gained significant improvement from neural approaches, especially large pre-trained language models (Wadden et al., 2019; Nguyen et al., 2016; Liu et al., 2018; Lin et al., 2020; Balali et al., 2020). Recently, event extraction at the document level gains more attention. Yang et al. (2018) proposed a two-stage framework for Chinese financial event extraction: 1) sentence-level sequence tagging, and 2) document-level key event detection and heuristic-based argument completion. Zheng et al. (2019) transforms tabular event data into entity-based directed acyclic graphs to tackle the *argument scattering* challenge. Du and Cardie (2020) employed a mutli-granularity reader to aggregate representations from different levels of granularity. However, none of these approaches handle entity coreference and event coreference jointly. Our work focus on extracting events at the scope of document, while jointly resolving both event and entity coreference.

Structured Prediction on Event Extraction Existing event extraction systems integrating structured prediction typically uses conditional random fields (CRFs) to capture dependencies between predicted events (Xu et al., 2019; Wang et al., 2018). However, CRF is only applicable to modeling linear dependencies, and has scalablility issue as the computation cost at least grows quadratically in the size of label. Another line of solutions incorporated beam search with structured prediction algorithms. Li et al. (2013) leveraged structured perceptron to learn from hand-crafted global features. Lin et al. (2020) adopted hand-crafted global features with a global scoring function and uses beam search for inference. While these structured prediction methods can model beyond linear dependencies and alleviate the scalability issue, it requires pre-defined orders for running beam search. In contrast, our method addresses the above two issues by adopting an efficient stuctured prediction algorithm, Deep Value Networks, which runs linear in the size of label and does not require pre-defined order for decoding.

3 Document-level Event Extraction

3.1 Task Definition

The input to the document-level event extraction task is a document of tokens $\mathcal{D} = \{d_0, d_1, ..., d_m\}$, with spans $\mathcal{S} = \{s_0, s_1, ...s_n\}$ generated by iterating k-grams in each sentence (Wadden et al., 2019). Our model aims to jointly solve event mention extraction, event coreference, and entity coreference.

Event Mention Extraction refers to the subtask of 1) identifying event triggers in $\mathcal{D}$ by predicting the event type for each token d_i. 2) Then, given each trigger, corresponding arguments in $\mathcal{S}$ and argument roles are extracted. This task is similar to the sentence-level event extraction task addressed by previous studies (Wadden et al., 2019; Lin et al., 2020). The difference is that we require extracting *full spans* of all name, nominal, and pronoun arguments, while these works focus on extracting *head spans* of *name* arguments. **Entity Coreference** aims to find which entity mentions refer to the same entity. Our model predicts the most likely antecedent span s_j for each span s_i. **Event Coreference** is to recognize event mentions that are coreferent to each other. Similar to entity coreference, we predict the most likely antecedent trigger d_j for each predicted trigger d_i. **Entity Extraction** is performed as an auxiliary subtask for richer representations. Each entity mention corresponds to a span s_i in $\mathcal{S}$.

3.2 Task Evaluation

Evaluation metrics used by previous sentence-level event extraction studies (Wadden et al., 2019; Zheng et al., 2019; Lin et al., 2020) are not suitable for our task as event coreference and entity coreference are not considered. Du and Cardie (2020) evaluates entity coreference using bipartite matching. However, it does not consider event coreference and less informative arguments (nominal and pronoun). As a solution, we propose two metrics: DocTrigger and DocArgument, to properly evaluate event extraction at the document level. The purpose is to conduct evaluation on

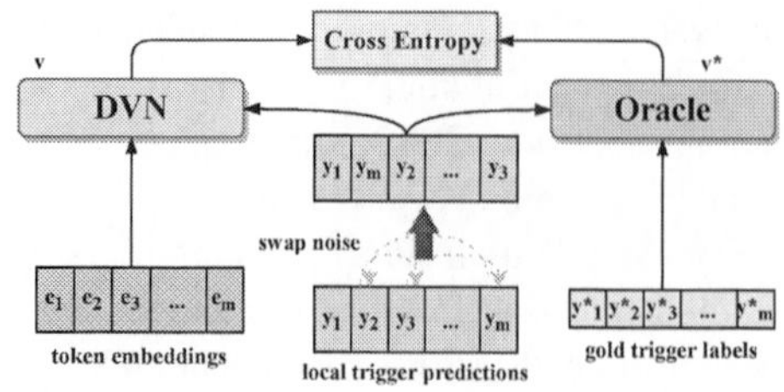

Figure 2: Use swap noise to enable DVN to continue learning from the oracle value function even when the local trigger classifier overfits on the training set.

event coreference clusters and argument coreference clusters. **DocTrigger** considers trigger span, event type, and event coreference. Triggers in the same event coreference chain are clustered together. The metric first aligns gold and predicted trigger clusters, and computes a matching score between each gold-predicted trigger cluster pair. A predicted trigger cluster gets full score if all the associated triggers are correctly identified. To enforce the constraint that one gold trigger cluster can only be mapped to at most one predicted trigger cluster, Kuhn–Munkres algorithm (Kuhn, 1955) is adopted. **DocArgument** considers argument span, argument role, and entity coreference. We define an argument cluster as an argument with its co-referent entity mentions. Similar to DocTrigger, DocArgument uses Kuhn–Munkres algorithm to align gold and predicted argument clusters, and compute a matching score between each argument cluster pair. An event extraction system should get full credits in DocArgument as long as it identifies the most informative co-referent entity mentions and does not predict false positive co-referent entity mentions.[1] Details of the evaluation metric are included in Appendix C.

4 Proposed Approach

We develop a base model that makes independent predictions for each subtask under a multi-task IE framework. The proposed end-to-end framework, DEED, then incorporates DVN into the base model to efficiently capture cross-event dependencies.

4.1 Base Model

Our Base model is built on a span-based IE framework, DyGIE++ (Wadden et al., 2019). DyGIE++ learns entity classification, entity corefernce, and event extraction jointly. The base model extends

[1]We set the weights for name, nominal, and pronoun to be 1, 0.5, and 0.25, inspired by Chen and Ng (2013).

the entity coreference module of DyGIE++ to handle event coreference.

Encoding Ideally, we want to encode all tokens in a document $\mathcal{D} = \{d_1, d_2, ..., d_m\}$ with embeddings that covers the context of the entire document. However, due to hardware limitation for long documents, each document is split into multi-sentences. Each multi-sentence corresponds to a chunk of consecutive sentences. We obtain rich contextualized embeddings for each multi-sentence of tokens $\boldsymbol{e} = \{\boldsymbol{e_1}, \boldsymbol{e_2}, ..., \boldsymbol{e_n}\}$ using BERT-BASE (Devlin et al., 2019).

Span Enumeration Conventional event extraction systems use BIO tag scheme to identify the starting and ending position of each trigger and entity. Nevertheless, this method fails to handle nested entities. As a solution, we enumerate all possible spans to generate event mention and entity mention candidates from uni-gram to k-gram.[2] Each span s_i is represented by corresponding head token $\boldsymbol{e_h}$, tail token $\boldsymbol{e_t}$ and the distance embeddings $\boldsymbol{c_{h,t}}$, denoted as $\boldsymbol{x_i} = [\boldsymbol{e_h}, \boldsymbol{e_t}, \boldsymbol{c_{h,t}}]$, following Wadden et al. (2019).

Classification We use task-specific feed-forward networks (FFN) to compute the label probabilities. Trigger extraction is performed on each token $\boldsymbol{y}_i^{trig} = \text{FFN}^{trig}(\boldsymbol{e_i})$, while entity extraction is done on each span $\boldsymbol{y}_i^{ent} = \text{FFN}^{ent}(\boldsymbol{x_i})$. For argument extraction, event coreference, and entity coreference, we score each pair of candidate spans $\boldsymbol{y}_{\boldsymbol{k}}^t = \text{FFN}^t([\boldsymbol{x_i}, \boldsymbol{x_j}])$, where t refers to a specific task. Cross-entropy loss is used to learn trigger extraction, argument extraction as follows

$$\mathcal{L}^t = \frac{1}{N^t} \sum_{i=1}^{N^t} \boldsymbol{y}_i^{t*} \log \boldsymbol{y}_i^t,$$

, where $\boldsymbol{y}^{t*}$ denotes the ground truth labels, N^t denotes the number of instances, and t denotes different tasks.

For entity coreference and event coreference, BASE optimizes marginal log-likelihood for all correct coreferent spans given candidate spans.

$$\mathcal{L}^t = \log \prod_{i=1}^{N} \sum_{j \,\in\, \text{COREF}(i)} \boldsymbol{y}_{(i,j)}^t,$$

where $\text{COREF}(i)$ denotes the gold set of spans coreferent with candidate span i, and t denotes different tasks. The total loss function for BASE is the weighted sum of all tasks:

$$\mathcal{L}^{\text{BASE}} = \sum_t \beta^t \mathcal{L}^t,$$

β^t is the loss weight for task t.

4.2 Cross-event Dependencies

A main issue for document-level event extraction is the increased complexity for capturing event dependencies. Due to larger number of events at the scope of document, efficiency is a key challenge to modeling inter-event interactions. We incorporate DVN (Gygli et al., 2017) into BASE to solve this issue given its advantage in computation efficiency.

Deep Value Networks DVN is an energy-based *structured prediction* architecture $v(\boldsymbol{x}, \boldsymbol{y}; \theta)$ parameterized over θ that learns to evaluate the compatibility between a structured prediction $\boldsymbol{y}$ and an input $\boldsymbol{x}$. The objective of $v(\boldsymbol{x}, \boldsymbol{y}; \theta)$ is to approximate an *oracle value function* $v^*(\boldsymbol{y}, \boldsymbol{y}^*)$, a function which measures the quality of the output $\boldsymbol{y}$ in comparison to the groundtruth $\boldsymbol{y}^*$, $s.t. \forall \boldsymbol{y} \in \mathcal{Y}, v(\boldsymbol{x}, \boldsymbol{y}; \theta) \approx v^*(\boldsymbol{y}, \boldsymbol{y}^*)$. The final evaluation metrics are usually used as the *oracle value function* $v^*(\boldsymbol{y}, \boldsymbol{y}^*)$. For simplicity, we drop the parameter notion θ , and use $v(\boldsymbol{x}, \boldsymbol{y})$ to denote DVN instead.

The inference aims to find $\hat{\boldsymbol{y}} = \texttt{argmax}_{\boldsymbol{y}} v(\boldsymbol{x}, \boldsymbol{y})$ for every pair of input and output. A local optimum of $v(\boldsymbol{x}, \boldsymbol{y})$ can be efficiently found by performing gradient ascent that runs linear in the size of label. Given DVN's higher scalability compared with other structured prediction algorithms, we leverage DVN to capture cross-event dependencies.

Deep Value Networks Integration Local trigger classifier predicts the *event type scores* for each token independently. DVN takes in predictions from local trigger classifiers $\boldsymbol{y}^{trig}$ and embeddings of all tokens $\boldsymbol{e}$ as inputs. Structured outputs $\hat{\boldsymbol{y}}^{trig}$ should correct errors made by the local trigger classifier due to uncaptured cross-event dependencies. $\hat{\boldsymbol{y}}^{trig}$ is obtained by performing h-iteration updates on local trigger predictions $\boldsymbol{y}^{trig}$ using gradient ascent,[3]

[2] k is empirically determined to be 12.

[3] We set h=20 for best empirical performance.

$$y^{t+1} = \mathcal{P}_{\mathcal{Y}}(y^t + \alpha \frac{d}{dy} v(e, y^t))$$
$$\hat{y}^{trig} = y^h, \tag{1}$$

where $y^1 = y^{trig}$, α denotes the inference learning rate, and $\mathcal{P}_{\mathcal{Y}}$ denotes a function that clamps inputs into the range $(0, 1)$. The most likely event type for token i is determined by computing $\texttt{argmax}(\hat{y}_i^{trig})$.

End-to-end DVN Learning We train DEED in an end-to-end fashion by directly feeding the local trigger predictions to both DVN and the oracle value function. The trigger classification F_1 metric adopted by previous works (Wadden et al., 2019; Lin et al., 2020) is used as the *oracle value function* $v^*(y^{trig}, y^{trig*})$. To accommodate continuous outputs, $v^*(y^{trig}, y^{trig*})$ needs to be relaxed. We relaxed the output label for each token from $[0, 1]$ to $(0, 1)$. Union and intersection set operations for computing the F_1 scores are replaced with element-wise minimum and maximum operations, respectively. The relaxed *oracle value function* is denoted as $\underline{v}^*(y_{trig}, y^*_{trig})$. The loss function for the trigger DVN is the following:

$$\mathcal{L}^{\text{DVN}} = \sum_{y^{trig}} -\underline{v}^*(y^{trig}, y^{trig*}) \log v(e, y^{trig}) - (1 - \underline{v}^*(y^{trig}, y^{trig*})) \log(1 - v(e, y^{trig})). \tag{2}$$

The total loss function for training DEED end-to-end is the summation of BASE loss and DVN loss,

$$\mathcal{L}^{\text{DEED}} = \mathcal{L}^{\text{BASE}} + \mathcal{L}^{\text{DVN}}.$$

Noise Injection However, in this training setup, DVN observes a large portion of high scoring examples at the later stage of training process when the local trigger classifier starts to overfit on the training examples. A naive solution is feeding random noise to train DVN in addition to the outputs of local trigger classifier. Yet, the distribution of these noise are largely distinct from the output of trigger classifier, and therefore easily distinguishable by DVN. Thus, we incorporate swap noise into the local trigger predictions, where $s\%$ of the local trigger outputs y^{trig} are swapped, as depicted in Figure 2.[4] This way, noisy local trigger predictions have similar distributions to the original trigger predictions. We also hypothesize that higher-confident predictions are often easier to identify, and swapping higher-confident trigger predictions may not help DVN learn. We experimented swapping only the lower-confident trigger predictions.

5 Experiments

5.1 Experimental Setup

Our models are evaluated on the ACE05 dataset, containing event, relation, entity, and coreference annotations. Experiments are conducted at the document level instead of sentence level as previous works (Wadden et al., 2019; Lin et al., 2020).

5.2 Baselines and Model Variations

We compare DEED with three baselines: (1) BASE, the base model described in Section 4.1; (2) BCRF extends BASE by adding a CRF layer on top of the trigger classifier; (3) OneIE$^+$ is a pipeline composed of the joint model presented in Lin et al. (2020) and coreference modules adapted from BASE. Lin et al. (2020) is the state-of-the-art sentence-level event extraction model that utilizes beam search and CRF with global features to model cross sub-task dependencies. For fair comparison, all models are re-trained using BERT-BASE (Devlin et al., 2019) as the encoder.

In addition to the original DEED model, we consider three variations of it, as discussed in Section 4.2. **DEED w/RN** incorporates random noise while learning DVN, whereas **DEED w/SN** integrates swap noise. **DEED w/SNLC** is an extension of **DEED w/SN**, where swap noise is only applied to lower-confident trigger predictions.

5.3 Overall Results

The overall results are summarized in Table 1. To measure the overall performance, a combined score (*Comb.*) is computed by multiplying DOCTRIGGER F_1 and DOCARGUMENT F_1. DEED and BCRF achieve huge improvement on all metrics over BASE, suggesting the importance of cross-event dependency modeling for our task. Adding random noise or swap noise to train DVN both improve upon the vanilla training method. OneIE$^+$ achieves the best DOCARGUMENT performance,

[4] s is empirically set to 20

	DocTrigger			DocArgument			
Model	Prec.	Rec.	F1	Prec.	Rec.	F1	Comb.
Base	71.25	60.94	65.69	43.75	48.65	46.07	17.13
BCrf	71.87	65.18	68.36	**49.84**	52.16	50.97	34.84
OneIE$^+$	71.96	62.04	66.63	49.64	**56.58**	**52.88**	35.23
DeeD	70.97	62.90	66.70	46.13	51.34	48.60	32.42
w/ RN	71.69	**65.76**	68.59	48.52	52.53	50.44	34.60
w/ SN	70.87	64.02	67.28	43.76	55.15	48.80	32.83
w/ SNLC	**73.89**	64.98	**69.14**	48.00	55.27	51.38	**35.52**

Table 1: Experimental results on ACE05 using document-level evaluation metrics. *RN*: random noise; *SN*: swap noise; *SNLC*: swap noise applying to lower-confident predicted triggers.

Model	Trig-I	Trig-C	Arg-I	Arg-C	Evt-Co	Ent-Co
BCrf	73.92	70.57	51.77	48.31	**54.02**	74.23
Base	71.97	68.17	47.95	44.57	43.95	71.88
OneIE$^+$	73.91	71.01	**57.19**	**53.89**	42.75	**77.00**
DeeD	73.68	69.62	52.35	48.24	53.85	75.77
w/ RN	72.33	68.20	51.33	48.66	49.86	74.39
w/ SN	74.19	69.54	51.27	48.10	48.94	75.60
w/ SNLC	**75.06**	**71.73**	55.12	52.09	50.11	76.98

Table 2: A breakdown of evaluation for each component in F1 evaluated on ACE05. *Trig*: trigger; *Arg*: argument;*I*: identification; *C*: classification; *Evt-Co*: event coreference; *Ent-Co*: entity coreferecne.

Model	Training (sec/ multi-sent)	Inference (sec/ doc)
Base	0.52	1.50
BCrf	2.55	9.10
OneIE$^+$	1.21	15.89
DeeD	0.71	1.52

Table 3: Comparison of training and inference time, evaluated on the training set and the dev set.

while **DeeD w/SNLC** achieves the highest DocTrigger score and combined score.

6 Analysis

6.1 Performance of Each Component

To understand the capabilities of each module, we show an evaluation breakdown on each component following previous works (Wadden et al., 2019; Lin et al., 2020) in Table 2.[5] Both BCrf and DeeD obtain significant performance gain over Base across all tasks. In terms of trigger-related tasks, *Trig-I* and *Trig-C*, **DeeD w/SNLC** achieves the highest scores. Yet, BCrf performs the best on *Evt-Co*. This explains the close performance of **DeeD w/SNLC** and BCrf on DocTrigger, as shown in Table 1. In terms of argument-related tasks, OneIE$^+$ achieves the best performance on *Arg-I* and *Arg-C*. This suggests that cross-subtask modeling can be important to improve argument extraction. *Arg-I* and *Arg-C* are much lower than the reported scores by previous studies (Wadden et al., 2019; Lin et al., 2020). This suggests the difficulty of extracting full span of pronoun and nominal arguments.

[5]These studies focus on extracting head span of name argument, while we extract full span of all types of arguments.

6.2 Computation Time

Table 3 describes the computation time of different models. DeeD only requires slightly more computation time in both training and inference time than Base. By contrast, compared to BCrf, DeeD is ~3.5x faster in training time and ~6x faster in inference time. This demonstrates the efficiency of our approach given the little increase in computation time and the significant performance gain comparable to BCrf detailed in Tables 1 and 2. We also added experiments with OneIE$^+$ as a reference, but the comparison focuses on end-to-end frameworks.

Training Method	Loss (Cross Entropy)
Original	0.3613
RN	0.7451
SN	0.2393
SNLC	0.2298

Table 4: The average DVN loss of different DEED training methods on the test set. The lower the loss, the closer between DVN and the *oracle value function*.

6.3 Value Function Approximation

To show that the performance gain of DEED is resulted from improved capabilities of DVN in judging the structure of predicted triggers, we investigate how close DVN approximates the oracle value function under different training settings. We use cross entropy loss as the distance function between the output of DVN and and output of the oracle value function on the test set. The lower the loss is, the closer between the output of DVN and the output of the oracle value function. Table 4 shows the approximation results. The SNLC variation (swap noise applying to lower-confident predicted triggers) yields the lowest loss comparing to the base model and other variations. Along with the results shown in Table 2, we show that lower DVN loss results in better trigger scores. This demonstrates that integrating noise into DVN training procedure is effective in learning better DVN and obtaining better overall performance.

6.4 Error Analysis

We manually compared gold and predicted labels of event mentions on the ACE05 test set and analyzed the mistakes made by our model. These errors are categorized as demonstrated in Figure 3.

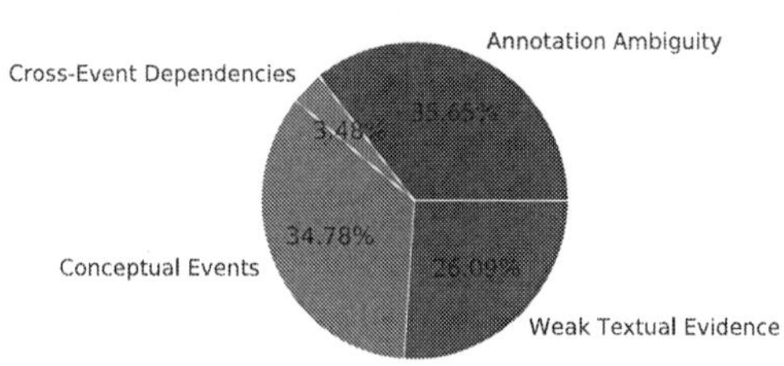

Figure 3: Distribution of errors made by DVN on the ACE05 test set.

Annotation ambiguity A significant portion of the false positive errors are caused by the ambiguity of the task. Such ambiguity can result in disagreement between human annotators. For example,

> Lebanese Prime Minister Rafiq Hariri submitted his *resignation* Tuesday and it was accepted by President Emile Lahoud.

In the sentence above, the trigger label for token *resignation* should be END-POSITION, according to the annotation guideline. Yet, it is not annotated as a trigger in gold annotation. In other cases, two sentences with similar structures contain inconsistent gold annotation, such as:

> Separately, *former* WorldCom CEO Bernard Ebbers failed on April 29 to make a first repayment of 25 million dollars ...

> *Former* senior banker Callum McCarthy begins what is one of the most important jobs in London 's financial world in September

The two examples above share similar context. However, the *former* in the first sentence is not involved with any event, whereas the *former* in the second sentence is annotated as an END-POSITION typed trigger.

Conceptual Events Another common source of false positive errors is extracting "conceptual" events, which did not happen or may happen in the future. For instance,

> ... former WorldCom CEO Bernard Ebbers failed on April 29 to make a first *repayment* of 25 million dollars ...

Our model predicts the word *repayment* as an TRANSFER-MONEY, which is true if it indeed happened, except it *failed*, as indicated in the beginning of the sentence. To handle this type of error, models need to be aware of the tense and whether there is a negative sentiment associated with the predicted events.

Weak Textual Evidence Our model commonly made false negative errors in cases where the textual information is vague.

> But both men observed an uneasy truce over US concerns about Russian *aid* to the nuclear program of Iran ...

In the above sentence, DVN fails to identify the token *aid* as a trigger of type TRANSFER-MONEY. In fact, it is hard to determine whether the *aid* is monetary or military given the context of the whole document. In this case, models have to be aware of information from other sources, such as knowledge bases or other news articles.

Cross-event Dependencies Although our model is able to correct many mistakes made by BASE that requires modeling of cross-event dependencies, as

		Within sentence	Cross sentence
BASE	Correct	161	126
	Incorrect	71	45
DEED	Correct	166	136
	Incorrect	66	35

Table 5: Trigger predictions comparison between BASE and DEED. *Cross sentence* refers to triggers with co-referent triggers that lie in different sentences.

demonstrated in Table 5, there are still a few cases where our model fails.

> ... after the city 's bishop committed *suicide* over the 1985 blasphemy law . Faisalabad 's Catholic Bishop John Joseph , who had been campaigning against the law , *shot* himself in the head outside a court in Sahiwal district when the judge ... himself in the head outside a court

In the above example, DVN correctly predict *suicide* as a DIE typed trigger, but falsely predict *shot* as type ATTACK instead of type DIE. If our model could capture the interactions between *suicide* and *shot*, it would be able to process this situation. There is still room to improve in cross-event dependency modeling.

7 Conclusion

In this paper, we investigate document-level event extraction that requires joint modeling of event and entity coreference. We propose a document-level event extraction framework, DEED, which uses DVN to capture cross-event dependencies, and explore different end-to-end learning methods of DVN. Experimental results show that DEED achieves comparable performance to competitive baseline models, while DEED is much favorable in terms of computation efficiency. We also found that incorporating noise into end-to-end DVN training procedure can result in higher DVN quality and better overall performance.

8 Ethics

Biases have been studied in many information extraction tasks, such as relation extraction (Gaut et al., 2020), named entity recognition (Mehrabi et al., 2020), and coreference resolution (Zhao et al., 2018a). Nevertheless, not many works investigate biases in event extraction tasks, particularly ACE05.

We analyze the portion of male pronouns (he, him, and his) and female pronouns (she and her) in the ACE05 dataset. In total, there are 2780 male pronouns, while only 970 female pronouns appear in the corpus. We would expect the trained model to perform better when extracting events where male arguments are involved, and make more mistakes for event involving female arguments due to the significant imbalance between male and female entity annotation. After analyzing the performance of **DEED w/ SNLC** on the test set, we found that it scores 54.90 and 73.80 on *Arg-C* F_1 for male and female pronoun arguments, respectively. Surprisingly, our model is better at identifying female pronoun arguments than male pronoun arguments.

While our proposed framework may not subject to gender biases in ACE05, whether such issue can occur when our model is deployed for public use is unknown. Rigorous studies on out-of-domain corpus is needed to answer this question.

Acknowledgements

We appreciate insightful feedback from PLUSLab members and the anonymous reviewers. This research was sponsored by the Intelligence Advanced Research Projects Activity (IARPA), via Contract No. 2019-19051600007. The views and conclusions of this paper are those of the authors and do not reflect the official policy or position of IARPA or the US government.

References

David Ahn. 2006. The stages of event extraction. In *Proceedings of the Workshop on Annotating and Reasoning about Time and Events*, pages 1–8, Sydney, Australia. Association for Computational Linguistics.

Ali Balali, Masoud Asadpour, Ricardo Campos, and Adam Jatowt. 2020. Joint event extraction along shortest dependency paths using graph convolutional networks. *Knowledge-Based Systems*, 210:106492.

Chen Chen and Vincent Ng. 2013. Linguistically aware coreference evaluation metrics. In *Proceedings of the Sixth International Joint Conference on Natural Language Processing*, pages 1366–1374, Nagoya, Japan. Asian Federation of Natural Language Processing.

Jacob Devlin, Ming-Wei Chang, Kenton Lee, and Kristina Toutanova. 2019. BERT: Pre-training of deep bidirectional transformers for language understanding. In *Proceedings of the 2019 Conference of the North American Chapter of the Association for Computational Linguistics: Human Language Technologies, Volume 1 (Long and Short Papers)*, pages 4171–

4186, Minneapolis, Minnesota. Association for Computational Linguistics.

Xinya Du and Claire Cardie. 2020. Document-level event role filler extraction using multi-granularity contextualized encoding. In *Proceedings of the 58th Annual Meeting of the Association for Computational Linguistics*, pages 8010–8020, Online. Association for Computational Linguistics.

Xinya Du, Alexander Rush, and Claire Cardie. 2020. Document-level event-based extraction using generative template-filling transformers. *arXiv preprint arXiv:2008.09249*.

Andrew Gaut, Tony Sun, Shirlyn Tang, Yuxin Huang, Jing Qian, Mai ElSherief, Jieyu Zhao, Diba Mirza, Elizabeth Belding, Kai-Wei Chang, and William Yang Wang. 2020. Towards understanding gender bias in relation extraction. In *Proceedings of the 58th Annual Meeting of the Association for Computational Linguistics*, pages 2943–2953, Online. Association for Computational Linguistics.

R. Grishman, D. Westbrook, and Adam Meyers. 2005. Nyu's english ace 2005 system description.

Prashant Gupta and Heng Ji. 2009. Predicting unknown time arguments based on cross-event propagation. In *Proceedings of the ACL-IJCNLP 2009 Conference Short Papers*, pages 369–372, Suntec, Singapore. Association for Computational Linguistics.

Michael Gygli, Mohammad Norouzi, and A. Angelova. 2017. Deep value networks learn to evaluate and iteratively refine structured outputs. In *ICML*.

Anwen Hu, Zhicheng Dou, Jian-Yun Nie, and Ji-Rong Wen. 2020. Leveraging multi-token entities in document-level named entity recognition. In *AAAI*, pages 7961–7968.

Kung-Hsiang Huang, Mu Yang, and Nanyun Peng. 2020. Biomedical event extraction with hierarchical knowledge graphs. In *Findings of the Association for Computational Linguistics: EMNLP 2020*, pages 1277–1285, Online. Association for Computational Linguistics.

Sarthak Jain, Madeleine van Zuylen, Hannaneh Hajishirzi, and Iz Beltagy. 2020. SciREX: A challenge dataset for document-level information extraction. In *Proceedings of the 58th Annual Meeting of the Association for Computational Linguistics*, pages 7506–7516, Online. Association for Computational Linguistics.

Robin Jia, Cliff Wong, and Hoifung Poon. 2019. Document-level n-ary relation extraction with multiscale representation learning. In *Proceedings of the 2019 Conference of the North American Chapter of the Association for Computational Linguistics: Human Language Technologies, Volume 1 (Long and Short Papers)*, pages 3693–3704, Minneapolis, Minnesota. Association for Computational Linguistics.

Meizhi Ju, Makoto Miwa, and Sophia Ananiadou. 2018. A neural layered model for nested named entity recognition. In *Proceedings of the 2018 Conference of the North American Chapter of the Association for Computational Linguistics: Human Language Technologies, Volume 1 (Long Papers)*, pages 1446–1459, New Orleans, Louisiana. Association for Computational Linguistics.

Harold W Kuhn. 1955. The hungarian method for the assignment problem. *Naval research logistics quarterly*, 2(1-2):83–97.

Manling Li, Alireza Zareian, Ying Lin, Xiaoman Pan, Spencer Whitehead, Brian Chen, Bo Wu, Heng Ji, Shih-Fu Chang, Clare Voss, Daniel Napierski, and Marjorie Freedman. 2020a. GAIA: A fine-grained multimedia knowledge extraction system. In *Proceedings of the 58th Annual Meeting of the Association for Computational Linguistics: System Demonstrations*, pages 77–86, Online. Association for Computational Linguistics.

Qi Li and Heng Ji. 2014. Incremental joint extraction of entity mentions and relations. In *Proceedings of the 52nd Annual Meeting of the Association for Computational Linguistics (Volume 1: Long Papers)*, pages 402–412, Baltimore, Maryland. Association for Computational Linguistics.

Qi Li, Heng Ji, and Liang Huang. 2013. Joint event extraction via structured prediction with global features. In *Proceedings of the 51st Annual Meeting of the Association for Computational Linguistics (Volume 1: Long Papers)*, pages 73–82, Sofia, Bulgaria. Association for Computational Linguistics.

Zhiheng Li, Zhihao Yang, Yang Xiang, Ling Luo, Yuanyuan Sun, and Hongfei Lin. 2020b. Exploiting sequence labeling framework to extract document-level relations from biomedical texts. *BMC bioinformatics*, 21:1–14.

Ying Lin, Heng Ji, Fei Huang, and Lingfei Wu. 2020. A joint neural model for information extraction with global features. In *Proceedings of the 58th Annual Meeting of the Association for Computational Linguistics*, pages 7999–8009, Online. Association for Computational Linguistics.

Xiao Liu, Zhunchen Luo, and Heyan Huang. 2018. Jointly multiple events extraction via attention-based graph information aggregation. In *EMNLP*.

Ninareh Mehrabi, Thamme Gowda, Fred Morstatter, Nanyun Peng, and Aram Galstyan. 2020. Man is to person as woman is to location: Measuring gender bias in named entity recognition. In *Proceedings of the 31st ACM Conference on Hypertext and Social Media*, HT '20, page 231–232, New York, NY, USA. Association for Computing Machinery.

Thien Huu Nguyen, Kyunghyun Cho, and Ralph Grishman. 2016. Joint event extraction via recurrent neural networks. In *Proceedings of the 2016 Conference of the North American Chapter of the Association for Computational Linguistics: Human Language Technologies*, pages 300–309, San Diego, California. Association for Computational Linguistics.

Pengda Qin, Weiran Xu, and William Yang Wang.

2018. Robust distant supervision relation extraction via deep reinforcement learning. In *Proceedings of the 56th Annual Meeting of the Association for Computational Linguistics (Volume 1: Long Papers)*, pages 2137–2147, Melbourne, Australia. Association for Computational Linguistics.

Gabriel Stanovsky, Julian Michael, Luke Zettlemoyer, and Ido Dagan. 2018. Supervised open information extraction. In *Proceedings of the 2018 Conference of the North American Chapter of the Association for Computational Linguistics: Human Language Technologies, Volume 1 (Long Papers)*, pages 885–895, New Orleans, Louisiana. Association for Computational Linguistics.

Laurence Urdang. 1968. *The Random House dictionary of the English language*. New York : Random House.

David Wadden, Ulme Wennberg, Yi Luan, and Hannaneh Hajishirzi. 2019. Entity, relation, and event extraction with contextualized span representations. In *EMNLP/IJCNLP*.

Yan Wang, Jian Wang, Hongfei Lin, Xiwei Tang, Shaowu Zhang, and Lishuang Li. 2018. Bidirectional long short-term memory with crf for detecting biomedical event trigger in fasttext semantic space. *BMC bioinformatics*, 19(20):507.

Meng Xu, Xin Zhang, and Lixiang Guo. 2019. Jointly detecting and extracting social events from twitter using gated bilstm-crf. *IEEE Access*, 7:148462–148471.

Bishan Yang and Tom M. Mitchell. 2016. Joint extraction of events and entities within a document context. In *Proceedings of the 2016 Conference of the North American Chapter of the Association for Computational Linguistics: Human Language Technologies*, pages 289–299, San Diego, California. Association for Computational Linguistics.

Hang Yang, Yubo Chen, Kang Liu, Yang Xiao, and Jun Zhao. 2018. DCFEE: A document-level Chinese financial event extraction system based on automatically labeled training data. In *Proceedings of ACL 2018, System Demonstrations*, pages 50–55, Melbourne, Australia. Association for Computational Linguistics.

Jieyu Zhao, Tianlu Wang, Mark Yatskar, Vicente Ordonez, and Kai-Wei Chang. 2018a. Gender bias in coreference resolution: Evaluation and debiasing methods. In *Proceedings of the 2018 Conference of the North American Chapter of the Association for Computational Linguistics: Human Language Technologies, Volume 2 (Short Papers)*, pages 15–20, New Orleans, Louisiana. Association for Computational Linguistics.

Yue Zhao, Xiaolong Jin, Yuanzhuo Wang, and Xueqi Cheng. 2018b. Document embedding enhanced event detection with hierarchical and supervised attention. In *Proceedings of the 56th Annual Meeting of the Association for Computational Linguistics (Volume 2: Short Papers)*, pages 414–419, Melbourne, Australia. Association for Computational Linguistics.

Shun Zheng, Wei Cao, Wei Xu, and Jiang Bian. 2019. Doc2EDAG: An end-to-end document-level framework for Chinese financial event extraction. In *Proceedings of the 2019 Conference on Empirical Methods in Natural Language Processing and the 9th International Joint Conference on Natural Language Processing (EMNLP-IJCNLP)*, pages 337–346, Hong Kong, China. Association for Computational Linguistics.

A Data Statistics

The statistics of ACE05 are shown in Table 6.We observe that the event coreference annotation is very sparse.

Split	Docs	Events	Entities	Ent-C	Evt-C
Train	529	4202	47569	6814	482
Dev	28	450	3423	553	45
Test	40	403	3673	577	58

Table 6: Data statistics of ACE05. *Ent-C* and *Evt-C* denote the number of entity and event coreference clusters, respectively.

B Implementation Details

We adopted part of the pre-processing pipelines from Wadden et al. (2019) for data cleaning and dataset splitting.

BASE, BCRF, and DVN are optimized with BERTADAM for 250 epochs with batch size of 16. BERT-BASE is fine-tuned with learning rate of 1e-4 and no decay, while the other components are trained with learning rate of 1e-3 and weight decay of 1e-2. Training is stopped if the dev set *Arg-C* F_1 score does not improve for 15 consecutive epochs. OneIE$^+$ is trained with the default parameters described in Lin et al. (2020). All experiments are conducted on a 12-CPU machine running CentOS Linux 7 (Core) and NVIDIA RTX 2080 with CUDA 10.1.

C Document-level Evaluation Metrics

D Development Set Performance

Algorithm 1 Document-level Trigger Evaluation Metric

```
function DocTrigger(gold events G, predicted events P)
    Let match = false-alarm = miss = hit = 0
    Let M be a trigger matching matrix.
    for g in G.triggers do
        for p in P.triggers do
            if ! SameEventType(g, p) then
                match = 0
            else
                match = Trig-I(p, g)
            end if
            M[g.idx, p.idx] = match
        end for
    end for
    assignments = Kuhn-Munkres(M)
    for i, j in assignments do
        if G.triggers[i] is null then
            false-alarm += 1
        else if P.triggers[j] is null then
            miss += 1
        else
            match += M[i][j]
            hit += 1
        end if
    end for
    return (match, false-alarm, miss, hit)
end function
```

Model	Trig-I	Trig-C	Arg-I	Arg-C	Evt-Co	Ent-Co
BASE	74.63	70.49	56.82	52.41	30.64	67.31
BCRF	76.53	72.89	59.62	54.47	33.16	68.72
OneIE[+]	76.78	73.56	**63.12**	**59.32**	35.81	**70.78**
DEED	77.11	72.31	62.42	55.80	31.90	69.57
w/ RN	75.74	70.94	61.45	55.18	34.88	68.56
w/ SN	**77.81**	**74.53**	61.90	55.52	**38.55**	69.48
w/ SNLC	76.76	72.13	62.78	57.45	31.32	**70.78**

Table 7: A breakdown of evaluation on the dev set for each model. The corresponding test set performance is shown in Table 2.

Algorithm 2 Document-level Argument Evaluation Metric

```
function DOCARGUMENT(gold events G, predicted events P)
    Let match = false-alarm = miss = hit = 0
    Let M be an argument matching matrix.
    for g in G.arguments do
        for p in P.arguments do
            M[i, j] = ARGMATCH(g, p)
        end for
    end for
    assignments = KUHN-MUNKRES(M)
    for i, j in assignments do
        if G.arguments[i] is null then
            false-alarm += 1
        else if P.arguments[j] is null then
            miss += 1
        else
            match += M[i][j]
            hit += 1
        end if
    end for
    return (match, false-alarm, miss, hit)
end function
```

Algorithm 3 Argument match called by Algorithm 2

```
function ARGMATCH(gold argument cluster g, predicted argument cluster p)
    if not SAMEROLE(g, p) or not
        not SAMEEVENTTYPE(g, p) then
        return 0
    end if
    BMA = BESTMATCHEDARGUMENT(p,g)
    w = GETWEIGHT(BMA)    ▷ The weights for name, nominal, pronoun are 1, 0.5, 0.25.
    false-alarm = |p − g|    ▷ Set operation
    return w × (1 − false-alarm / |p|)
end function
```

Gender and Representation Bias in GPT-3 Generated Stories

Li Lucy
University of California, Berkeley
lucy3_li@berkeley.edu

David Bamman
University of California, Berkeley
dbamman@berkeley.edu

Abstract

Using topic modeling and lexicon-based word similarity, we find that stories generated by GPT-3 exhibit many known gender stereotypes. Generated stories depict different topics and descriptions depending on GPT-3's perceived gender of the character in a prompt, with feminine characters[1] more likely to be associated with family and appearance, and described as less powerful than masculine characters, even when associated with high power verbs in a prompt. Our study raises questions on how one can avoid unintended social biases when using large language models for storytelling.

1 Introduction

Advances in large language models have allowed new possibilities for their use in storytelling, such as machine-in-the-loop creative writing (Clark et al., 2018; Kreminski et al., 2020; Akoury et al., 2020) and narrative generation for games (Raley and Hua, 2020). However, fictional stories can reinforce real stereotypes, and artificially generated stories are no exception. Language models mimic patterns in their training data, parroting or even amplifying social biases (Bender et al., 2021).

An ongoing line of research examines the nature and effects of these biases in natural language generation (Sheng et al., 2020; Wallace et al., 2019; Shwartz et al., 2020). Language models generate different occupations and levels of respect for different genders, races, and sexual orientations (Sheng et al., 2019; Kirk et al., 2021). Abid et al. (2021) showed that GPT-3's association of Muslims and violence can be difficult to diminish, even when prompts include anti-stereotype content.

Our work focuses on representational harms in generated narratives, especially the reproduction of gender stereotypes found in film, television, and books. We use GPT-3, a large language model that has been released as a commercial product and thus has potential for wide use in narrative generation tasks (Brown et al., 2020; Brockman et al., 2020; Scott, 2020; Elkins and Chun, 2020; Branwen, 2020). Our experiments compare GPT-3's stories with literature as a form of domain control, using generated stories and book excerpts that begin with the same sentence.

Douloti understood some and didn't understand some. But he didn't care to understand. It was enough for him to know the facts of the situation and why his mother had left ...
Douloti understood some and didn't understand some. But more, she could tell that Nenn had sympathy for one who had given up life. Sister Nenn went on with her mending ...

Figure 1: GPT-3 can assign different gender pronouns to a character across different generations, as shown in this example using a prompt, in bold, pulled from Mahasweta Devi's *Imaginary Maps*.

We examine the topic distributions of books and GPT-3 stories, as well as the amount of attention given to characters' appearances, intellect, and power. We find that GPT-3's stories tend to include more masculine characters than feminine ones (mirroring a similar tendency in books), and identical prompts can lead to topics and descriptions that follow social stereotypes, depending on the prompt character's gender. Stereotype-related topics in prompts tend to persist further in a story if the character's gender aligns with the stereotype. Finally, using prompts containing different verbs, we are able to steer GPT-3 towards more intellectual, but not more powerful, characters. Code and materials to support this work can be found at https://github.com/lucy3/gpt3_gender.

2 Data

Our prompts are single sentences containing main characters sampled from 402 English contemporary fiction books, which includes texts from the

[1] We use "feminine character" to refer to characters with feminine pronouns, honorifics, or names, and ditto for "masculine character". See §3.1 for details.

Proceedings of the 3rd Workshop on Narrative Understanding, pages 48–55
June 11, 2021.

Black Book Interactive Project, global Anglophone fiction, Pulitzer Prize winners, and bestsellers reported by *Publisher's Weekly* and the *New York Times*. We use BookNLP to find main characters and sentences containing them (Bamman et al., 2014). We define a main character as someone who is within their book's top 2% most frequent characters and mentioned at least 50 times. Every prompt is longer than 3 tokens, does not contain feminine or masculine pronouns, is from the main narrative and not dialogue, and contains only one single-token character name. This results in 2154 characters, with 10 randomly selected prompts each.

We use the GPT-3 API to obtain 5 text completions per prompt, with the `davinci` model, a temperature of 0.9, and a limit of 1800 tokens. A high temperature is often recommended to yield more "creative" responses (Alexeev, 2020; Branwen, 2020). We also pull excerpts that begin with each prompt from the original books, where each excerpt length is the average length of stories generated by that prompt. This human-authored text provides a control that contains the same main character names and initial content as GPT-3 data. The collection of generated stories contains over 161 million tokens, and the set of book excerpts contains over 32 million tokens.

3 Text processing methods

We use BookNLP's tokenizer and dependency parser on our data (Underwood et al., 2018; Bamman et al., 2014), followed by coreference resolution on named entities using the model annotated and trained on literature by Bamman et al. (2020). Pronoun chains containing the same character name within the same story are combined.

3.1 Gender inference

Depending on the context, gender may refer to a person's self-determined identity, how they express their identity, how they are perceived, and others' social expectations of them (Cao and Daumé III, 2020; Ackerman, 2019). Gender inference raises many ethical considerations and carries a risk of harmful misgendering, so it is best to have individuals self-report their gender (Larson, 2017). However, fictional characters typically do not state their genders in machine-generated text, and GPT-3 may gender a character differently from the original book. Our study focuses on how GPT-3 may perceive a character's gender based on textual features. Thus, we infer conceptual gender, or gender used by a perceiver, which may differ from the gender experienced internally by an individual being perceived (Ackerman, 2019).

First, we use a character's pronouns (*he/him/his*, *she/her/hers*, *their/theirs*) as a rough heuristic for gender. For book character gender, we aggregate pronouns for characters across all excerpts, while for generated text, we assign gender on a per-story basis. Since coreference resolution can be noisy, we label a character as feminine if at least 75% of their pronouns are *she/her*, and a character as masculine if at least 75% of their pronouns are *he/his*. The use of pronouns as the primary gendering step labels the majority of main characters (Figure 2). This approach has several limitations. Gender and pronoun use can be fluid, but we do not determine which cases of mixed-gender pronouns are gender fluidity rather than coreference error. Coreference models are also susceptible to gender biases (Rudinger et al., 2018), and they are not inclusive of nonbinary genders and pronouns (Cao and Daumé III, 2020).

Out of 734,560 characters, 48.3% have no pronouns. For these characters, we perform a second step of estimating expected conceptual gender by name, first using a list of gendered honorifics if they appear.[2] Then, if a name has no pronouns or honorifics, we use U.S. birth names from 1990 to 2019 (Social Security Administration, 2020), labeling a name as a gender if at least 90% of birth names have that gender. This step also has limitations. The gender categories of names are not exact, and the association between a name and gender can change over time (Blevins and Mullen, 2015). Some cultures do not commonly gender names, and U.S. name lists do not always generalize to names from other countries. Still, humans and NLP models associate many names with gender and consequently, with gender stereotypes (Bjorkman, 2017; Caliskan et al., 2017; Nosek et al., 2002; Moss-Racusin et al., 2012). We assume that GPT-3 also draws on social connotations when generating and processing names. We hope that future work can further improve the respectful measurement of gender in fiction.

All book excerpts and generated stories are more likely to have masculine characters, and in ones with feminine main characters in the prompt, there is a slightly smaller gap between feminine and mas-

[2]The full of list of honorifics is in our Github repo.

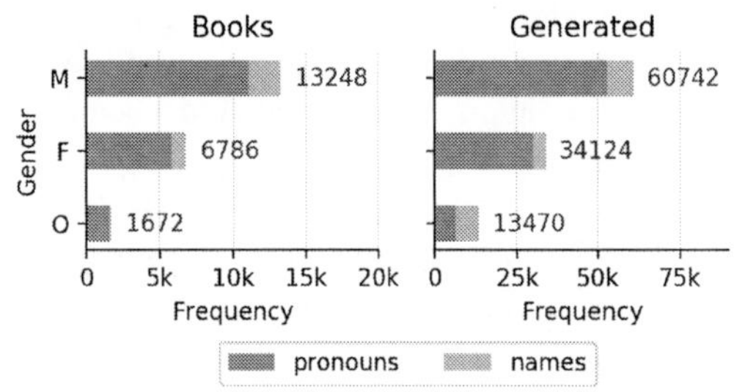

Figure 2: Frequency of masculine (*M*), feminine (*F*), and other (*O*) main prompt characters in our datasets. Bars are colored by gendering method.

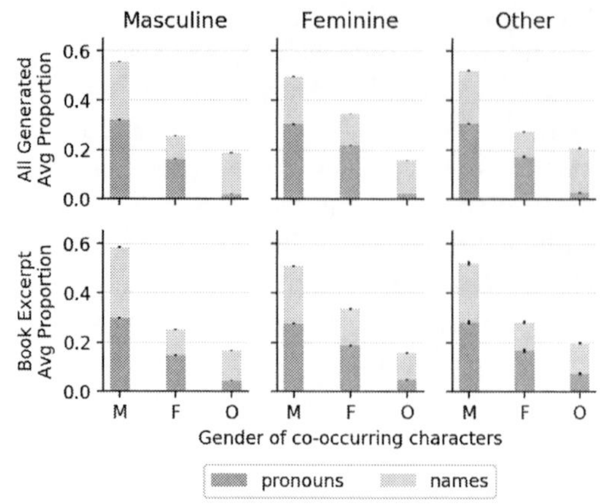

Figure 3: On average, there are more masculine characters in each GPT-3 story or book excerpt. Each column is the gender of the prompt character, and the bars are colored by gendering method. Error bars are 95% confidence intervals.

culine characters (Figure 3). This pattern persists even when only looking at pronoun-gendered characters, who are referred to multiple times and are likely to play larger roles. Our results echo previous work that show that English literature pays more attention to men in text (Underwood et al., 2018; Kraicer and Piper, 2018; Johns and Dye, 2019).

3.2 Matched stories

Prompts containing main characters of different genders may also contain different content, which can introduce confounding factors when isolating the effect of perceived gender on generated stories. We also run all our experiments on a subset of 7334 paired GPT-3 stories. Every prompt does not contain gendered pronouns and is used to generate multiple stories. GPT-3 may assign different gender pronouns to the main character in the same prompt across different stories (Table 1). We find cases where this occurs, randomly pairing stories with the same prompt, where one has the main character associated with feminine pronouns and another has them associated with masculine pronouns. In this setup, we exclude stories where the main character in the prompt is gendered by name.

4 Topic differences

Given this dataset of book excerpts and stories generated by GPT-3, we carry out several analyses to understand the representation of gender within them. We focus on overall content differences between stories containing prompt characters of different genders in this current section, and lexicon-based stereotypes in §5.

4.1 Method

Topic modeling is a common unsupervised method for uncovering coherent collections of words across narratives (Boyd-Graber et al., 2017; Goldstone and Underwood, 2014). We train latent Dirichlet allocation (LDA) on unigrams and bigrams from book excerpts and generated stories using MALLET, with 50 topics and default parameters. We remove character names from the text during training. For each topic t, we calculate $\Delta T(t) = P(t|F) - P(t|M)$, where $P(t|M)$ is the average probability of a topic occurring in stories with masculine main characters, and $P(t|F)$ is the analogous value for feminine main characters.

4.2 Results

Table 1 shows that generated stories place masculine and feminine characters in different topics, and in the subset of matched GPT-3 stories, these differences still persist (Pearson $r = 0.91$, $p < 0.001$). Feminine characters are more likely to be discussed in topics related to family, emotions, and body parts, while masculine ones are more aligned to politics, war, sports, and crime. The differences in generated stories follow those seen in books (Pearson $r = 0.84$, $p < 0.001$). Prompts with the same content can still lead to different narratives that are tied to character gender, suggesting that GPT-3 has internally linked stereotypical contexts to gender. In previous work, GPT-3's predecessor GPT-2 also places women in caregiving roles (Kirk et al., 2021), and character tropes for women emphasize maternalism and appearance (Gala et al., 2020).

We also use our trained LDA model to infer topic probabilities for each prompt, and examine prompts

topic	high probability words	all GPT-3	matched GPT-3
life	really, time, want, going, sure, lot, feel, little, life, things	0.018	0.010
family	baby, little, sister, child, girl, want, children, father, mom, mama	0.014	0.007
appearance	woman, girl, black, hair, white, women, looked, look, face, eyes	0.007	0.006
politics	people, country, government, president, war, american, world, chinese, political, united states	-0.008	-0.003
war	men, war, soldiers, soldier, general, enemy, camp, fight, battle, fighting	-0.008	-0.006
machines	plane, time, air, ship, machine, pilot, space, computer, screen, control	-0.008	-0.004

Table 1: Feminine and masculine main characters are associated with different topics, even in the matched prompt setup. These topics have the biggest ΔT in all GPT-3 stories, and these differences are statistically significant (t-test with Bonferroni correction, $p < 0.05$).

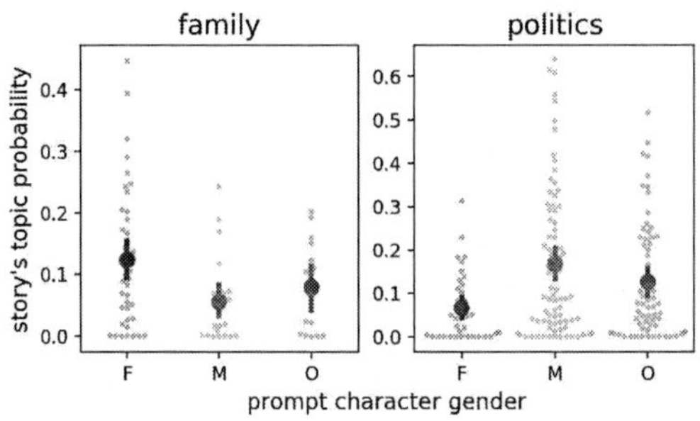

Figure 4: Prompt character gender is related the probability of a generated story continuing the *family* and *politics* topics. Each dot is a GPT-3 story, and the larger dots are means with 95% confidence intervals.

with a high (> 0.15) probability of a topic with gender bias, such as *politics* or *family*. We chose this threshold using manual inspection, and prompts that meet this threshold tended to have at least one topic-related word in them. When prompts contain the *family* topic, the resulting story tends to continue or amplify that topic more so if the main character is feminine (Figure 4). The reverse occurs when prompts have a high probability of *politics*: the resulting story is more likely to continue the topic if the main character is masculine. So, even if characters are in a prompt with anti-stereotypical content, it is still challenging to generate stories with topic probabilities at similar levels as a character with the stereotype-aligned gender.

5 Lexicon-based stereotypes

Now, we measure how much descriptions of characters correspond to a few established gender stereotypes. Men are often portrayed as strong, intelligent, and natural leaders (Smith et al., 2012; Sap et al., 2017; Fast et al., 2016b; Gala et al., 2020). Popular culture has increased its attention towards women in science, politics, academia, and law (Long et al., 2010; Inness, 2008; Flicker, 2003). Even so, depictions of women still foreground their physical appearances (Hoyle et al., 2019), and portray them as weak and less powerful (Fast et al., 2016b; Sap et al., 2017). Thus, our present study measures three dimensions of character descriptions: appearance, intellect, and power.

5.1 Method

Words linked to people via linguistic dependencies can be used to analyze descriptions of people in text (Fast et al., 2016b; Hoyle et al., 2019; Lucy et al., 2020; Bamman et al., 2013; Sap et al., 2017). These words can be aligned with lexicons curated by human annotators, such as Fast et al. (2016b)'s categories of adjectives and verbs, which were used to measure gender stereotypes in online fiction.

We train 100-dimensional word2vec embeddings (Mikolov et al., 2013) on lowercased, punctuationless generated stories and books, using default parameters in the `gensim` Python package. We extract adjectives and verbs using the dependency relations `nsubj` and `amod` attached to main character names and their pronouns in non-prompt text. For masculine and feminine characters, we only use their gender-conforming pronouns.

To gather words describing appearance, we combine Fast et al. (2016b)'s lexicons for *beautiful* and *sexual* (201 words). For words related to intellect, we use Fast et al. (2016a)'s Empath categories containing the word *intellectual* (98 words). For measuring power, we take Fast et al. (2016b)'s lexicons for *strong* and *dominant* (113 words), and contrast them with a union of their lexicons for *weak*, *dependent*, *submissive*, and *afraid* (141 words).

Counting lexicon word frequency can overemphasize popular words (e.g. *want*) and exclude related words. Therefore, we calculate semantic similarity instead. For appearance and intellect, we compute the average cosine similarity of a verb or adjective to every word in each lexicon. For power, we take a different approach, because antonyms tend be close in semantic space (Mrkšić et al., 2016). Previous work has used differences between antonyms to create semantic axes and compare words to these axes (Kozlowski et al., 2019; Turney and Littman, 2003; An et al., 2018). Let a

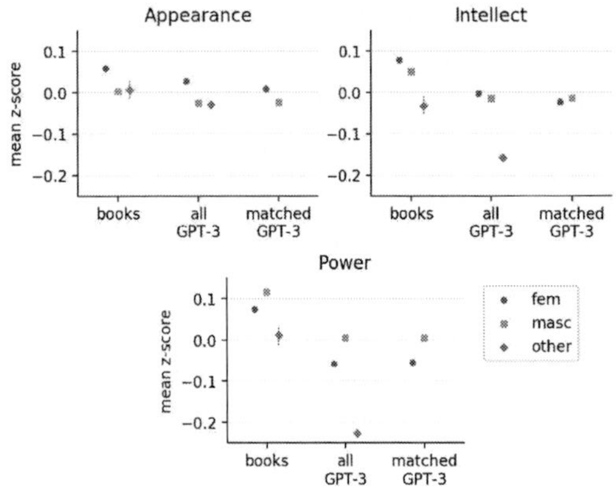

Figure 5: Appearance, intellect, and power scores across genders in books and GPT-3-generated stories. Error bars are 95% confidence intervals. All differences between feminine and masculine characters are significant (Welch's t-test, $p < 0.001$), except for intellect in matched GPT-3 stories.

be a word in the lexicon related to strength and b be a word embedding from the lexicon related to weakness. We use An et al. (2018)'s SEMAXIS to calculate word x's score:

$$S(x) = \cos\left(x, \frac{1}{|A|}\sum_{a\in A} a - \frac{1}{|B|}\sum_{b\in B} b\right),$$

where a positive value means x is stronger, and a negative value means x is weaker. We z-score all three of our metrics, and average the scores for all words associated with characters of each gender.

5.2 Results

Book characters have higher power and intellect than generated characters, but relative gender differences are similar between the two datasets (Figure 5). As hypothesized, feminine characters are most likely to be described by their appearance, and masculine characters are most powerful. The gender differences between masculine and feminine characters for appearance and power persist in matched GPT-3 stories, suggesting that GPT-3 has internally linked gender to these attributes. The patterns for intellect show that feminine characters are usually highest, though the insignificant difference in matched GPT-3 stories ($p > 0.05$) suggests that this attribute may be more affected by other content than gender.

We also test the ability of prompts to steer GPT-3 towards stronger and more intellectual characters. We examine character descriptions in stories generated by prompts in which characters are the subject of high power verbs from Sap et al. (2017)'s connotation frame lexicon, which was created for the study of characters in film. We also examine GPT-3 stories with prompts where characters use cognitive verbs from Bloom's Taxonomy, which is used to measure student learning, such as *summarize*, *interpret*, or *critique* (Anderson et al., 2001). We match verbs based on their lemmatized forms.

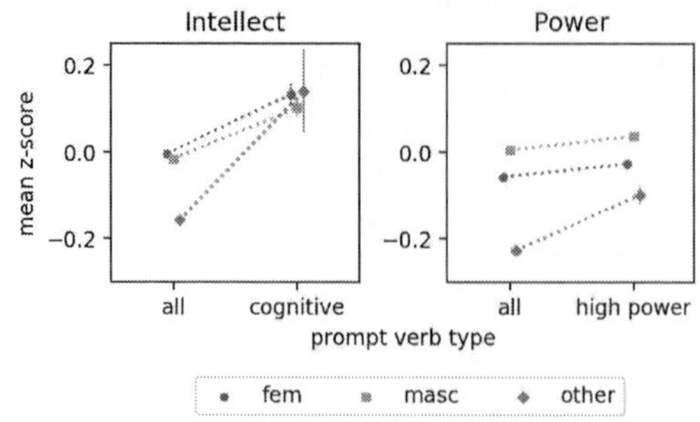

Figure 6: A comparison of stories generated by all prompts with stories generated by prompts where characters are linked to cognitive or high power verbs. Error bars are 95% confidence intervals.

We find that prompts containing cognitive verbs result in descriptions with higher intellect scores (Figure 6). Prompts containing high power verbs, however, do not lead to similar change, and non-masculine characters with high power verbs still have lower power on average than all masculine characters. Traditional power differentials in gender may be challenging to override and require more targeted prompts.

6 Conclusion

The use of GPT-3 for storytelling requires a balance between creativity and controllability to avoid unintended generations. We show that multiple gender stereotypes occur in generated narratives, and can emerge even when prompts do not contain explicit gender cues or stereotype-related content. Our study uses prompt design as a possible mechanism for mitigating bias, but we do not intend to shift the responsibility of preventing social harm from the creators of these systems to their users. Future studies can use causal inference and more carefully designed prompts to untangle the factors that influence GPT-3 and other text generation models' narrative outputs.

7 Acknowledgments

We thank Nicholas Tomlin, Julia Mendelsohn, and Emma Lurie for their helpful feedback on earlier versions of this paper. This work was supported by funding from the National Science Foundation (Graduate Research Fellowship DGE-1752814 and grant IIS-1942591).

References

Abubakar Abid, Maheen Farooqi, and James Zou. 2021. Persistent anti-Muslim bias in large language models. *arXiv preprint arXiv:2101.05783*.

Lauren Ackerman. 2019. Syntactic and cognitive issues in investigating gendered coreference. *Glossa: A Journal of General Linguistics*, 4(1).

Nader Akoury, Shufan Wang, Josh Whiting, Stephen Hood, Nanyun Peng, and Mohit Iyyer. 2020. STORIUM: A Dataset and Evaluation Platform for Machine-in-the-Loop Story Generation. In *Proceedings of the 2020 Conference on Empirical Methods in Natural Language Processing (EMNLP)*, pages 6470–6484, Online. Association for Computational Linguistics.

Vladimir Alexeev. 2020. GPT-3: Creative potential of NLP. Towards Data Science.

Jisun An, Haewoon Kwak, and Yong-Yeol Ahn. 2018. SemAxis: A lightweight framework to characterize domain-specific word semantics beyond sentiment. In *Proceedings of the 56th Annual Meeting of the Association for Computational Linguistics (Volume 1: Long Papers)*, pages 2450–2461, Melbourne, Australia. Association for Computational Linguistics.

L.W. Anderson, B.S. Bloom, D.R. Krathwohl, P. Airasian, K. Cruikshank, R. Mayer, P. Pintrich, J. Raths, and M. Wittrock. 2001. *A Taxonomy for Learning, Teaching, and Assessing: A Revision of Bloom's Taxonomy of Educational Objectives*. Longman.

David Bamman, Olivia Lewke, and Anya Mansoor. 2020. An annotated dataset of coreference in English literature. In *Proceedings of the 12th Language Resources and Evaluation Conference*, pages 44–54, Marseille, France. European Language Resources Association.

David Bamman, Brendan O'Connor, and Noah A. Smith. 2013. Learning latent personas of film characters. In *Proceedings of the 51st Annual Meeting of the Association for Computational Linguistics (Volume 1: Long Papers)*, pages 352–361, Sofia, Bulgaria. Association for Computational Linguistics.

David Bamman, Ted Underwood, and Noah A. Smith. 2014. A Bayesian mixed effects model of literary character. In *Proceedings of the 52nd Annual Meeting of the Association for Computational Linguistics (Volume 1: Long Papers)*, pages 370–379, Baltimore, Maryland. Association for Computational Linguistics.

Emily M. Bender, Timnit Gebru, Angelina McMillan-Major, and Shmargaret Shmitchell. 2021. On the dangers of stochastic parrots: Can language models be too big? 🦜. In *Proceedings of the 2021 ACM Conference on Fairness, Accountability, and Transparency*, FAccT '21, page 610–623, New York, NY, USA. Association for Computing Machinery.

Bronwyn M Bjorkman. 2017. Singular *they* and the syntactic representation of gender in English. *Glossa: A Journal of General Linguistics*, 2(1).

Cameron Blevins and Lincoln Mullen. 2015. Jane, john... leslie? a historical method for algorithmic gender prediction. *DHQ: Digital Humanities Quarterly*, 9(3).

Jordan Boyd-Graber, Yuening Hu, and David Mimno. 2017. Applications of topic models. *Foundations and Trends® in Information Retrieval*, 11(2-3):143–296.

Gwern Branwen. 2020. GPT-3 creative fiction.

Greg Brockman, Mira Murati, Peter Welinder, and OpenAI. 2020. OpenAI API. OpenAI Blog.

Tom Brown, Benjamin Mann, Nick Ryder, Melanie Subbiah, Jared D Kaplan, Prafulla Dhariwal, Arvind Neelakantan, Pranav Shyam, Girish Sastry, Amanda Askell, Sandhini Agarwal, Ariel Herbert-Voss, Gretchen Krueger, Tom Henighan, Rewon Child, Aditya Ramesh, Daniel Ziegler, Jeffrey Wu, Clemens Winter, Chris Hesse, Mark Chen, Eric Sigler, Mateusz Litwin, Scott Gray, Benjamin Chess, Jack Clark, Christopher Berner, Sam McCandlish, Alec Radford, Ilya Sutskever, and Dario Amodei. 2020. Language models are few-shot learners. In *Advances in Neural Information Processing Systems*, volume 33, pages 1877–1901. Curran Associates, Inc.

Aylin Caliskan, Joanna J. Bryson, and Arvind Narayanan. 2017. Semantics derived automatically from language corpora contain human-like biases. *Science*, 356(6334):183–186.

Yang Trista Cao and Hal Daumé III. 2020. Toward gender-inclusive coreference resolution. In *Proceedings of the 58th Annual Meeting of the Association for Computational Linguistics*, pages 4568–4595, Online. Association for Computational Linguistics.

Elizabeth Clark, Anne Spencer Ross, Chenhao Tan, Yangfeng Ji, and Noah A. Smith. 2018. Creative writing with a machine in the loop: Case studies on slogans and stories. In *23rd International Conference on Intelligent User Interfaces*, IUI '18, page 329–340, New York, NY, USA. Association for Computing Machinery.

Katherine Elkins and Jon Chun. 2020. Can GPT-3 pass a writer's Turing Test? *Journal of Cultural Analytics*.

Ethan Fast, Binbin Chen, and Michael S Bernstein. 2016a. Empath: Understanding topic signals in large-scale text. In *Proceedings of the 2016 CHI Conference on Human Factors in Computing Systems*, pages 4647–4657.

Ethan Fast, Tina Vachovsky, and Michael Bernstein. 2016b. Shirtless and dangerous: Quantifying linguistic signals of gender bias in an online fiction writing community. In *Proceedings of the International AAAI Conference on Web and Social Media*, volume 10.

Eva Flicker. 2003. Between brains and breasts—women scientists in fiction film: On the marginalization and sexualization of scientific competence. *Public Understanding of Science*, 12(3):307–318.

Dhruvil Gala, Mohammad Omar Khursheed, Hannah Lerner, Brendan O'Connor, and Mohit Iyyer. 2020. Analyzing gender bias within narrative tropes. In *Proceedings of the Fourth Workshop on Natural Language Processing and Computational Social Science*, pages 212–217, Online. Association for Computational Linguistics.

Andrew Goldstone and Ted Underwood. 2014. The quiet transformations of literary studies: What thirteen thousand scholars could tell us. *New Literary History*, 45(3):359–384.

Alexander Miserlis Hoyle, Lawrence Wolf-Sonkin, Hanna Wallach, Isabelle Augenstein, and Ryan Cotterell. 2019. Unsupervised discovery of gendered language through latent-variable modeling. In *Proceedings of the 57th Annual Meeting of the Association for Computational Linguistics*, pages 1706–1716, Florence, Italy. Association for Computational Linguistics.

Sherrie A. Inness. 2008. *Geek Chic: Smart Women in Popular Culture*. Palgrave Macmillan.

Brendan T. Johns and Melody Dye. 2019. Gender bias at scale: Evidence from the usage of personal names. *Behavior Research Methods*, 51(4).

Hannah Kirk, Yennie Jun, Haider Iqbal, Elias Benussi, Filippo Volpin, Frederic A. Dreyer, Aleksandar Shtedritski, and Yuki M. Asano. 2021. How true is gpt-2? an empirical analysis of intersectional occupational biases.

Austin C. Kozlowski, Matt Taddy, and James A. Evans. 2019. The geometry of culture: Analyzing the meanings of class through word embeddings. *American Sociological Review*, 84(5):905–949.

Eve Kraicer and Andrew Piper. 2018. Social characters: The hierarchy of gender in contemporary English-language fiction. *Cultural Analytics*.

Max Kreminski, Melanie Dickinson, Michael Mateas, and Noah Wardrip-Fruin. 2020. Why are we like this?: The AI architecture of a co-creative storytelling game. In *International Conference on the Foundations of Digital Games*, FDG '20, New York, NY, USA. Association for Computing Machinery.

Brian Larson. 2017. Gender as a variable in natural-language processing: Ethical considerations. In *Proceedings of the First ACL Workshop on Ethics in Natural Language Processing*, pages 1–11, Valencia, Spain. Association for Computational Linguistics.

Marilee Long, Jocelyn Steinke, Brooks Applegate, Maria Knight Lapinski, Marne J. Johnson, and Sayani Ghosh. 2010. Portrayals of male and female scientists in television programs popular among middle school-age children. *Science Communication*, 32(3):356–382.

Li Lucy, Dorottya Demszky, Patricia Bromley, and Dan Jurafsky. 2020. Content analysis of textbooks via natural language processing: Findings on gender, race, and ethnicity in Texas U.S. history textbooks. *AERA Open*, 6(3):2332858420940312.

Tomas Mikolov, Greg Corrado, Kai Chen, and Jeffrey Dean. 2013. Efficient estimation of word representations in vector space. In *Proceedings of the International Conference on Learning Representations (ICLR)*, pages 1–12.

Corinne A. Moss-Racusin, John F. Dovidio, Victoria L. Brescoll, Mark J. Graham, and Jo Handelsman. 2012. Science faculty's subtle gender biases favor male students. *Proceedings of the National Academy of Sciences*, 109(41):16474–16479.

Nikola Mrkšić, Diarmuid Ó Séaghdha, Blaise Thomson, Milica Gašić, Lina M. Rojas-Barahona, Pei-Hao Su, David Vandyke, Tsung-Hsien Wen, and Steve Young. 2016. Counter-fitting word vectors to linguistic constraints. In *Proceedings of the 2016 Conference of the North American Chapter of the Association for Computational Linguistics: Human Language Technologies*, pages 142–148, San Diego, California. Association for Computational Linguistics.

Brian A Nosek, Mahzarin R Banaji, and Anthony G Greenwald. 2002. Harvesting implicit group attitudes and beliefs from a demonstration web site. *Group Dynamics: Theory, Research, and Practice*, 6(1):101.

Rita Raley and Minh Hua. 2020. Playing with unicorns: AI dungeon and citizen NLP. *Digital Humanities Quarterly*, 14(4).

Rachel Rudinger, Jason Naradowsky, Brian Leonard, and Benjamin Van Durme. 2018. Gender bias in coreference resolution. In *Proceedings of the 2018 Conference of the North American Chapter of the Association for Computational Linguistics: Human Language Technologies, Volume 2 (Short Papers)*, pages 8–14, New Orleans, Louisiana. Association for Computational Linguistics.

Maarten Sap, Marcella Cindy Prasettio, Ari Holtzman, Hannah Rashkin, and Yejin Choi. 2017. Connotation frames of power and agency in modern films. In *Proceedings of the 2017 Conference on Empirical Methods in Natural Language Processing*, pages 2329–2334, Copenhagen, Denmark. Association for Computational Linguistics.

Kevin Scott. 2020. Microsoft teams up with OpenAI to exclusively license GPT-3 language model. The Official Microsoft Blog.

Emily Sheng, Kai-Wei Chang, Prem Natarajan, and Nanyun Peng. 2020. Towards Controllable Biases in Language Generation. In *Findings of the Association for Computational Linguistics: EMNLP 2020*, pages 3239–3254, Online. Association for Computational Linguistics.

Emily Sheng, Kai-Wei Chang, Premkumar Natarajan, and Nanyun Peng. 2019. The woman worked as a babysitter: On biases in language generation. In *Proceedings of the 2019 Conference on Empirical Methods in Natural Language Processing and the 9th International Joint Conference on Natural Language Processing (EMNLP-IJCNLP)*, pages 3407–3412, Hong Kong, China. Association for Computational Linguistics.

Vered Shwartz, Rachel Rudinger, and Oyvind Tafjord. 2020. "you are grounded!": Latent name artifacts in pre-trained language models. In *Proceedings of the 2020 Conference on Empirical Methods in Natural Language Processing (EMNLP)*, pages 6850–6861, Online. Association for Computational Linguistics.

Stacy L Smith, Marc Choueiti, Ashley Prescott, and Katherine Pieper. 2012. Gender roles & occupations: A look at character attributes and job-related aspirations in film and television. *Geena Davis Institute on Gender in Media*, pages 1–46.

Social Security Administration. 2020. Popular baby names: Beyond the top 1000 names. National Data.

Peter D. Turney and Michael L. Littman. 2003. Measuring praise and criticism: Inference of semantic orientation from association. *ACM Trans. Inf. Syst.*, 21(4):315–346.

William E Underwood, David Bamman, and Sabrina Lee. 2018. The transformation of gender in English-language fiction. *Journal of Cultural Analytics*, 1(1).

Eric Wallace, Shi Feng, Nikhil Kandpal, Matt Gardner, and Sameer Singh. 2019. Universal adversarial triggers for attacking and analyzing NLP. In *Proceedings of the 2019 Conference on Empirical Methods in Natural Language Processing and the 9th International Joint Conference on Natural Language Processing (EMNLP-IJCNLP)*, pages 2153–2162, Hong Kong, China. Association for Computational Linguistics.

Transformer-based Screenplay Summarization Using Augmented Learning Representation with Dialogue Information

Myungji Lee[1] **Hongseok Kwon**[2] **Jaehun Shin**[1]
WonKee Lee[1] **Baikjin Jung**[1] **Jong-Hyeok Lee**[1 2]
[1]Department of Computer Science and Engineering
[2]Graduate School of Artificial Intelligence
POSTECH, Republic of Korea
{mjlee7, hkwon, jaehun.shin}@postech.ac.kr
{wklee, bjjung, jhlee}@postech.ac.kr

Abstract

Screenplay summarization is the task of extracting informative scenes from a screenplay. The screenplay contains turning point (TP) events that change the story direction and thus define the story structure decisively. Accordingly, this task can be defined as the TP identification task. We suggest using dialogue information, one attribute of screenplays, motivated by previous work that discovered that TPs have a relation with dialogues appearing in screenplays. To teach a model this characteristic, we add a dialogue feature to the input embedding. Moreover, in an attempt to improve the model architecture of previous studies, we replace LSTM with Transformer. We observed that the model can better identify TPs in a screenplay by using dialogue information and that a model adopting Transformer outperforms LSTM-based models.

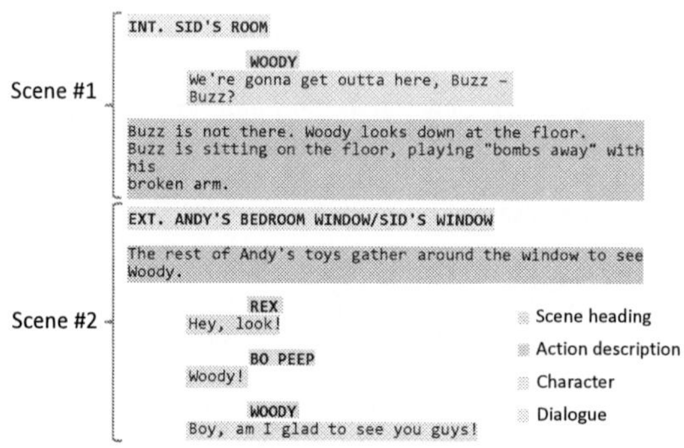

Figure 1: An excerpt from "Toy Story." A screenplay consists of scenes. A scene is an event that takes place at the same time or place. Every scene starts with a scene heading (starts with "INT." or "EXT.") and is followed by action descriptions and dialogues. 'Scene heading' denotes when and where actions take place. 'Action description' explains who and what are in the scene. 'Character' is the speaker. 'Dialogue' is a spoken utterance.

1 Introduction

Text summarization is one major task in NLP that seeks to produce concise texts containing only the essential information in the original texts. Although most researches have been focusing on summarizing news articles (Narayan et al., 2018; See et al., 2017), as various contents with different structures increase these days, there has been growing interests in applying text summarization to various domains, including social media (Sharifi et al., 2010; Kim and Monroy-Hernandez, 2016), dialogue (Goo and Chen, 2018), scientific articles (Cohan and Goharian, 2017; Yasunaga et al., 2019), books (Mihalcea and Ceylan, 2007), screenplays (or scripts) (Gorinski and Lapata, 2015; Papalampidi et al., 2020a). Among them, this paper focuses on screenplay summarization.

A screenplay is a type of literary text, which typically contains around 120 pages and has a strictly structured format (Figure 1). It usually contains various storytelling elements, such as a story, dialogues, characters' actions, and what the camera sees, thereby elaborating a complex story. In a real-life situation, filmmakers and directors hire script readers to select a script that seems to be a popular movie among numerous candidate scripts. They create a coverage per script, a report of about four pages containing a logline (the indicative summary), a synopsis (the informative summary), recommendations, ratings, and comments.

The goal of screenplay summarization is to help speeding up script browsing; to provide an overview of the script's contents and storyline; and to reduce the reading time (Gorinski and Lapata, 2015). As shown in Figure 2, to make this long narrative-text summarization feasible, early work in screenplay summarization (Gorinski and Lapata, 2015; Papalampidi et al., 2020a) defined the task as extracting a sequence of scenes that represents informative summary (i.e., scene-level extractive summarization).

To this end, Papalampidi et al. (2019, 2020b)

Proceedings of the 3rd Workshop on Narrative Understanding, pages 56–61
June 11, 2021.

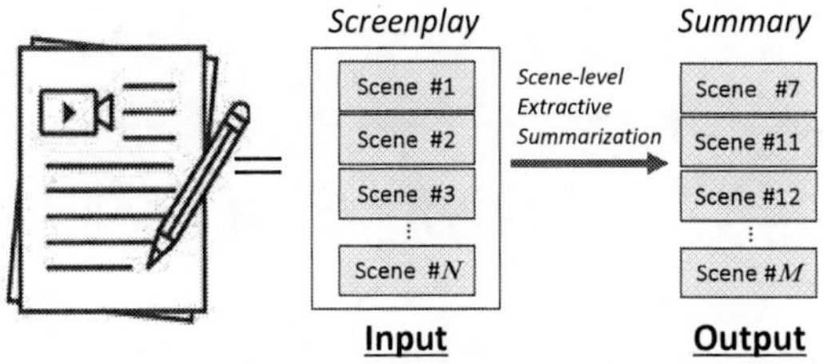

Figure 2: Screenplay summarization is defined as scene-level extractive summarization (Gorinski and Lapata, 2015; Papalampidi et al., 2020a).

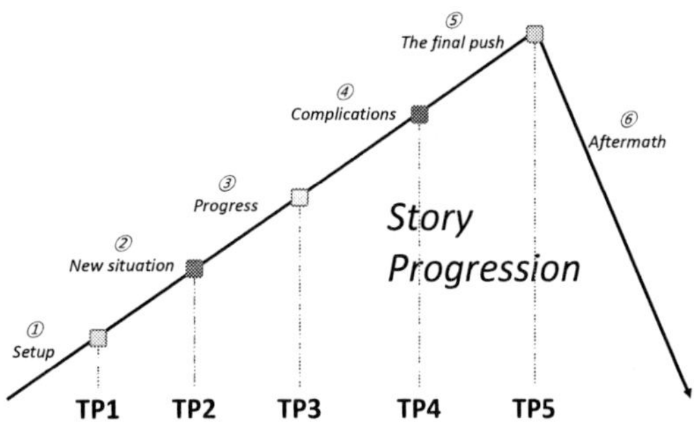

Figure 3: A well-structured story consists of six stages. TPs divide a story into multiple sections and define the screenplay's structure. There are five TPs in a story (Cutting, 2016; Hauge, 2017; Papalampidi et al., 2019).

assumed that such scenes compose a set of events, called turning points (TPs), which change the story's direction and thus determine the progression of the story (Figure 3). The definition of each TP is shown in Table 1.

Following their assumption, we propose two methods to identify TPs better: 1) we suggest using dialogue information included in screenplays (Figure 1) as a training feature, considering one previous study revealed that there is a relation between TPs and the frequency of conversations (Cutting, 2016) in a screenplay; 2) we attempt to use Transformer (Vaswani et al., 2017) instead of LSTM, which have been dominantly used in previous studies (Papalampidi et al., 2019, 2020b), because Transformer has generally shown to be beneficial in capturing long-term dependencies; we can expect that Transformer will summarize long and complex screenplays better.

TP1: Opportunity
Introductory event that occurs after presentation of setting and background of main characters
TP2: Change of Plans
Main goal of story is defined; action begins to increase
TP3: Point of No Return
Event that pushes the main characters to fully commit to their goal
TP4: Major Setback
Event where everything falls apart, temporarily or permanently
TP5: Climax
Final event of the main story, moment of resolution and "biggest spoiler"

Table 1: Definition of TPs (Papalampidi et al., 2019).

2 Background and Related Work

2.1 Topic-Aware Model

Topic-Aware Model (TAM) (Papalampidi et al., 2019) is one screenplay summarization model that identifies TPs to use them for an informative summary. The key feature of this model is that it takes sentence-level inputs and uses Bi-LSTM to generate their latent representations; it produces scene representations by applying self-attention to the sentence representations belonging to each scene and applying a context-interaction layer to capture the similarity among scenes. At last, TPs are selected among all scene representations. Our proposed model is also inspired by this work, and our work aims to improve this study.

2.2 GraphTP

Another TP identification model is GraphTP (Papalampidi et al., 2020b), which uses Bi-LSTM and Graph Convolution Network (GCN) (Duvenaud et al., 2015) to encode direct interactions among scenes, thereby better capturing long-term dependencies. Specifically, they represent a screenplay as a sparse graph, and then the GCN produces scene representations that reflect information of neighboring scenes. It shows comparable performance with TAM. In our experiments, we adopt TAM and GraphTP as baselines.

3 Method

3.1 Input Augmentation

Recall that screenplay summarization can be defined as identifying TPs, where the story stage's transition occurs. Therefore, we suggest using dialogue information related to the story stage's transition to identify TPs better. The motivation for this method is that a previous study (Cutting, 2016) that analyzed movies found that there is a pattern in which the frequency of conversations changes according to the story stage (Figure 3); there are few conversations until the end of the setup; then the frequency of conversations stay constant for the progress and complication; and finally, it decreases during the beginning of the final push but increases again in the aftermath. This study implies that dialogue information can be a good hint to capture screenplays' story stage transition. However, to our knowledge, there has been no previous work that attempts to utilize such information for screenplay summarization, that is, most previous studies (Papalampidi et al., 2019, 2020b) do not consider employing various elements included in a screenplay.

We expect that adding dialogue information as an additional training feature will help a model predict TP scenes from screenplays better. Therefore, we first extract the binary label d_i from a screenplay by inspecting whether a specific sentence is notated as a dialogue. We then concatenated the sentence embedding (x_i) and the binary label (d_i) to design a new augmented input $[x_i; d_i]$.

3.2 Architecture

It has been generally known that RNN-based architectures, which were used also in aforementioned previous studies (Papalampidi et al., 2019, 2020b), do not capture long-range dependencies well due to the vanishing gradient problem. Also in the case of screenplay summarization, because screenplays are normally long and complex, we speculate that there is a limit to generating a summary by using LSTM. Therefore, we propose a screenplay-summarization model to which Transformer (Vaswani et al., 2017) is applied, which is widely used for various NLP tasks and well known for having less computational complexity and better capturing long-term dependencies.

In detail, we propose a hierarchical screenplay encoder using Transformer (Figure 4). First, it receives a sentence-level input; we use Universal

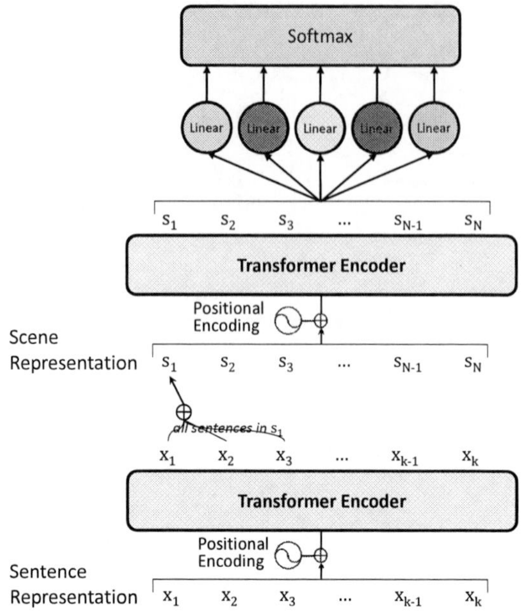

Figure 4: Proposed architecture using Transformer encoders.

Sentence Encoder (USE) (Cer et al., 2018) as in TAM. After the sentence representations become contextualized by the first Transformer encoder, all the sentence representations belonging to the scene are added up to form the scene representation that is fed into the second Transformer encoder. The second Transformer encoder produces the final scene vectors and inputs them into five different linear layers, one classifier per TP, each of which projects the vectors to a scalar value. Lastly, a softmax layer produces five probability distributions over all scenes that indicate how relevant each scene is to the TPs. We then select one scene with the highest probability per TP; each selected scene joins together with its neighbors into three consecutive scenes, which compose the final summary.

4 Experiments

4.1 Dataset

For both training and evaluating our model, we use TRIPOD (Papalampidi et al., 2019) dataset. This dataset contains screenplays and their TPs; the TPs in the test set are manually annotated by human experts whereas those in the training set are pseudo-TPs. Statistics of the dataset are presented in Table 2.

TRIPOD	Train	Test
screenplays	84	15
scenes	11,320	2,083
turning points	420	75
per screenplay		
tokens	23.0k (6.6)	20.9k (4.5)
sentences	3.0k (0.9)	2.8k (0.6)
scenes	133.0 (61.1)	138.9 (50.7)
per scene		
tokens	173.0 (235.0)	150.5 (198.3)
sentences	22.2 (31.5)	19.9 (26.9)
sentence tokens	7.8 (6.0)	7.6 (6.4)

Table 2: Statistics of TRIPOD (Papalampidi et al., 2019).

4.2 Experimental Setting

For our experiments, we adapted source codes in two repositories[1] [2] Papalampidi et al. (2020b); Liu and Lapata (2019) to implement our model. We set the training hyperparameters as follows: $L = 1$, $H = 128$, $A = 4$, and $P_{drop} = 0.0$, where L is the number of layers, H is the hidden size, A is the number of heads, and P_{drop} is the dropout rate. We consider two previous methods that receive raw sentence representations as inputs as the baseline systems: TAM (Papalampidi et al., 2019) and GraphTP (Papalampidi et al., 2020b). During training, because TRIPOD does not contain a validation set, we conducted n-fold cross-validation with $n = 5$ to extract the validation set from the existing test set. Finally, we averaged out the test results of the five models to obtain the final test results.

4.3 Evaluation Metric

To evaluate our model, we used the TP identification evaluation metrics proposed by Papalampidi et al. (2019): Total Agreement (TA), Partial Agreement (PA), and Distance (D). Those Metrics are defined as follows.

TA is the ratio of TP scenes that are correctly identified (Eq. 1). In the equation, S_i is a set of scenes that is predicted as a certain TP in a screenplay, G_i is the ground-truth set of scenes corresponding to that TP event, T is the number of TPs, in our case $T = 5$, and L is the number of

[1] https://github.com/ppapalampidi/GraphTP

[2] https://github.com/nlpyang/PreSumm

Input	Model	TA ↑	PA ↑	D ↓
sentence	TAM	8.15	9.33	10.59
	GraphTP	7.41	**10.67**	9.24
	Transformer	**10.37**	**10.67**	**9.12**
sentence + dialogue	TAM	7.41	9.33	9.97
	GraphTP	**13.33**	**14.67**	11.61
	Transformer	11.11	12.00	**9.82**

Table 3: Total Agreement (TA), Partial Agreement (PA), and mean distance (D). The first two rows are the baselines. A **boldface** score is the best score in its column.

Model	# of parameters	Training time (ratio)
TAM	40.1k	1.12
GraphTP	41.6k	1.45
Transformer	46.3k	1.00

Table 4: The number of parameters and training time of models. Numbers in 'Training time' are ratios to the training time of our proposed model set at 1.

screenplays contained in the test set.

$$TA = \frac{1}{T \cdot L} \sum_{i=1}^{T \cdot L} \frac{|S_i \cap G_i|}{|S_i \cup G_i|} \tag{1}$$

PA is the ratio of TP events about which more than one ground-truth TP scenes are identified (Eq. 2).

$$PA = \frac{1}{T \cdot L} \sum_{i=1}^{T \cdot L} [|S_i \cap G_i| \neq \phi] \tag{2}$$

D is the average distance between all pairs of predicted TP scenes (S_i) and ground-truth TP scenes (G_i) (Eq. 3, 4), where N is the number of scenes in a screenplay.

$$d\,[S_i, G_i] = \frac{1}{N} \min_{s \in S_i, g \in G_i} |s - g| \tag{3}$$

$$D = \frac{1}{T \cdot L} \sum_{i=1}^{T \cdot L} d\,[S_i, G_i] \tag{4}$$

TA and PA indicate how correctly a model predicts TPs, and D indicates how well the model has learned TP positions. It can be seen that TA and PA represent the model's prediction bias, and D represents variance, so we can suppose that there is a trade-off between D and TA or PA. Also, when the TA and PA scores are similar, it means that the model has a high accuracy.

4.4 Result Analysis

Input Augmentation It is revealed that the models trained with augmented inputs outperform those trained only with raw inputs by the TA and PA scores (Table 3). This result supports our assumption that dialogue information will be helpful in finding TPs because the TA and PA scores, which indicate whether TPs are correctly identified, have improved. As aforementioned in Section 4.3, the D score has an inverse relationship with TA in that it represents the variance of model predictions. On the other hand, TAM shows a relatively poor TA score; it seems that dialogue information hardly improves the performance of a model that does not capture long-term dependencies well. One possible reason is that dialogue information provides the model with information that the model already knows even though it does not capture long-term dependencies well. For more accurate explanation, further analyses are required.

Architecture In the case of raw sentence inputs, our proposed architecture based on Transformer outperforms the two baseline systems consistently. The result implies that the model that captures long-term dependencies well can improve the performance of summarizing long and complex texts, as we have expected. Because the model's performance has improved over the baseline by all metrics, our proposed architecture can be considered as an adequate model for TP identification, compared to the baselines. Also, even though our model contains a few more parameters than the two baselines, it has faster training speed, especially compared to GraphTP, showing a difference of almost 40% or more (Table 4).

When we fed dialogue-augmented inputs into the model, the TA and PA scores have improved. Although, when we used dialogue-augmented inputs, GraphTP recorded better performance by TA and PA, for D, our model shows much better results. This result means that the model predicts whether a given scene is a TP or not becomes more accurately whereas it does not predict well across all TPs (i.e., TP1 to TP5), but for a given scene, the model predicts certain TPs very well and some other TPs very bad. Therefore, the dialogue feature provides helpful information for TP identification that GraphTP lacks even though it is helpful for some TPs but redundant and even disturbing for some other TPs. This suggests that there is high possibility that not all TPs (i.e., TP1 to TP5) are included in the output summary. In this regard, we can conclude that our proposed model makes more confident predictions.

5 Conclusion

In this paper, we suggest using dialogue information as an additional training feature and propose a Transformer-based architecture for TP identification. Our experimental results present that dialogue information has a positive effect on the prediction accuracy on whether the scene is TP or not. However, the opposite was the case for the sequence-based model; further analyses are needed. In addition, the results indicate that using Transformer instead of LSTM significantly improves the overall performance in identifying TP scenes by encoding long-term dependencies among scenes better. We believe that using unique attributes in screenplays, such as dialogues, can help improving the model performance and when summarizing texts that have complex structures including screenplays, Transformer , which handles long histories robustly, is effective. In the future, we plan to go through the human evaluating process to see how dialogue information affects the output summary's informativeness, especially which one is identified better than another, and how the trade-off among automatic evaluation metrics affects the summary output.

Acknowledgement

We appreciate all of the reviewers giving their invaluable comments on this paper. This work was supported by Institute of Information & communications Technology Planning & Evaluation (IITP) grant funded by the Korea government (MSIT) (No.2019-0-01906, Artificial Intelligence Graduate School Program (POSTECH)).

References

Daniel Cer, Yinfei Yang, Sheng yi Kong, Nan Hua, Nicole Limtiaco, Rhomni St. John, Noah Constant, Mario Guajardo-Cespedes, Steve Yuan, Chris Tar, Yun-Hsuan Sung, Brian Strope, and Ray Kurzweil. 2018. Universal sentence encoder.

Arman Cohan and Nazli Goharian. 2017. Scientific document summarization via citation contextualization and scientific discourse. *International Journal on Digital Libraries*, 19:287–303.

James E. Cutting. 2016. Narrative theory and the dynamics of popular movies. *Psychonomic Bulletin Review*, 23:1713—-1743.

David Duvenaud, Dougal Maclaurin, Jorge Aguilera-Iparraguirre, Rafael Gómez-Bombarelli, Timothy Hirzel, Alán Aspuru-Guzik, and Ryan P. Adams. 2015. Convolutional networks on graphs for learning molecular fingerprints.

C. Goo and Y. Chen. 2018. Abstractive dialogue summarization with sentence-gated modeling optimized by dialogue acts. In *2018 IEEE Spoken Language Technology Workshop (SLT)*, pages 735–742.

Philip John Gorinski and Mirella Lapata. 2015. Movie script summarization as graph-based scene extraction. In *Proceedings of the 2015 Conference of the North American Chapter of the Association for Computational Linguistics: Human Language Technologies*, pages 1066–1076, Denver, Colorado. Association for Computational Linguistics.

Michael Hauge. 2017. *Storytelling Made Easy: Persuade and Transform Your Audiences, Buyers, and Clients – Simply, Quickly, and Profitably*. Indie Books International.

Joy Kim and Andres Monroy-Hernandez. 2016. Storia: Summarizing social media content based on narrative theory using crowdsourcing. In *Proceedings of the 19th ACM Conference on Computer-Supported Cooperative Work amp; Social Computing*, CSCW '16, page 1018–1027, New York, NY, USA. Association for Computing Machinery.

Yang Liu and Mirella Lapata. 2019. Text summarization with pretrained encoders. *CoRR*, abs/1908.08345.

R. Mihalcea and H. Ceylan. 2007. Explorations in automatic book summarization. In *EMNLP-CoNLL*.

Shashi Narayan, Shay B. Cohen, and Mirella Lapata. 2018. Don't give me the details, just the summary! topic-aware convolutional neural networks for extreme summarization. *CoRR*, abs/1808.08745.

Pinelopi Papalampidi, Frank Keller, Lea Frermann, and Mirella Lapata. 2020a. Screenplay summarization using latent narrative structure.

Pinelopi Papalampidi, Frank Keller, and Mirella Lapata. 2019. Movie plot analysis via turning point identification.

Pinelopi Papalampidi, Frank Keller, and Mirella Lapata. 2020b. Movie summarization via sparse graph construction.

Abigail See, Peter J. Liu, and Christopher D. Manning. 2017. Get to the point: Summarization with pointer-generator networks. *CoRR*, abs/1704.04368.

B. Sharifi, M. Hutton, and J. Kalita. 2010. Experiments in microblog summarization. *2010 IEEE Second International Conference on Social Computing*, pages 49–56.

Ashish Vaswani, Noam Shazeer, Niki Parmar, Jakob Uszkoreit, Llion Jones, Aidan N. Gomez, Lukasz Kaiser, and Illia Polosukhin. 2017. Attention is all you need.

Michihiro Yasunaga, Jungo Kasai, Rui Zhang, A. R. Fabbri, Irene Li, D. Friedman, and Dragomir R. Radev. 2019. Scisummnet: A large annotated corpus and content-impact models for scientific paper summarization with citation networks. In *AAAI*.

Plug-and-Blend: A Framework for Controllable Story Generation with Blended Control Codes

Zhiyu Lin
Georgia Institute of Technology
North Ave NW, Atlanta, GA 30332
zhiyulin@gatech.edu

Mark O. Riedl
Georgia Institute of Technology
North Ave NW, Atlanta, GA 30332
riedl@cc.gatech.edu

Abstract

We describe a Plug-and-Play controllable language generation framework, Plug-and-Blend, that allows a human user to input multiple control codes (topics). In the context of automated story generation, this allows a human user loose or fine grained control of the topics that will appear in the generated story, and can even allow for overlapping, blended topics. We show that our framework, working with different generation models, controls the generation towards given continuous-weighted control codes while keeping the generated sentences fluent, demonstrating strong blending capability.

1 Introduction

Recent advancement in very large pre-trained neural language models (e.g. (Radford et al., 2019; Brown et al., 2020)) have enabled a new generation of applications that make use of the text generation capability they provide, ranging from auto-completion of e-mails to solving complicated math equations. However these very large pre-trained neural language models are also difficult to **control** beyond providing a prompt for a generated continuation. This makes very large language models ill-suited for *co-creative* tasks wherein a human works with a language model in an iterative fashion to produce novel content, such as stories or poems. Co-creative tasks require an ability to not only prompt the language model but to guide the generation with, for example, style, context, or topic constraints.

Conditional generation is a family of text generation methods that attempt to provide controllability by either directly modifying the model to accept control signals or posing constraints in the generation process. Conditional text generation techniques add an extra input feature (Ficler and Goldberg, 2017) and fine-tuning with additional information embedded (Fang et al., 2021; Hosseini-Asl et al., 2020; Keskar et al., 2019; Khalifa et al., 2020; Hu et al., 2017; Wu et al., 2020; Ficler and Goldberg, 2017; Chan et al., 2020), or by sideloading additional discriminators along with a pre-trained model, without changing base model parameters holisticly (Dathathri et al., 2020; Madotto et al., 2020; Duan et al., 2020; Mai et al., 2020).

We seek "plug-and-play" approaches to controllable text generation wherein new language models can be slotted into existing generative systems; new language models are being developed and it becomes intractable to update and retrain controlled generation architectures. Plug-and-play techniques such as (Krause et al., 2020; Pascual et al., 2020) aim to only intervene with the outputs—a vector of logits—of a generative language model. This becomes especially important as the latest iteration of very large pre-trained language models such as GPT-3 (Brown et al., 2020) restrict access to the hidden states and layer weights of models. As language models improve, they can be easily incorporated into existing, controllable generation frameworks.

We present *Plug-and-Blend* [1], an efficient plug-and-play generative framework for controllable text generation that (a) works with the logit outputs of any language model; (b) facilitates fine control of generated sentences by allowing continuous bias towards specific control codes; and (c) allows multiple control codes representing style and topic constraints to be provided in overlapping contexts. These control codes can be blended together to generate content that meets multiple style or topic constraints. We describe that these key capabilities empower latent space walking in the hyperspace of generated sentences, and show a simple content planning technique that utilizes this feature to generate paragraphs regarding user intentions in a co-authoring. We present our work in the context

[1] Code available at https://github.com/xxbidiao/plug-and-blend

Proceedings of the 3rd Workshop on Narrative Understanding, pages 62–71
June 11, 2021.

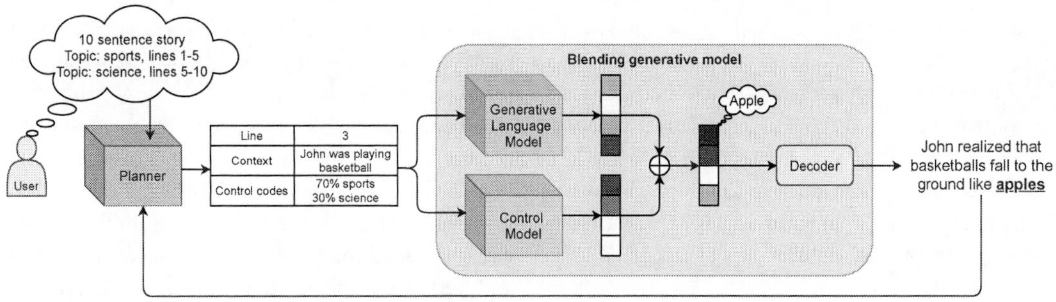

Figure 1: Illustration of overall architecture of our framework

of automated story generation wherein a human author provides a prompt as well as a high-level control specification for topics.

2 Related Work

2.1 Plug-and-Play Conditional Generation

Researchers aim for "plug-and-play" (PnP) frameworks (Dathathri et al., 2020) which can be used along an existing generative LM (referred to as the "base LM") with minimum or no interference between the PnP components and the base LM.

Comparing to non-plug-and-play methods ("white-box" approaches), these frameworks can be roughly classified into three categories. *Gray-box* approaches access and modify some non-input-output layer computations, usually the hidden representation, hence "plugging" an additional model in the middle of the base LM (Dathathri et al., 2020; Madotto et al., 2020; Duan et al., 2020; Mai et al., 2020). *Black-box* approaches including "Prompt Engineering" that aim to change the prompts fed into the base LM at inference time (Wallace et al., 2019; Li and Liang, 2021). *Guided generation* targets at building a controllable "guiding" model that shifts the output from base LM at inference time (Krause et al., 2020; Pascual et al., 2020).

The generation model we propose is an extension of GeDi (Krause et al., 2020). Adding to the complete decoupling of generation and controlling, we enhanced it with additional capabilities to support multi-topic generation with continuous weighting, supporting the downstreaming applications while keeping its capability to transfer to different base LMs.

2.2 Controllable Story Generation

Neural story generation systems train or fine-tune a language model on story data. Sampling from a language model trained on story data tends to result in text output that looks like stories as well. However, sampling from $P_\theta(x_t|x_{<t})$ (See Section 3) is uncontrolled in the sense that one does not have any influence over the output after the initial context prompt.

A number of story generation systems have attempted to condition the generation with some form of high-level plan. Storytelling systems such as (Akoury et al., 2020; Yao et al., 2019) embeds topic constraints directly into the model. These system extract a set of topics from a dataset that must be incorporated into the story. PlotMachines (Rashkin et al., 2020) allows a human user to specify topics that can be incorporated into a story in any order. Wang et al. (2020) generate a story by interpolating between a start event and an end event in a slot filling fashion, targeted the same goal. Our work differs in two ways. First, we allow blending of topics such that a single line in a story can meet more than one topic provided by a human user. Second, we have developed a black-box plug-and-play system that works with different LMs.

3 Preliminaries

Generative Language Models (LMs), specifically continuation models, take a context ("prompt") and generate a continuation by predicting the next tokens. This is achieved by optimizing the model parameters θ that best estimates the probability density of a sequence of word tokens $x_{1:T} = \{x_1, \ldots, x_T\}$ represented as an auto-regressive factorization

$$P_\theta(x_{1:T}) = \prod_{t=1}^{T} P_\theta(x_t \mid x_{<t}). \quad (1)$$

By iteratively predicting a distribution on the next token given the previous tokens, a continuation can be generated by repeatedly sampling $P_\theta(x_t \mid x_{<t})$

and attach the selected token back to the "previous" tokens for the next step.

Sequences generated this way are not controlled; To control the generated sequence, an **attribute** represented as a class variable (Keskar et al., 2019) that could describe sentiment or topics can be introduced to equation (1) to form a Class-Conditional Language Model (CC-LM):

$$P_\theta(x_{1:T} \mid c) = \prod_{t=1}^{T} P_\theta(x_t \mid x_{<t}, c) \quad (2)$$

where c represents the class variable, or "control code", that describes an **attribute** of the sequence $x_{1:T}$. However, since c and $x_{1:T}$ are entangled in equation (2), naively optimizing P_θ requires a new CC-LM to be trained.

To decouple the conditional generation component, c, from the unconditional part, $P_{LM}(x_{1:T})$, (Krause et al., 2020) proposed the GeDi framework and an algorithm to enable a separate controlling model to guide the generation process of a base language model. Instead of tackling $P_\theta(x_{1:T} \mid c)$ directly, they train a contrastive discriminator model on the side to estimate

$$P_\theta(c \mid x_{1:t}) = \alpha P(c) \prod_{j=1}^{t} P_\theta(x_j \mid x_{<j}, c) \quad (3)$$

where α is the normalization constant $\alpha = 1/(\sum_{c' \in \{c,\bar{c}\}} \prod_{j=1}^{t} P(c') P_\theta(x_j \mid x_{<j}, c'))$, and c and c' are contrastive control codes (c and not-c). At the decoding stage of the generation process, one can guide the generation by using $P_\theta(c \mid x_{1:t})$ as a posterior to the output probability distribution of the base LM:

$$\begin{aligned} &P(x_t \mid x_{<t}, c) \propto \\ &\quad P_{LM}(x_t \mid x_{<t}) P_\theta(c \mid x_t, x_{<t})^{\omega} \end{aligned} \quad (4)$$

where ω is a parameter for control strength, with larger values biasing generation more strongly towards c. CC-LMs trained this way do not require access to any internal data of the base LM, and works independently of it.

4 The Plug-and-Blend Framework

Our *Plug-and-Blend* framework consists of two components (See figure 1): (1) a *blending generative Model* that is responsible for plug-and-play controlled continuations using the control specifications; and (2) a *planner* that plans and assigns control specifications based on control sketches.

A *control sketch* is a high-level specification of what topics should be present in the story and what portions of the story each topic should approximately appear in. This provides a human co-creator the ability to guide the generator loosely, with a broad range per topic, or tightly, with a narrow range per topic. We envision a co-creative loop wherein the human user provides a control sketch and iteratively updates the control sketch based on generation results, refining the topics and refining the ranges for the topics. The user interface for eliciting control sketches from a human is outside the scope of this paper and experiments about the co-creative loop are left for future work. The next sections provide the algorithmic support for control sketches.

4.1 Blending Generative Model

The blending generative model generates the sentence continuation. It consists of two parts, a (1) plug-and-play language model and (2) a control model. Given a prompt $x_{<t}$, the plug-and-play language model produces a vector of logits $P_{LM}(x_t \mid x_{<t})$. The control model biases the output of the language model toward particular tokens associated with the topics of the control codes $c \in C$ based on the desired strengths of each topic $\omega^*_{c \in C} \in \Omega$. Together the two models iteratively find the best token x_t that reflects both natural language composition and control bias presented by c and ω. A larger ω^*_c means more steering towards the topic represented by control code c.

Inspired by the application of generative adversarial networks to latent space walking, we treat $P_\theta(c \mid x_t, x_{<t})$ (described in section 3) as a heuristic of **direction** that increases $P(x_t \mid x_{<t}, c)$ in a $|V|$-dimensional latent space, where V is the language model's vocabulary. For example, consider two different control codes c_1 and c_2 instantiating equation (4). To apply both control codes in the generation process, we use the heuristic

$$\begin{aligned} &P(x_t \mid x_{<t}, c_1, c_2) \propto P_{LM}(x_t \mid x_{<t}) \times \\ &\quad P_\theta(c_1 \mid x_t, x_{<t})^{\omega_1} P_\theta(c_2 \mid x_t, x_{<t})^{\omega_2} \end{aligned} \quad (5)$$

to combine the effect of both posterior distributions into one universal posterior. ω_1 and ω_2 in this case represents control strength for each control code, c_1 and c_2 respectively, and can be different, enabling continuous blending between topics. This process can be repeated with a set of control codes $C = \{c_1, \ldots, c_n\}$ with weights $\Omega = \{\omega_1, \ldots, \omega_n\}$.

Formally, at the decoding stage of the generation process, a control model compute controlled probability using the following equation:

$$P(x_t \mid x_{<t}, C) = \\ P_{LM}(x_t \mid x_{<t}) \prod_{c^* \in C} P_\theta (c^* \mid x_t, x_{<t})^{\omega_c^*} \quad (6)$$

where the control strengths of individual control codes are normalized with $\sum_c \omega_c^* = \omega$, where ω is total control strength.[2] This can be efficiently computed by batching input sequences appended by different control codes, with little overhead compared to the original GeDi (Krause et al., 2020) framework.

4.2 Planner

The human user provides a high-level control sketch of the story, consisting of the number of sentences, N, a set of topics, C, and a range of lines to which to apply the topic, $r := (s, e)$ where $s \leq e$. See figure 2 for example sketches. Sketches can have their range r overlap such that multiple topics can be applied to the same lines of the story.

Given the control sketch, the planner produces a control configuration C_n, Ω_n for each sentence position $n = \{0, \ldots, N-1\}$. The control configuration for each sentence is passed to the blending generative model along with previous generated sentences as prompt.

We interpret a control sketch as story arc on a specific topic, which typically contains a transition, an engagement and a phase-out, the planner should give highest control strength to the midpoint of the area, $m := (s+e)/2$, and lower strength towards the start and end of the span of the area; We capture this as a Gaussian distribution.

Formally, the following equation translates the sketch into a control configuration for each position $n \in N$:

$$\omega_{c,n}^{+} = f(\mathcal{N}(m, (\sigma/(e-s+\epsilon)^2))(n-m) \quad (7)$$

where $f(\cdot)$ indicates probability density function, ϵ is an infinitesimal, and σ is a tunable parameter representing overall transition smoothness, where higher σ grants smoother transitions in the cost of reduced topic engagement for midpoint. Since there can be multiple control sketches and they can be of the same control code, we apply each individual sketch in the order they are presented and normalize after each application so that $\Sigma_n \omega_{c,n} = 1$.

5 Experiments

For our experiments, we use the GPT2-large model fine-tuned on ROCStories (Mostafazadeh et al., 2016) as our base language model. Fine-tuning GPT2 on ROCStories results in a model that generates short stories about common everyday situations. We pair the language model with a pre-trained GeDi (which in turn is based on GPT-2-medium) trained on AG-news[3] as the guiding model. Across all setups, at generation time, we use greedy decoding with repetition penalty described in Keskar et al. (2019), and only use the first sentence generated as the output, discarding every token after it if any.

Since there is no ground truth for any generated sequence, metrics such as BLEU and other n-gram-based metrics are not applicable. This poses a unique challenge in evaluating our system, limiting us to unsupervised metrics. In this section, we report evaluation of our blending generative model from two aspects:

- Fluency: measuring how our generated sequence forms natural language; and
- Control fidelity: measuring how our generated sequence respects the requested control codes and strength.

5.1 Blending Fluency

To evaluate fluency of sequences generated by our blending generation model, we use perplexity of *base* language model. The intuition is that if generated sentences have low average perplexity when evaluated by the base LM then they are consistent with sentences we would find in the English language, as represented by the data used to train the base LM. This in turn results in fluent-appearing sentences.

To generate sequences from our model, we used 100 sentences from a held-out evaluation set of ROCStories not seen at fine-tuning time. ROCStories contains five-sentence stories; we always pick the first sentence. That sentence becomes our prompt and is paired with all possible combinations of two topic choices chosen from "Business", "Science", "Sports", or "World". These are the topics that the GeDi model are optimized for. Our control sketch gives equal blending weighting for all topics. We vary the control strength using the following

[2] This is not the only way to formalize this heuristic; We found this to be effective and efficient.

[3] http://groups.di.unipi.it/~gulli/AG_corpus_of_news_articles.html

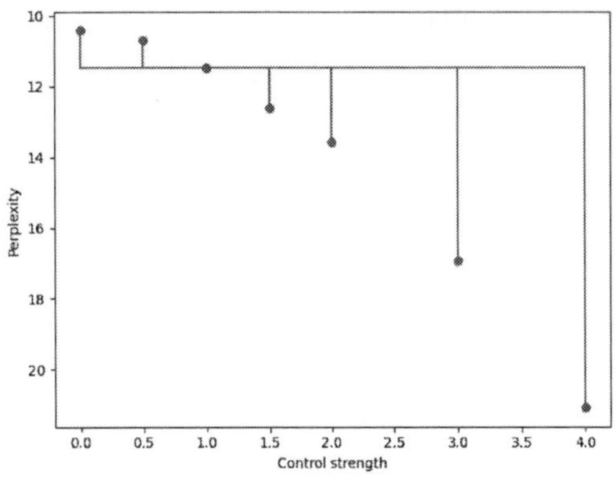

Figure 2: Perplexity (lower is better) of generated sequences with 2 topics. Baseline performance set at $1x$ of (Krause et al., 2020)-suggested control strength.

increments: $[0, 0.5, 1, 1.5, 2, 3, 4]x$, where 0 represents an uncontrolled base LM and $4x$ represents 400% of the control strength hyperparameter used by Krause et al. (2020).

Figure 2 shows the average perplexity of generated sequences, measured by the Base LM. We observe that average perplexity increases with stronger control, signaling a departure of generated sequences from what the base LM would generate, and a potential decrease in fluency. This is to be expected as the control is biasing the generated text more and more toward the use of words that are consistent with a particular topic and away from general word frequency. While perplexity increase is more or less linear in the range of 0 to 2x strength, once above 2x strength, it can be better described as exponential, hinting a stabler capability to generate fluent sentences in the region of 0 to 2x control strength.

5.2 Control Fidelity

Control fidelity is how well the generator responds to multiple control codes applied at once (see Krause et al. (2020) for experiments applying one control code at a time; we do not replicate them in this paper). For story generation, multiple control codes can be applied to the same sentence in a story at different weights. We perform experiments in a latent space walking setting, to measure content changes of generated sentences under the same prompt, same control codes but different relative control strength, in an unsupervised way.

Given a particular prompt line in a story and two control topics c_1 and c_2, we re-generate the same line multiple times under different control strengths for each topic. Specifically we set ω_{c_1} to 0%, 25%, 50%, 75% or 100% and $\omega_{c_2} = 1 - \omega_{c_1}$ to represent a range of different possible blends of topics in the same line. See table 1 for an example. Since we know the control parameters used to generate these sentences, in which c_1 receives more and more control strength relative to c_2, we expect to see sentences that are increasingly about topic c_1 and decreasingly about topic c_2. These sentences do not comprise a story sequence, but are different alternative sentences for the same line in a story under different topic control specifications.

To determine whether a given generated sentence was representative of a topic, we score each generated sentence with an off-the-shelf BART-based zero-shot classifier (Wolf et al., 2020)[4] with c_1 and c_2, in raw text form, as possible classes. We then compare the order of the sentences as determined by the classifier to the ground truth order of increasing control strength of c_1. We report the correlation of order between these two sequences using Kendall's τ-a metric. A perfectly strictly increasing classifier score will grant a τ-a score of 1 for a sequence. If the sentences have some reordering based on classification score, τ-a is reduced. A score of 0 indicates a random ordering and and a score of -1 indicates a sequence that is exactly in opposite order. Table 1 shows the classifier scores for the possible next sentences under different control strengths; the classifier scores are not monotonically decreasing, resulting in a τ-a score of 0.8.

Figure 3 shows a heat-map of the average τ-a score of sequences of sentences generated with different control code pairs and different total control strength (percentages). For each combination of parameters, 100 sequences of 5 sentences are generated and evaluated. Comparing to the baseline, which is the evaluation metric applied to order-randomized stories in ROCStories dataset, we observe universal statistical significance ($p < .01$) in improvement in τ-a metric. That is, without a control bias, rank ordering is random. As we increase the total control strength, the rank order of generated sentences more closely matches the ground truth order.

Some topic combinations (For example, Science-Sports) work better than others (For example, Science-World); the "World" category appears to include a lot of overlapping vocabulary usage with

[4]pipeline("zero-shot-classifier")

Prompt: The people gathered to protest the court's ruling last week.

c_1 = Sports ω_{c_1}	c_2 = Business ω_{c_2}	Generated Sentence	Classifier score c_1	Classifier score c_2
100%	0%	Coach Leeman was in a wheelchair and had been taken to hospital for treatment.	86%	14%
75%	25%	Coach Reebok was one of them.	65%	35%
50%	50%	The players were joined by a few of them.	84%	16%
25%	75%	The company that owns the team was fined $1,000 for violating a rule prohibiting employees from using their own equipment.	37%	63%
0%	100%	Bankruptcy Judge William H. said that the bank had failed to pay its creditors and was in default on $1 billion of loans it owed them.	24%	76%

Comparing column 1 with column 4, Kendall's τ-a $= 0.8$ for this generated sequence.

Table 1: An example sequence of sentences generated for evaluation of control fidelity. The first two columns indicate the requested control strengths for two topics, sports and business. The generated sentence results from the prompt and the control weights (all numbers are $2x$ the default control strength). The last two columns indicate the probability that each line is either Sports or Business based on a BART-based topic classifier. We expect to see the classifier score for c_1 decrease as the classifier score for c_2 increases.

the other categories. Note that a perfect Kendall's τ-a of 1.0 is likely impossible because our zero-shot topic classifier will introduce some noise to the ranking. However, the results show us that the plug-and-blend technique (a) significantly increases the likelihood that topics will be incorporated into sentences, and (b) is sensitive to blended topics.

Figure 4 shows the same experiment as above, but with a non-fine-tuned version of GPT2-large. This shows that the plug-and-blend technique works on language models that haven't been fine-tuned on ROCStories. The prompts are still selected from ROCStories, however, for comparison, but are not as representative of the untuned model. In this condition, the text generated will not read as sentences in stories. We observe similar improvements over the baseline, demonstrating the ability of our method in keeping the strong adaptation capability.

5.3 Planner Experiments

In this section, we qualitatively demonstrate the capability of our pipeline by analyzing the generated paragraphs using simulated user inputs described as sets of control sketches.

Table 2 (left column) shows three sets of control sketches with overlapping topic ranges. For example, sketch 1 requests a 10-line story that covers the topic of sports for the first 6 lines and covers the topic of science for the last 6 lines (topics overlap in the middle). For each control sketch we generate 10-line stories ($N = 10$) using the hyper-parameter $\sigma = 1$ (see Equation 7). We use a neutral prompt consisting of only the word "Recently" as the context to generate the first line or if the generator ever generates an empty line. The remainder of lines use up to 2 sentences generated for the previous context.

Table 2 (right column) shows the generated stories for each control sketch. We bold the sentence where it is most clear that the topic has changed. Figure 5 shows how the heuristic transforms each control sketch into bias weights. The figure shows ω_{c_1} for c_1 = Sports showing how the planner decreases the probability density bias for the topic (the probability density for the second topic, ω_{c_2}, is the mirror image).

With slight differences in the input control sketches, we observe very different generated stories, with the transition between sports and science happening later. One can see from Figure 5 why this would be the case: the probability density for the first topic becomes increasingly stronger for the first lines of the story as the control sketch requests the second topic later.

Because each sentence is biased by the previous sentences in addition to the control sketch, the sentence where the topic appears to switch often comes later than the point of earliest topic overlap. The requirement that each sentence continue the previous context creates a sense of momentum from the previous context and thus from the previous topic.

Incoherent transitions may still happen. In the story in Table 2 for sketch 3 shows one such incoherent transition due to the generation of an end-of-text token. Our implementation uses the initial prompt in this case, causing a portion of the story to not be contextualized by the earlier story sentences. Our ROCStories-tuned language model, based on

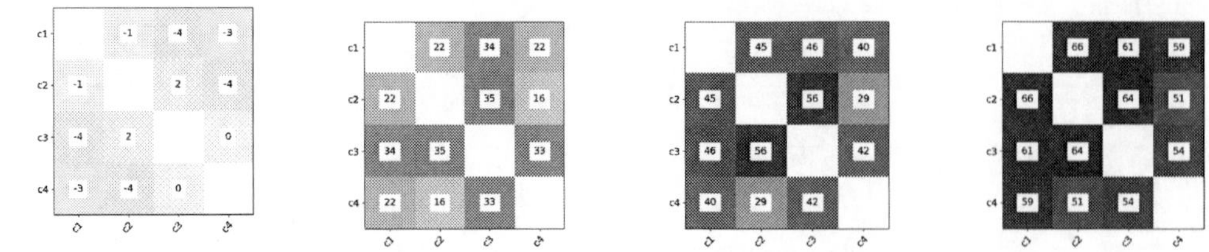

(a) Baseline on order-shuffled stories in ROCStories dataset. (b) Total control strength $1x$. (c) Total control strength $2x$. (d) Total control strength $4x$.

Figure 3: average τ-a (higher meaning better control fidelity) under different Total control strength for the tuned model with topics: (c1) Business, (c2) Science, (c3) Sports, (c4) World, comparing to uncontrolled baseline. Heat map strength is given as percentages ($-100\% \ldots 100\%$).

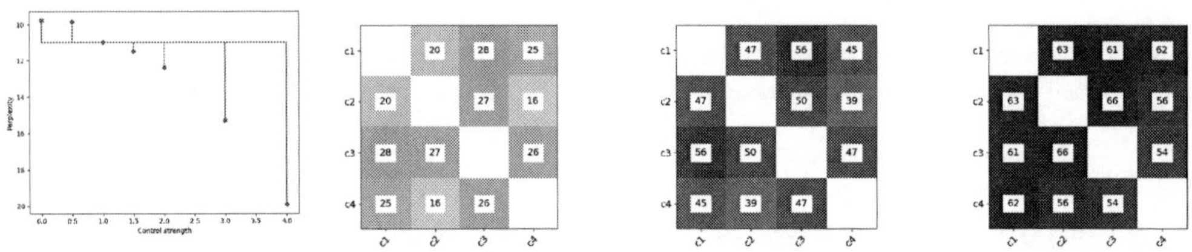

(a) Perplexity of generated sequences. (b) Total control strength 1x. (c) Total control strength 2x. (d) Total control strength 4x.

Figure 4: Experiment results for the untuned model. Refer to Figure 3a for baseline comparison.

5-sentence stories, tends to predict end-of-text earlier than models trained on longer stories.

6 Discussion

Our experiments suggest that there is a trade-off between control fidelity and fluency. As Figures 2 and 3 show, a higher total control strength results in overall better τ-a scores, meaning more sensitivity and ability to correctly differentiate between topic blends, but worse perplexity, risking less fluent language. In practice, an iterative deepening algorithm where multiple control strengths are used to generate multiple candidate sentences per line, can be used. Control strength modifiers of $1x$, $2x$, $3x$, $4x$, etc. can be tried and the best generated sentence, as measured by perplexity (or any other task-specific metric), is selected. This can, just like how multiple control codes are handled, be implemented very efficiently.

The current planner is heuristic. Empirically we find the heuristic to create good blends. We envision a planner that can be parameterized and learn from demonstrations. Reinforcement learning, in which the context and control sketches work as world states, can choose control configurations as actions. Feedback (reward) from the user would be necessary. This would incorporate the plug-and-blend technique into a human-in-the-loop creative process wherein the generator learns blending preferences from the human creator (Guzdial et al., 2018).

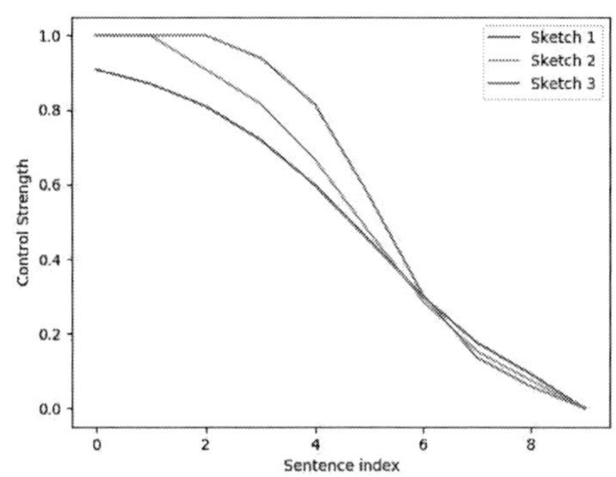

Figure 5: Control strength generated by the planner for the first control code used for each control sketch in Table 2. The control strength for the second control code is the mirror of each.

In this paper we have made no assumptions about how control sketches are acquired from the human user. We envision a processes whereby the human co-creator has an idea of what the final product—in this case a story—should be and can express that vision at the level of how topics manifest through the story. Supporting a co-creative

Control Sketches	Generated Paragraph
Sketch 1 $c_1 = \text{Sports}, \{0 \rightarrow 5\}$ $c_2 = \text{Science}, \{\mathbf{4} \rightarrow 10\}$	Jackie Robinson was playing in the NBA. He had just been drafted by the Cleveland Cavaliers. He decided to play for a team that was trying to win a championship. "I'm gonna go out there and beat them," he said "They're going to be great." "Yeah, they're good," he said "they'll be great." **He added that his wife had been working on the project for about a year.** **He was happy to see her progress.** She was able to get some work done and she started getting more comfortable with it. She had a lot of fun doing it! She also got her own computer, which is now in the living room.
Sketch 2 $c_1 = \text{Sports}, 0 \rightarrow 5$ $c_2 = \text{Science}, \mathbf{5} \rightarrow 10$	Jackie Robinson was playing in the NBA. He had just played basketball for a few years. He was looking forward to his first game of the season. He decided to play with his friends and play against them in the court. He got a lot of feedback from everyone who played against him, including some that were very excited about it! I was really happy when I saw how he played. I also had to admit that my favorite player was the guy who beat me in the finals. **The computer game Super Mario 64 is a great game, but it's not perfect.** **I played it on my laptop and found that I couldn't play it properly because of some bugs.** The problem was that the graphics were bad, so I had to use an emulator instead of playing the game.
Sketch 3 $c_1 = \text{Sports}, 0 \rightarrow 5$ $c_2 = \text{Science}, \mathbf{6} \rightarrow 10$	Jackie Robinson was playing in the NBA. He had just played basketball for a few years. He was looking forward to his first game of the season. He decided to play with his friends and play against them in the court. He had a lot of fun playing against them, but he didn't want to lose any time. So he played with his friends for about an hour before going home and playing again. He was very happy when they got home and started playing again! I think it's a good idea to have some fun with your kids, especially if you're not too busy. I'm sure that you'll enjoy this post as much as I did! **my daughter was diagnosed with a rare form of cancer.**

Table 2: Generated Examples with different Control-Sketches. Sentences in **bold** show a topic transition.

human-AI interaction, the human user can update the control sketch and re-generate parts (or all) of the story by changing the range of topics or choosing different topics. The control model will need to support different topics at different levels of granularity; currently the control model only supports four topics, which is sufficient for conducting experiments to characterize the plug-and-blend technique but not for full co-creativity.

7 Conclusions

In this paper, we present Plug-and-Blend, a plug-and-play framework that enhances a base LM, enables controllable generation with continuous-weighted control codes, along with capability of generating paragraphs based on control sketches, all without access to internal knowledge of this base LM. These capabilities will fuel a new generation of controllable generation applications with the key assets of decoupling between the controllable component and the generative component, and easiness of adapting to new advancements in the field of generative LMs.

8 Acknowledgment

This material is based upon work supported by the Office of Naval Research (ONR) under Grant #N00014-14-1-0003.

References

Nader Akoury, Shufan Wang, Josh Whiting, Stephen Hood, Nanyun Peng, and Mohit Iyyer. 2020. STORIUM: A Dataset and Evaluation Platform for Machine-in-the-Loop Story Generation. In *Proceedings of the 2020 Conference on Empirical Methods in Natural Language Processing (EMNLP)*, pages 6470–6484, Online. Association for Computational Linguistics.

Tom B. Brown, Benjamin Mann, Nick Ryder, Melanie Subbiah, Jared Kaplan, Prafulla Dhariwal, Arvind Neelakantan, Pranav Shyam, Girish Sastry, Amanda Askell, Sandhini Agarwal, Ariel Herbert-Voss, Gretchen Krueger, Tom Henighan, Rewon Child, Aditya Ramesh, Daniel M. Ziegler, Jeffrey Wu, Clemens Winter, Christopher Hesse, Mark Chen, Eric Sigler, Mateusz Litwin, Scott Gray, Benjamin Chess, Jack Clark, Christopher Berner, Sam McCandlish, Alec Radford, Ilya Sutskever, and Dario Amodei. 2020. Language Models are Few-Shot Learners.

Alvin Chan, Yew-Soon Ong, Bill Pung, Aston Zhang, and Jie Fu. 2020. CoCon: A Self-Supervised Approach for Controlled Text Generation. *arXiv:2006.03535 [cs]*. ArXiv: 2006.03535.

Sumanth Dathathri, Andrea Madotto, Janice Lan, Jane Hung, Eric Frank, Piero Molino, Jason Yosinski, and Rosanne Liu. 2020. Plug and Play Language Models: A Simple Approach to Controlled Text Generation. *International Conference on Learning Representations*, (2020). ArXiv: 1912.02164.

Yu Duan, Canwen Xu, Jiaxin Pei, Jialong Han, and Chenliang Li. 2020. Pre-train and Plug-in: Flexible Conditional Text Generation with Variational Auto-Encoders. *Proceedings of the 58th Annual Meeting of the Association for Computational Linguistics*, (2020):253–262. ArXiv: 1911.03882.

Le Fang, Tao Zeng, Chaochun Liu, Liefeng Bo, Wen Dong, and Changyou Chen. 2021. Transformer-based Conditional Variational Autoencoder for Controllable Story Generation. *arXiv:2101.00828 [cs]*. ArXiv: 2101.00828.

Jessica Ficler and Yoav Goldberg. 2017. Controlling Linguistic Style Aspects in Neural Language Generation. *Proceedings of the Workshop on Stylistic Variation*, (2017):94–104. ArXiv: 1707.02633.

Matthew Guzdial, Nicholas Liao, and Mark Riedl. 2018. Co-Creative Level Design via Machine Learning. *Fifth Experimental AI in Games Workshop*. ArXiv: 1809.09420.

Ehsan Hosseini-Asl, Bryan McCann, Chien-Sheng Wu, Semih Yavuz, and Richard Socher. 2020. A Simple Language Model for Task-Oriented Dialogue. *Advances in Neural Information Processing Systems*, 33.

Zhiting Hu, Zichao Yang, Xiaodan Liang, Ruslan Salakhutdinov, and Eric P. Xing. 2017. Toward Controlled Generation of Text. In *Proceedings of the 34th International Conference on Machine Learning*, volume 70 of *Proceedings of Machine Learning Research*, pages 1587–1596, International Convention Centre, Sydney, Australia. PMLR.

Nitish Shirish Keskar, Bryan McCann, Lav R. Varshney, Caiming Xiong, and Richard Socher. 2019. CTRL: A Conditional Transformer Language Model for Controllable Generation. *arXiv:1909.05858 [cs]*. ArXiv: 1909.05858.

Muhammad Khalifa, Hady Elsahar, and Marc Dymetman. 2020. A Distributional Approach to Controlled Text Generation. *arXiv:2012.11635 [cs]*. ArXiv: 2012.11635.

Ben Krause, Akhilesh Deepak Gotmare, Bryan McCann, Nitish Shirish Keskar, Shafiq Joty, Richard Socher, and Nazneen Fatema Rajani. 2020. GeDi: Generative Discriminator Guided Sequence Generation. *arXiv:2009.06367 [cs]*. ArXiv: 2009.06367.

Xiang Lisa Li and Percy Liang. 2021. Prefix-Tuning: Optimizing Continuous Prompts for Generation. *arXiv:2101.00190 [cs]*. ArXiv: 2101.00190.

Andrea Madotto, Etsuko Ishii, Zhaojiang Lin, Sumanth Dathathri, and Pascale Fung. 2020. Plug-and-Play Conversational Models. *arXiv:2010.04344 [cs]*. ArXiv: 2010.04344.

Florian Mai, Nikolaos Pappas, Ivan Montero, Noah A. Smith, and James Henderson. 2020. Plug and Play Autoencoders for Conditional Text Generation. In *Proceedings of the 2020 Conference on Empirical Methods in Natural Language Processing (EMNLP)*, pages 6076–6092, Online. Association for Computational Linguistics.

Nasrin Mostafazadeh, Nathanael Chambers, Xiaodong He, Devi Parikh, Dhruv Batra, Lucy Vanderwende, Pushmeet Kohli, and James Allen. 2016. A Corpus and Evaluation Framework for Deeper Understanding of Commonsense Stories. *Proceedings of the 2016 Conference of the North {A}merican Chapter of the Association for Computational Linguistics: Human Language Technologies*, pages 839–849. ArXiv: 1604.01696.

Damian Pascual, Beni Egressy, Florian Bolli, and Roger Wattenhofer. 2020. Directed Beam Search: Plug-and-Play Lexically Constrained Language Generation. *arXiv:2012.15416 [cs]*. ArXiv: 2012.15416.

Alec Radford, Jeffrey Wu, Rewon Child, David Luan, Dario Amodei, and Ilya Sutskever. 2019. Language Models are Unsupervised Multitask Learners. page 24.

Hannah Rashkin, Asli Celikyilmaz, Yejin Choi, and Jianfeng Gao. 2020. PlotMachines: Outline-conditioned generation with dynamic plot state tracking. In *Proceedings of the 2020 Conference on Empirical Methods in Natural Language Processing (EMNLP)*, pages 4274–4295, Online. Association for Computational Linguistics.

Eric Wallace, Shi Feng, Nikhil Kandpal, Matt Gardner, and Sameer Singh. 2019. Universal Adversarial Triggers for Attacking and Analyzing NLP. *Proceedings of the 2019 Conference on Empirical Methods in Natural Language Processing and the 9th International Joint Conference on Natural Language Processing (EMNLP-IJCNLP)*, (2019):2153–2162. ArXiv: 1908.07125.

Su Wang, Greg Durrett, and Katrin Erk. 2020. Narrative Interpolation for Generating and Understanding Stories. *arXiv:2008.07466 [cs]*. ArXiv: 2008.07466.

Thomas Wolf, Lysandre Debut, Victor Sanh, Julien Chaumond, Clement Delangue, Anthony Moi, Pierric Cistac, Tim Rault, Rémi Louf, Morgan Funtowicz, Joe Davison, Sam Shleifer, Patrick von Platen, Clara Ma, Yacine Jernite, Julien Plu, Canwen Xu,

Teven Le Scao, Sylvain Gugger, Mariama Drame, Quentin Lhoest, and Alexander M. Rush. 2020. HuggingFace's Transformers: State-of-the-art Natural Language Processing. *arXiv:1910.03771 [cs]*. ArXiv: 1910.03771.

Zeqiu Wu, Michel Galley, Chris Brockett, Yizhe Zhang, Xiang Gao, Chris Quirk, Rik Koncel-Kedziorski, Jianfeng Gao, Hannaneh Hajishirzi, Mari Ostendorf, and Bill Dolan. 2020. A Controllable Model of Grounded Response Generation. *arXiv:2005.00613 [cs]*. ArXiv: 2005.00613.

Lili Yao, Nanyun Peng, Ralph Weischedel, Kevin Knight, Dongyan Zhao, and Rui Yan. 2019. Plan-And-Write: Towards Better Automatic Storytelling. *Proceedings of the AAAI Conference on Artificial Intelligence*, 33(1):7378–7385. ArXiv: 1811.05701.

Automatic Story Generation: Challenges and Attempts

Amal Alabdulkarim *, **Siyan Li** *, **Xiangyu Peng** *
Georgia Institute of Technology
Atlanta, GA 30332
{amal, lisiyansylvia, xpeng62}@gatech.edu

Abstract

Automated storytelling has long captured the attention of researchers for the ubiquity of narratives in everyday life. The best human-crafted stories exhibit coherent plot, strong characters, and adherence to genres, attributes that current states-of-the-art still struggle to produce, even using transformer architectures. In this paper, we analyze works in story generation that utilize machine learning approaches to (1) address story generation controllability, (2) incorporate commonsense knowledge, (3) infer reasonable character actions and (4) generate creative language.

1 Introduction and Motivation

Storytelling is central to human communication. People use stories to communicate effectively with one another. As humans, we engage with well-told stories and comprehend more information from stories (Suzuki et al., 2018). However, when it comes to automatic storytelling, computers still have a long way to go. The field of automated story generation, or computational narrative, has received more attention because of recent technological enhancements. The importance of computational narrative is that it can improve human interaction with intelligent systems. Storytelling helps computers communicate with humans (Riedl, 2016), and automated story generation drives improvements in natural language processing. Computational narrative research involves story understanding, story representation, and story generation. In this survey, we will focus on the story generation capabilities of computational systems.

Many surveys were written on different facets of computational storytelling. (Gervás, 2009) provides a chronological summary of storytelling systems focusing on computational creativity, measured using metrics including the stories' novelty and the users' involvement in the storytelling process. (Riedl and Bulitko, 2013) focuses on interactive intelligence, a digital interactive storytelling experience where users interact with the computational system to build storylines. The survey paper touches on generating narrative structures and character building. (Riedl, 2016) discusses human-centered computational narrative and how it can improve artificial intelligence applications. The paper shed some light on machine learning challenges concerned with story generation and commonsense reasoning. Nevertheless, it does not go into these challenges in-depth as it is not its primary focus point.

Past survey papers focused primarily on story generation using specific approaches or on specific sub-problems in story generation. For example, (Kybartas and Bidarra, 2017) summarizes progress in the areas of plot and space generation without much discussion around neural language models. (Hou et al., 2019) examine different deep learning models used in story generation and categorize them by their goals. However, there is still motivation to organize a survey in a different manner. The process of automatically generating a logically-coherent and interesting narrative is complex. Therefore, it might be more beneficial detailing the major problems present in the field and techniques used to address them rather than summarizing different types of models. For people who are new in the field, our survey should serve as a decent starting point for conducting innovative research in the field.

Some of the survey papers, albeit comprehensive, do not include the latest development in story generation because of transformers. (Riedl and Bulitko, 2013) chronicles interactive narrative prior to 2013, yet the discussed approaches do not include large-scale neural language models, which we have access to now and has been fueling new research in

* Equal contributions

Proceedings of the 3rd Workshop on Narrative Understanding, pages 72–83
June 11, 2021.

the field. Another example would be the paper by (Gervás, 2009), where the author comments on storytelling systems and different evaluation criteria for creativity; similarly, all of the systems consist of planning and no neural approaches.

We acknowledge that more survey papers exist with different areas of focus within the domain of computational narratives, such as Narrative theories (Cavazza and Pizzi, 2006), Interactive Intelligence (Luo et al., 2015), Drama Management (Roberts and Isbell, 2008), Plan-based story generation (Young et al., 2013).

It has been demonstrated that the field of automated story generation has a gap in up-to-date survey papers. Our paper, by laying out all the prominent research problems in story generation and previous literature addressing these issues, will fill this gap.

The scope of this survey paper is to explore the challenges in automatic story generation. We hope to contribute in the following ways:

1. Explore how previous research in story generation addressed those challenges.

2. Discuss future research directions and new technologies that may aid more advancements.

3. Shed light on emerging and often overlooked challenges such as creativity and discourse.

There are several important background concepts crucial to understanding the problem of story generation. Automated story generation is a process involving the use of computer systems to create written stories, often involving artificial intelligence (AI). Story generation requires story understanding and representation, which are usually handled by natural language processing. Hence, the first concentration in this paper is content encoding and comprehension. A system is conventionally defined as capable of story comprehension if it, given a textual story, can read and answer questions about it (Lehnert et al., 1983; Reeves, 1991). Recently, state-of-the-art neural text generation models (such as GPT-2 (Radford et al., 2019)), are used to generate stories. These models are trained on the WebText corpus, a collection of texts scraped from the internet. Hence, the key challenge of applying these language models to story generation is to ensure that the generated story remains on topic and maintains entity and event consistencies. In our paper, we consider the following two concepts as crucial starting points: Controllability – having human inputs influence the generation results (Section 2.1), and commonsense – narrative systems with pre-existing knowledge that would help generate coherent stories (Section 2.2).

2 Method

2.1 Controllability in Story Generation

The controllability problem in story generation is the user input's ability to influence the generation results. Such influence often takes the form of a plot the user wishes the system to adhere to when producing a new narrative. Controlling story generation is a significant challenge that gained more attention in the last few years due to the limitations of neural-based story generation approaches. Most modern story generators use Neural based techniques that need little to no manual modeling to generate stories. Neural based models solve the lack of novelty issues found in the symbolic systems due to their unstructured generation. Yet, this advance comes at the cost of less controllability and plot coherence. In this section, we shed light on a few approaches to the problem of controllability, discuss their strengths and weaknesses, and compare their methodologies.

Reinforcement Learning. (Tambwekar et al., 2019) aimed at controlling the story plot by controlling its ending and events order. They proposed a deep reinforce approach to controlled story generation with a reward shaping technique to optimize the pre-trained sequence to sequence model in (Martin et al., 2017). Their reward function encompasses two main parts, the distance to the goal verb and the story verb frequency. They evaluated their model on plot coherence and goal achievement, length, and perplexity. Their method was better than their base model alone. However, this approach requires training the model for every new goal, which can be inconvenient for the users. Another drawback to this model is it uses the sequence to sequence model in (Martin et al., 2017), which generates stories as sequences of objects encapsulating the sentence components (verb and subject) that require translation to full sentences.

Model Fusion. (Fan et al., 2018) attempts to solving the plot controllability problem by dividing the generation process into two levels of hierarchy a premise and a story. The premise provides an overall sketch of the story, which was utilized to write the story. This fusion model combines a convolutional sequence to sequence model with a self-attention mechanism to improve generated story quality. A convolutional network first generates a writing prompt which then, becomes the input to the sequence to sequence model and guide it in generating a story conditioned on the prompt. Their model was superior in both human evaluations and perplexity scores than a traditional sequence to sequence method. Conditioning on the generated premise makes the generated story plot consistent and has an improved long-term dependency. Overall, this approach improves the shortcomings of the previous work by writing the stories directly and being conditioned for different prompts without retraining. Yet this model also has its limitations. First, it relies heavily on random sampling for the generation, which is prone to errors. Second, it suffers from text repetition in the generated stories. Lastly, the generated prompts are generic and less interesting than human written writing prompts, which often generates boring stories.

Plan and Write. (Yao et al., 2019) proposed the Plan-and-write story generation framework. The authors leveraged some of the characteristics of symbolic planning and integrated it into a neural system. Their work improves the previous literature in that it uses the titles to generate controlled storylines rather than the auto-generated writing prompts directly. They utilize storyline planning to improve the generated stories' quality and coherence and thus control the generation. They explore several story planning strategies to see their effect on story generation. This framework takes as an input the title of the story and then generates a storyline. The storyline and the title are then used as input to control the story generation in a sequence to sequence model. They also proposed two metrics to evaluate their model, inter-story repetition, and intra-story repetition. The evaluations showed that the model is more superior to the used conditional language model baselines. Those evaluations also showed that the model suffers from several major problems: repetition, going off-topic, and logical inconsistencies. It also utilizes a sequential language model to approximate the story plot, which simplifies the structure and depth of a good story plot, suggesting that generating coherent and logical story plots is still far from being solved.

Generation by Interpolation. (Wang et al., 2020) introduced a generation-by-interpolation story generation model. While previously introduced methods require minimal human input, they still suffer from logical inconsistencies and off-topic wandering. The generation by interpolation model is designed to overcome these challenges. It is an ending-guided model that is better than storyline-guided models because, in the storyline-guided, the model can easily be misled by a very general prompt. In contrast, an ending-guided model can use a single ending sentence to develop a good story plot. Their ending-guided method centers on conditioning the generation on the first and last sentences of the story. Where a GPT-2 model (Radford et al., 2019) generates several candidates for a storyline, and then these candidates are ranked based on their coherence scores using a RoBERTa model(Liu et al., 2019). Then the sentence with the highest coherence with the first and last sentence is chosen and then generated. Their evaluations demonstrate the informativeness of the ending guide and the effectiveness of the coherence ranking approach. The generated stories were of higher quality and better coherence than previous state-of-the-art models. The model's human evaluations suggested that good stories' assessment needs better and deeper evaluation metrics to match how humans define an excellent story, for example, measuring how the organization of events and characters can constitute better narratives. Lastly, using a transformer-language-model-based system improved the model's coherence and repetition. However, it showed that it could not manage commonsense inference beyond a small extend and thus established the need to integrate more human knowledge into the model.

Plot Machines. (Rashkin et al., 2020) proposed a transformer-language-model-based system that generates multi-paragraph stories conditioned on specified outlines for these stories. This model shows improvements in the narrative over the previous work. The approach utilizes memory state tracking and discourse structures to better control the generated story plot and keep track of the generated lines to maintain the coherence. The outlines are represented with an unordered list of high-level, multi-word descriptions of events occurring in the story. At every step, the model generates based on the representation of the given outline, the high-level discourse representation, the preceding story context, and the previous memory. Discourse representation is an encoding of the type of paragraph the current paragraph is, including introduction (_i_), body (_b_), and conclusion (_c_), which is appended to the outline representations at every time step. The preceding story context is the same as the hidden state vectors output by the transformer's attention blocks upon feeding generated sentences into a static GPT-2 model. Finally, the memory is a concatenated vector containing both the generated tokens and an encoded state of the story. When evaluated based on human preferences, the proposed system outperforms baseline models, including Fusion (Radford et al., 2018), GPT-2 (Radford et al., 2019), and Grover (Zellers et al., 2019) in metrics measuring logical ordering, narrative flow, and the level of repetitiveness. In PlotMachines, the conditioning of generation depended on a general outline that includes events and phrases for ease of extraction. Even with the better performance in PlotMachines, the stories can benefit from incorporating a comprehensive plot outline such as the output of an event-based planning system that can improve the generated stories' depth and interestingness.

Narrative controllability is still an open challenge for automatic story generation. Albeit being an active research area in natural language generation, we can attribute some of its problems to the new technologies that were essentially used to improve it, which manifested after introducing neural-based systems to story generation models. As summarized in table 1 in appendix A, narrative controllability approaches are typically ending-focused or storyline-focused. In the ending focused, the goal is to generate a story with a specific desired ending. An example of these such systems are (Tambwekar et al., 2019; Wang et al., 2020). Whereas in the storyline focused, the generated stories would follow an outline of the plot. (Rashkin et al., 2020; Yao et al., 2019; Fan et al., 2018) are examples of such systems. Both approaches reflect different controllability goals which needs to be addressed when comparing generation systems. We also notice a shift from Seq2Seq models (Tambwekar et al., 2019; Fan et al., 2018; Yao et al., 2019) to transformer based architecture in newer models (Rashkin et al., 2020; Wang et al., 2020).

After examining those solutions we notice that there are three main challenges that needs to be solved. First, rigid controls lead to low creativity and interestingness. Second, the evaluation metrics for the controllability of automatic story generation systems are neither sufficient nor unified, making it harder to evaluate and compare systems. Third, despite the controls added to the generation process, we still need to improve the coherence and logical plot generation. Those challenges are an open invitation for more research in controllability.

2.2 Commonsense Knowledge in Story Generation

Commonsense is regarded obvious to most humans(Cambria et al., 2011), and comprises shared knowledge about how the world works (Nunberg, 1987). Commonsense serves as a deep understanding of language. Two major bottlenecks here are how to acquire commonsense knowledge and incorporate it into state-of-the-art story-telling generation systems.

2.2.1 Benchmarks

Before integrating commonsense knowledge into neural language models, the models often are trained on commonsense knowledge bases, datasets containing information detailing well-known facts or causal relationships. We will first introduce these benchmarks, which target commonsense.

ConceptNet. ConceptNet by Speer et al. (2017) is a large semantic knowledge graph that connects words and phrases of natural language with labeled edges, describing general human knowledge and how it is expressed in natural language. The data is in form of triples of their start node, relation label, and end node. For example, the assertion that "a dog has a tail" can be represented as (dog, HasA, tail). It lays the foundation of incorporating real-world knowledge into a variety of AI projects and applications. What's more, many new benchmarks extract from ConceptNet and serve other utilities.

CommonsenseQA. CommonsenseQA by (Talmor et al., 2019) is a benchmark extracting from ConceptNet's multiple target concepts, which have the same semantic relation, to a single source concept. It provides a challenging new dataset for commonsense question answering. Each question requires one to disambiguate a target concept from three connected concepts in ConceptNet. The best pre-trained LM tuned on question answering, can only get 55.9% accuracy on CommonsenseQA, possessing important challenge for incorporating commonsense into large language model.

ATOMIC. (Sap et al., 2019a) presented ATlas Of MachIne Commonsense (ATOMIC), an atlas for commonsense knowledge with 877K textual descriptions of nine different types *If-then* relations. Instead of capturing general commonsense knowledge like ConceptNet, ATOMIC focuses on sequences of events and the social commonsense relating to them. The purpose of the dataset is to allow neural networks abstract commonsense inferences and make predictions on previously unseen events. The dataset is in the form of <`event, relation, event`> and is organized into nine categories such as xIntent (PersonX's intention) and xEffect (effect on PersonX). For instance, "PersonX makes PersonY a birthday cake xEffect PersonX gets thanked".

GLUCOSE. ATOMIC is person centric, hence it can not be used in sentences describing events. Mostafazadeh et al. (2020) constructs GLUCOSE (GeneraLized and COntextualized Story Explanations), a large-scale dataset of implicit commonsense causal knowledge, which sentences can describe any event/state. Each GLUCOSE entry is organized into a story-specific causal statement paired with an inference rule generalized from the statement. Given a short story and a sentence X in the story, GLUCOSE captures ten dimensions of causal explanations related to X. GLUCOSE shares the same purpose with ATOMIC.

SocialIQA. SocialIQA(Sap et al., 2019b) is the a large-scale benchmark for commonsense reasoning about social situations, which provides 38k multiple choice questions. Each question consists of a brief context, a question about the context, and three answer options. It covers various types of inference about people's actions being described in situational contexts. The purpose of SocialIQA is to reason about social situations.

There are also many other benchmarks involved in commonsense domain. **MCScript**(Ostermann et al., 2018) provides narrative texts and questions, collected based on script scenarios.**OpenBookQA**(Mihaylov et al., 2018) is a question answering dataset, modeled after open book exams for assessing human understanding of a subject. **Cosmos QA**(Huang et al., 2019) provides 35k problems with multiple-choice, which require commonsense-based reading comprehension.

What's more, technique of generating commonsense datasets are also developed. For example, Davison et al. (2019) proposed a method for generating commonsense knowledge by transforming relational triples into masked sentences, and then using a large, pre-trained bidirectional language model to rank a triple's validity by the estimated pointwise mutual information between the two entities. Schwartz et al. (2017) and Trinh and Le (2018) demonstrate a similar approach to using language models for tasks requiring commonsense, such as the Story Cloze Task and the Winograd Schema Challenge, respectively (Mostafazadeh et al., 2016; Levesque et al., 2012).

2.2.2 Frameworks

Three ways of applying these benchmarks on commonsense story generation are (1) fine-tuning pretrained language models (LM) on commonsense benchmarks, (2) perceptions of causality after generating stories, and (3) incorporating benchmarks into language models encoding.

An intuition is to utilize commonsense knowledge is to train language model on commonsense datasets. Yang et al. (2019) integrates external commonsense knowledge to BERT (Devlin et al., 2019) to enhance language representation for reading comprehension. Guan et al. (2020) fine-tuned GPT-2(Radford et al., 2019) on on knowledge-augmented data, ATOMIC and ConceptNet, for a better performance for commonsense story generation. They firstly transform ConceptNet and ATOMIC into readable natural language sentences and then post-trained on these transformed sentences by minimizing the negative likelihood of predicting the next token. Mao et al. (2019) and (Guan et al., 2020) also fine-tuned GPT-2 on ConceptNet and the BookCorpus(Kiros et al., 2015). They achieve a less perplexity and higher BLEU score, however, these knowledge-enhanced pre-training model for commonsense story generation are still far from generating stories with long-range coherence.

Instead of directly training language models on commonsense datasets, which improves LM's logicality and grammaticality, an alternative of incorporating commonsense into language model is to analyze perceptions of causality or overall story quality.

(Bosselut et al., 2019) extended upon the work ATOMIC by Sap et al. (2019a) and ConceptNet by Speer et al. (2017) and trained a GPT model (Radford et al., 2018) on commonsense knowledge tuples, in the format of <`phrase subject, relationship, phrase object`>. The resulting model, **COMeT**, is capable of generating new commonsense triples on novel phrases. With this feature, automatic generated story can be evaluated easily. The model has been proven to be efficient in learning commonsense knowledge tuples, as in humans deem most COMeT-generated triples from novel phrases to be correct. It provides a easy way of making inferece on generated text. However, it is Sentence-level Commonsense inferences, which is only able to deal with short sentences, within 18 tokens. Story generation is usually in need of a paragraph-level commonsense inference because combining with context, the inference could be completely different.

In order to incorporates paragraph-level information to generate coherent commonsense inferences from narratives, Gabriel et al. (2020) proposed a discourse-aware model **PARA-COMeT**. PARA-COMeT firstly created commonsense datasets by (1) using COMeT to provides inference on sentences in ROCStories corpus (Mostafazadeh et al., 2016) and (2) transform inference into natural language by human-written templates, (3) then filter out those with low coherence with narrative. PARA-COMeT consists of (1) a memory-less model, focusing on extracting semantic knowledge from the context, and (2) a model augmented with recurrent memory, used for incorporating episodic knowledge. Compared with COMeT, PARA-COMeT demonstrated the effectiveness of generating more implicit and novel discourse-aware inferences in paragraph level.

Ammanabrolu et al. (2020) also developed proposed **C**ausal, **C**ommonsense **P**ot **O**rdering(CCPO) on COMeT. CCPO establishs plot points by (1) extracting all the coreference clusters from a given textual story plot using a pre-trained neural coreference resolution model(Clark and Manning, 2016), and (2)extract a set of ¡subject, relation, object¿ triples from the story text using OpenIE(Angeli et al., 2015). Then a plot graph between each two plot points is generated by keep recursively querying commonsense inference on these two plot points. The automatic story is generated based on the plot graphs. CCPO successfully improves perceptions of local and global coherence in terms of causality, however its performance is restricted by commonsense inference models.

Another common method is incorporating commonsense knowledge graph into the model encoding process. Guan et al. (2019) incorporates commonsense knowledge graph by applying features from ConceptNet(Speer et al., 2017) and graph attention(Veličković et al., 2018) on building knowledge context vectors to represent the graph. They significantly improve the ability of neural networks to predict the end of a story. Mihaylov and Frank (2018) also incorporate external commonsense knowledge into a neural cloze-style reading comprehension model.

2.3 Other Challenges in Story Generation

There are issues in the story generation field that are yet to be heavily researched upon. The current emphasis of mainstream story generation research is to produce narratives with reasonable structures and plots and less on the cherries on top: fascinating and driven characters, consistent styles, and creative language and plot. Some researchers have ventured potential approaches to these currently outstanding problems, as detailed below.

2.3.1 Characters and Entities

How characters are motivated and interact with each other influence the progression of a story. Different approaches have been taken to model how focusing on characters can produce higher-quality generated narratives, some from the perspective of character affect, and some from entity representation in narrative generation.

EnGen (Clark et al., 2018) presented an entity-based generation model EnGen, which produces narratives relying on: (1) the current sentence; (2) the previous sentence, encoded by a Seq2Seq model (S2SA); (3) dynamic, up-to-date representations of all the entities in the narrative. The entity representation vectors are based on EntityNLM (Ji et al., 2017), and the vectors are updated every time their corresponding entities are mentioned. The model was evaluated on a series of tasks, including a novel mention generation task, where the model fills a slot with all previous mentions of entities, including coreferences. Similarly, the automated sentence selection task examines EnGen's ability to distinguish between the ground truth continuation sentence and a distraction sentence. EnGen is able to out-perform both S2SA and EntityNLM for these tasks. Another task involved Mechanical Turk workers reading sentences generated by both EnGen and S2SA on the same prompts and deciding which continuation is more fluent. Out of the 50 prompt passages, Turkers preferred the EnGen stories for 27 of them, and S2SA for the rest 23, although most of the human evaluations yield similar results between the two models. Incorporating character or entity information into the context for generation can improve model performance on some automated and human-evaluated tasks. The authors contended that this design improves the fluency of the generated texts. However, the lengths of the generated segments for the human-evaluation task are very short, usually fragments of sentences. Therefore, it is unlikely that these generated texts help propel the plot. Furthermore, the paper does not indicate how the entity representations model character interactions and how these interactions contribute to the stories.

Using Character Affinities A dive into character interactions in particular is detailed in (Méndez et al., 2016), where the authors attempted to model character interactions using numerical affinity values. Character relationships are categorized into four types: foe (lowest affinity), indifferent (medium affinity), friend (higher affinity), and mate (highest affinity). The system consists of a Director Agent, which sets up the environment for interactions to occur, and a set of Character Agents, each representing a character. The authors defines that each Character Agent interacts with the character's foes, friends, and mates. Actions pertinent to different interactions are templated using defined interaction protocols and are relatively restricted in terms of scope. These actions are independent and can be added upon each other to alter the affinity values. The primary parameter of concern in this model is the affinity between characters, a factor related to character emotions. Although this modeling approach has been suggested for narrative generation, the authors did not provide examples of stories generated using this character affinity model. Instead, the authors presented affinity changes for different Character Agents in the story to illustrate how different affinity threshold values for foe interactions affect the affinity evolution in the narratives. The model might be considered useful for modeling character interactions, yet the effect affinity changes have on the story plot remains unclear.

EC-CLF (Brahman and Chaturvedi, 2020) proposed a method for story generation conditioned on emotion arc of the protagonist by using reinforcement learning to train a GPT-2 model. The authors suggested two emotion consistency rewards: EC-EM and EC-CLF. EC-EM calculates how well the generated story aligns with the given arc using character reaction inferences from COMET (Bosselut et al., 2019); it is a modified Levensthtein distance that considers the cosine similarities between words from the given arc and the COMET inferences. EC-CLF, on the other hand, involves training a BERT (Devlin et al., 2019) classifier to identify the emotion in the generated sentences; the reward value is the probability of the desired emotions throughout the narrative from the classifier head. For human-evaluated tasks such as assessing emotion faithfulness and content quality, RL-CLF (GPT-2 trained with EC-CLF reward) outperformed baselines including GPT-2 trained with the emotion arc as an additional input to the narrative examples (EmoSup) and GPT-2 trained on the reward function EC-EM. This work augmented current state-of-the-art models with the ability to generate narratives with the protagonist's emotion changes following a specified emotion arc. It is an example of how character emotions can be used to inform story progression and improve narrative quality. Despite the enhancement of generation quality, the model still only focuses on one character instead of interactions between characters.

SRL + Entity (Fan et al., 2019) generated action-driven narratives by adapting the following pipeline: (1) based on the prompt given, produce an action plan with where all entities are represented with placeholder tags; (2) create an entity-anonymized story from the action plan; (3) output the full story after replacing the anonymized, generalized entities with natural language entities. Every entry in the action sequence consists of a predicate, which is a verb, and a series of arguments, which are the entities involved in the action. This representation allows models to learn more in-depth and generalizable relationships between different verbs and characters. A convolutional Seq2Seq model is trained on the prompts from the WRITINGPROMPTS dataset (Fan et al., 2018) and their corresponding action sequences. The network has an attention head dedicated to past verbs to improve verb diversity in generations.Human preference studies showed that the novel model generated more coherent narratives than the *Fusion* model from (Fan et al., 2018); additionally, the new model had more diversity in the generated verbs. The technique of abstraction and generalization can be proven useful in the story generation process, since abstractions reveal more widely-applicable rules in storytelling. Again, it is not clear if character interactions are implicitly learned by the models in this work, therefore further investigation would be required to determine if this work is suitable for multi-agent narrative generation.

In this section, we examine four works in the sub-field of character and entity-focused automated narrative generation. Generally, representing entities in certain format can improve the quality of the plotline, and character emotions can help inform the story generation process. Interactions between multiple characters are currently not the focus of the field, but it should be for potential future research.

2.3.2 Creativity

Creativity in human-authored narratives manifests in ways including figures of speech, character traits, and the environment for the narrative to occur in. (Martin et al., 2016) developed a system for improvisational interactive storytelling based on a plot graph as a general guideline for the generated storyline. Recent introduction to transformer-based language models has inspired people generating novel contents using these language models [1], including using GPT-2 to generate fantasy descriptions with explicit subjects and weblinks (Austin, 2019). Nonetheless, there has still not been much specific research into further improving the creativity of transformer-based language models.

3 Conclusion and Future Work

This survey discussed several directions in automatic story generation research and their respective challenges, and summarized research attempts at solving them. The research in automatic story generation is far from done. With automated story generation, such challenges include controlling the story content, commonsense knowledge, inferring reasonable character actions, and creativity. This survey provides a dive into some of these active research problems.

In Section 2.1, we summarized a few approaches addressing the problem of story generation controllability. We noticed that the papers we reviewed shared one of two goals, either controlling the story outline or controlling the story ending. We also observed an emerging trend towards using transformer-based language models for story generation.

In Section 2.2, we introduced methods to incorporate commonsense knowledge into story generation systems and frameworks with such integrated commonsense knowledge. Frequent approaches include: (1) Fine-tuning on commonsense datasets, (2) analyzing perceptions of causality and (3) incorporating commonsense knowledge graph into encoders. These methods are able to increase the overall story quality. However, no methods can ensure the generation of reasonable and coherent stories. One potential path to major improvements in this area would be to combine all of these different approaches.

In Section 2.3, we provided insight into some less-researched areas at the moment, including characters in generated narratives and the creativity of generated stories. Incorporating representations of entities into the generation process seems to improve the coherence of the plot, and character affect can help navigate the generation space as well. Extending the work in character affect from single character to multi characters can perhaps further enhance the generated narratives. There has not been much emphasis on the creativity of generated texts.

Additionally, we highlight a few future research problems that are worth exploring:

1. In the controllability systems we examined, we noticed that the stories become less interesting when the generation process is more controlled. There is a trade-off between narrative creativity and structural coherence of narratives.

2. The evaluation metrics used are generally the metrics used for other natural language generation tasks such as BLEU, perplexity, and ROUGE. Those metrics are weak and do not perform well for this task. Moreover, the story generation domain needs different metrics to capture story-specific characteristics. Such as measures for creativity and interestingness. Besides, there is a need to develop more robust and unified metrics to facilitate comparisons between systems.

3. The problems of plot incoherence and illogical plot generation are far from being solved. Both are still very active research areas and can be an interesting future research direction.

4. Instead of sentence-level and paragraph-level commonsense inference, a story-level commonsense inference could increase the accuracy of inference and provides a better tool for generating a more logic coherent story.

[1] https://www.gwern.net/GPT-3

References

Prithviraj Ammanabrolu, Wesley Cheung, William Broniec, and Mark O Riedl. 2020. Automated storytelling via causal, commonsense plot ordering. *arXiv preprint arXiv:2009.00829*.

Gabor Angeli, Melvin Jose Johnson Premkumar, and Christopher D Manning. 2015. Leveraging linguistic structure for open domain information extraction. In *Proceedings of the 53rd Annual Meeting of the Association for Computational Linguistics and the 7th International Joint Conference on Natural Language Processing (Volume 1: Long Papers)*, pages 344–354.

John Austin. 2019. The book of endless history: Authorial use of gpt2 for interactive storytelling. In *International Conference on Interactive Digital Storytelling*, pages 429–432. Springer.

Antoine Bosselut, Hannah Rashkin, Maarten Sap, Chaitanya Malaviya, Asli Celikyilmaz, and Yejin Choi. 2019. Comet: Commonsense transformers for automatic knowledge graph construction. pages 4762–4779.

Faeze Brahman and Snigdha Chaturvedi. 2020. Modeling protagonist emotions for emotion-aware storytelling. *arXiv preprint arXiv:2010.06822*.

Erik Cambria, Yangqiu Song, Haixun Wang, and Amir Hussain. 2011. Isanette: A common and common sense knowledge base for opinion mining. In *2011 IEEE 11th International Conference on Data Mining Workshops*, pages 315–322. IEEE.

Marc Cavazza and David Pizzi. 2006. Narratology for Interactive Storytelling: A Critical Introduction. In *Technologies for Interactive Digital Storytelling and Entertainment*, Lecture Notes in Computer Science, pages 72–83, Berlin, Heidelberg. Springer.

Elizabeth Clark, Yangfeng Ji, and Noah A. Smith. 2018. Neural text generation in stories using entity representations as context. In *Proceedings of the 2018 Conference of the North American Chapter of the Association for Computational Linguistics: Human Language Technologies, Volume 1 (Long Papers)*, pages 2250–2260, New Orleans, Louisiana. Association for Computational Linguistics.

Kevin Clark and Christopher D Manning. 2016. Deep reinforcement learning for mention-ranking coreference models. In *Proceedings of the 2016 Conference on Empirical Methods in Natural Language Processing*, pages 2256–2262.

Joe Davison, Joshua Feldman, and Alexander M Rush. 2019. Commonsense knowledge mining from pretrained models. In *Proceedings of the 2019 Conference on Empirical Methods in Natural Language Processing and the 9th International Joint Conference on Natural Language Processing (EMNLP-IJCNLP)*, pages 1173–1178.

Jacob Devlin, Ming-Wei Chang, Kenton Lee, and Kristina Toutanova. 2019. Bert: Pre-training of deep bidirectional transformers for language understanding. In *Proceedings of the 2019 Conference of the North American Chapter of the Association for Computational Linguistics: Human Language Technologies, Volume 1 (Long and Short Papers)*, pages 4171–4186.

Angela Fan, Mike Lewis, and Yann Dauphin. 2018. Hierarchical neural story generation. pages 889–898.

Angela Fan, Mike Lewis, and Yann Dauphin. 2019. Strategies for structuring story generation. In *Proceedings of the 57th Annual Meeting of the Association for Computational Linguistics*, pages 2650–2660.

Saadia Gabriel, Chandra Bhagavatula, Vered Shwartz, Ronan Le Bras, Maxwell Forbes, and Yejin Choi. 2020. Paragraph-level commonsense transformers with recurrent memory. *arXiv preprint arXiv:2010.01486*.

Pablo Gervás. 2009. Computational approaches to storytelling and creativity. *AI Magazine*, 30(3):49–49.

Jian Guan, Fei Huang, Zhihao Zhao, Xiaoyan Zhu, and Minlie Huang. 2020. A knowledge-enhanced pretraining model for commonsense story generation. *Transactions of the Association for Computational Linguistics*, 8:93–108.

Jian Guan, Yansen Wang, and Minlie Huang. 2019. Story ending generation with incremental encoding and commonsense knowledge. In *Proceedings of the AAAI Conference on Artificial Intelligence*, volume 33, pages 6473–6480.

Chenglong Hou, Chensong Zhou, Kun Zhou, Jinan Sun, and Sisi Xuanyuan. 2019. A survey of deep learning applied to story generation. In *Smart Computing and Communication*, pages 1–10, Cham. Springer International Publishing.

Lifu Huang, Ronan Le Bras, Chandra Bhagavatula, and Yejin Choi. 2019. Cosmos qa: Machine reading comprehension with contextual commonsense reasoning. In *Proceedings of the 2019 Conference on Empirical Methods in Natural Language Processing and the 9th International Joint Conference on Natural Language Processing (EMNLP-IJCNLP)*, pages 2391–2401.

Yangfeng Ji, Chenhao Tan, Sebastian Martschat, Yejin Choi, and Noah A Smith. 2017. Dynamic entity representations in neural language models. In *Proceedings of the 2017 Conference on Empirical Methods in Natural Language Processing*, pages 1830–1839.

Ryan Kiros, Yukun Zhu, Russ R Salakhutdinov, Richard Zemel, Raquel Urtasun, Antonio Torralba, and Sanja Fidler. 2015. Skip-thought vectors. In *Advances in neural information processing systems*, pages 3294–3302.

B. Kybartas and R. Bidarra. 2017. A survey on story generation techniques for authoring computational narratives. *IEEE Transactions on Computational Intelligence and AI in Games*, 9(3):239–253.

Wendy G Lehnert, Michael G Dyer, Peter N Johnson, CJ Yang, and Steve Harley. 1983. Boris—an experiment in in-depth understanding of narratives. *Artificial intelligence*, 20(1):15–62.

Hector Levesque, Ernest Davis, and Leora Morgenstern. 2012. The winograd schema challenge. In *Thirteenth International Conference on the Principles of Knowledge Representation and Reasoning*. Citeseer.

Yinhan Liu, Myle Ott, Naman Goyal, Jingfei Du, Mandar Joshi, Danqi Chen, Omer Levy, Mike Lewis, Luke Zettlemoyer, and Veselin Stoyanov. 2019. Roberta: A robustly optimized bert pretraining approach. *arXiv preprint arXiv:1907.11692*.

Linbo Luo, Wentong Cai, Suiping Zhou, Michael Lees, and Haiyan Yin. 2015. A review of interactive narrative systems and technologies: a training perspective. *SIMULATION*, 91(2):126–147. Publisher: SAGE Publications Ltd STM.

Huanru Henry Mao, Bodhisattwa Prasad Majumder, Julian McAuley, and Garrison Cottrell. 2019. Improving neural story generation by targeted common sense grounding. In *Proceedings of the 2019 Conference on Empirical Methods in Natural Language Processing and the 9th International Joint Conference on Natural Language Processing (EMNLP-IJCNLP)*, pages 5990–5995.

Lara J Martin, Prithviraj Ammanabrolu, Xinyu Wang, William Hancock, Shruti Singh, Brent Harrison, and Mark O Riedl. 2017. Event representations for automated story generation with deep neural nets. *arXiv preprint arXiv:1706.01331*.

Lara J. Martin, Brent Harrison, and Mark O. Riedl. 2016. Improvisational computational storytelling in open worlds. In *Interactive Storytelling*, pages 73–84, Cham. Springer International Publishing.

Gonzalo Méndez, Pablo Gervás, and Carlos León. 2016. On the use of character affinities for story plot generation. In *Knowledge, Information and Creativity Support Systems*, pages 211–225. Springer.

Todor Mihaylov, Peter Clark, Tushar Khot, and Ashish Sabharwal. 2018. Can a suit of armor conduct electricity? a new dataset for open book question answering. In *Proceedings of the 2018 Conference on Empirical Methods in Natural Language Processing*, pages 2381–2391.

Todor Mihaylov and Anette Frank. 2018. Knowledgeable reader: Enhancing cloze-style reading comprehension with external commonsense knowledge. In *Proceedings of the 56th Annual Meeting of the Association for Computational Linguistics (Volume 1: Long Papers)*, pages 821–832.

Nasrin Mostafazadeh, Nathanael Chambers, Xiaodong He, Devi Parikh, Dhruv Batra, Lucy Vanderwende, Pushmeet Kohli, and James Allen. 2016. A corpus and evaluation framework for deeper understanding of commonsense stories. *arXiv preprint arXiv:1604.01696*.

Nasrin Mostafazadeh, Aditya Kalyanpur, Lori Moon, David Buchanan, Lauren Berkowitz, Or Biran, and Jennifer Chu-Carroll. 2020. Glucose: Generalized and contextualized story explanations. *arXiv preprint arXiv:2009.07758*.

Geoffrey Nunberg. 1987. Position paper on commonsense and formal semantics. In *Theoretical Issues in Natural Language Processing 3*.

Simon Ostermann, Ashutosh Modi, Michael Roth, Stefan Thater, and Manfred Pinkal. 2018. Mcscript: A novel dataset for assessing machine comprehension using script knowledge. In *Proceedings of the Eleventh International Conference on Language Resources and Evaluation (LREC 2018)*.

Alec Radford, Karthik Narasimhan, Tim Salimans, and Ilya Sutskever. 2018. Improving language understanding by generative pre-training.

Alec Radford, Jeffrey Wu, Rewon Child, David Luan, Dario Amodei, and Ilya Sutskever. 2019. Language models are unsupervised multitask learners. *OpenAI Blog*, 1(8).

Hannah Rashkin, Asli Celikyilmaz, Yejin Choi, and Jianfeng Gao. 2020. Plotmachines: Outline-conditioned generation with dynamic plot state tracking. *arXiv preprint arXiv:2004.14967*.

John Fairbanks Reeves. 1991. Computational morality: A process model of belief conflict and resolution for story understanding.

Mark O. Riedl. 2016. Computational Narrative Intelligence: A Human-Centered Goal for Artificial Intelligence. *arXiv:1602.06484 [cs]*. ArXiv: 1602.06484.

Mark Owen Riedl and Vadim Bulitko. 2013. Interactive narrative: An intelligent systems approach. *Ai Magazine*, 34(1):67–67.

David L Roberts and Charles L Isbell. 2008. A Survey and Qualitative Analysis of Recent Advances in Drama Management. page 15.

Maarten Sap, Ronan Le Bras, Emily Allaway, Chandra Bhagavatula, Nicholas Lourie, Hannah Rashkin, Brendan Roof, Noah A Smith, and Yejin Choi. 2019a. Atomic: An atlas of machine commonsense for if-then reasoning. In *Proceedings of the AAAI Conference on Artificial Intelligence*, volume 33, pages 3027–3035.

Maarten Sap, Hannah Rashkin, Derek Chen, Ronan Le Bras, and Yejin Choi. 2019b. Social iqa: Commonsense reasoning about social interactions. In *Proceedings of the 2019 Conference on Empirical*

Methods in Natural Language Processing and the 9th International Joint Conference on Natural Language Processing (EMNLP-IJCNLP), pages 4453–4463.

Roy Schwartz, Maarten Sap, Ioannis Konstas, Leila Zilles, Yejin Choi, and Noah A Smith. 2017. The effect of different writing tasks on linguistic style: A case study of the roc story cloze task. In *Proceedings of the 21st Conference on Computational Natural Language Learning (CoNLL 2017)*, pages 15–25.

Robyn Speer, Joshua Chin, and Catherine Havasi. 2017. Conceptnet 5.5: an open multilingual graph of general knowledge. In *Proceedings of the Thirty-First AAAI Conference on Artificial Intelligence*, pages 4444–4451.

Wendy A. Suzuki, Mónica I. Feliú-Mójer, Uri Hasson, Rachel Yehuda, and Jean Mary Zarate. 2018. Dialogues: The Science and Power of Storytelling. *The Journal of Neuroscience*, 38(44):9468–9470.

Alon Talmor, Jonathan Herzig, Nicholas Lourie, and Jonathan Berant. 2019. Commonsenseqa: A question answering challenge targeting commonsense knowledge. In *Proceedings of the 2019 Conference of the North American Chapter of the Association for Computational Linguistics: Human Language Technologies, Volume 1 (Long and Short Papers)*, pages 4149–4158.

Pradyumna Tambwekar, Murtaza Dhuliawala, Lara J Martin, Animesh Mehta, Brent Harrison, and Mark O Riedl. 2019. Controllable neural story plot generation via reward shaping. pages 5982–5988.

Trieu H Trinh and Quoc V Le. 2018. A simple method for commonsense reasoning. *arXiv preprint arXiv:1806.02847*.

Petar Veličković, Guillem Cucurull, Arantxa Casanova, Adriana Romero, Pietro Liò, and Yoshua Bengio. 2018. Graph attention networks. In *International Conference on Learning Representations*.

Su Wang, Greg Durrett, and Katrin Erk. 2020. Narrative interpolation for generating and understanding stories. *arXiv preprint arXiv:2008.07466*.

An Yang, Quan Wang, Jing Liu, Kai Liu, Yajuan Lyu, Hua Wu, Qiaoqiao She, and Sujian Li. 2019. Enhancing pre-trained language representations with rich knowledge for machine reading comprehension. In *Proceedings of the 57th Annual Meeting of the Association for Computational Linguistics*, pages 2346–2357.

Lili Yao, Nanyun Peng, Ralph Weischedel, Kevin Knight, Dongyan Zhao, and Rui Yan. 2019. Plan-and-Write: Towards Better Automatic Storytelling. *Proceedings of the AAAI Conference on Artificial Intelligence*, 33:7378–7385.

R Michael Young, Stephen Ware, Brad Cassell, and Justus Robertson. 2013. Plans and Planning in Narrative Generation: A Review of Plan-Based Approaches to the Generation of Story, Dis- course and Interactivity in Narratives. page 24.

Rowan Zellers, Ari Holtzman, Hannah Rashkin, Yonatan Bisk, Ali Farhadi, Franziska Roesner, and Yejin Choi. 2019. Defending against neural fake news. In *Advances in Neural Information Processing Systems*, pages 9054–9065.

A Controllability Approaches

Model/System	Architecture	Condition	Goal
Reinforcement Learning	Reinforcement Learning on a Seq2Seq model	Goal Event	Generate a specific ending
Model Fusion	Generation on two levels: CNN to generate prompt, Seq2Seq to generate story from prompt	Generated Prompt	Generate with a storyline
Plan and Write	Two Seq2Seq models for plot and story generation	Title	Generate with a storyline
Generation by Interpolation	GPT-2 model for sentence generation and a RoBERTa coherence ranker	End sentence	Generate a specific ending
Plot Machines	end-to-end trainable transformer built on top of the GPT with memory representation	Outline	Generate with a storyline

Table 1: Summary of controllability approaches

Fabula Entropy Indexing: Objective Measures of Story Coherence

Louis Castricato, Spencer Frazier, Jonathan Balloch, and Mark O. Riedl
Georgia Tech
{lcastric, sfrazier7, balloch}@gatech.edu, {riedl}@cc.gatech.edu

Abstract

Automated story generation remains a difficult area of research because it lacks strong objective measures. Generated stories may be linguistically sound, but in many cases suffer poor narrative coherence required for a compelling, logically-sound story. To address this, we present Fabula Entropy Indexing (FEI), an evaluation method to assess story coherence by measuring the degree to which human participants agree with each other when answering true/false questions about stories. We devise two theoretically grounded measures of reader question-answering entropy, the entropy of world coherence (EWC), and the entropy of transitional coherence (ETC), focusing on global and local coherence, respectively. We evaluate these metrics by testing them on human-written stories and comparing against the same stories that have been corrupted to introduce incoherencies. We show that in these controlled studies, our entropy indices provide a reliable objective measure of story coherence.

1 Introduction

Automated story generation is one of the grand challenges of generative artificial intelligence. AI storytelling is a crucial component of the human experience. Humans have always used storytelling to entertain, share experiences, educate, and to facilitate social bonding. For an intelligent system to be unable to generate a coherent story limits its ability to interact with humans in naturalistic ways.

There have been a number of techniques explored for story generation; these include symbolic planning, case-based reasoning, neural language models and others. Despite extensive research, automated story generation remains a difficult task.

One of the reasons why automated story generation is such a difficult area of research is due to weak objective validation measures. Traditional automated measures of natural language quality—perplexity and n-gram based methods such as BLEU (Papineni et al., 2002)—are insufficient in creative generation domains such as story generation. These metrics assume that generated language can only be good if is resembles testing data or a given target story. This precludes the possibility that stories may be good yet be completely novel. Indeed, the goal of story generation is usually the construction of novel stories.

In the absence of automated evaluation metrics, the alternative is to use human participant studies. Human participants, typically recruited via crowdsourcing platforms (e.g Mechanical Turk or Prolific), are asked to read the stories generated by various systems and provide subjective rating or rankings. Questionnaires may ask participants to rate or rank the overall quality of stories, but may also ask specific questions about features of stories such as fluency or coherence. Coherence is particularly difficult feature of stories to measure because the term "coherence" can mean different things to different participants.

In this paper, we introduce a technique for **objective** human participant evaluation, called *Fabula Entropy Indexing* (FEI). FEI provides a structure for metrics that more objectively measure story coherence based on human question-answering. A *fabula* is a narratological term referring to the reader's inferred story world that a story takes place in, whether it be similar to the real world or a fantasy or science fiction world. The reader may of course be surprised by certain events but other events may seem implausible or contradictory, thus disrupting coherence. As they read, humans form cognitive structures to make sense of a story, which in turn can be used to answer simple true/false questions about the story. As such, an *incoherent* story results in readers making random guesses about the answers to these questions. FEI metrics thus measure the entropy of the answers—how much the answers disagree with each other—which directly

Proceedings of the 3rd Workshop on Narrative Understanding, pages 84–94
June 11, 2021. ©2021 Association for Computational Linguistics

correlates with the coherence of the story.

We introduce two such FEI metrics: *Entropy of Transitional Coherence* (ETC) and *Entropy of World Coherence* (EWC), measuring (respectively) sequential coherence between events in a story, and the internal coherence of the *story world*: the facts about characters, objects, and locations that distinguish a story. The correlation between human question-answering and these metrics are grounded in narratological[1] theories.

To validate the measure, we test our metrics on human-written stories as well as corrupted versions of those stories. For the corrupted stories, we artificially reduce the coherence by altering elements of the story. We show that FEI metrics evaluate non-corrupted human-written stories as having low entropy and corrupted stories as having higher entropy.

2 Background and Related Work

2.1 Automated Story Generation

Early story and plot generation systems relied on symbolic planning (Meehan, 1976; Lebowitz, 1987; Cavazza et al., 2003; Porteous and Cavazza, 2009; Riedl and Young, 2010; Ware and Young, 2011) or case-based reasoning (Pérez y Pérez and Sharples, 2001; Peinado and Gervás, 2005; Turner, 2014). An increasingly common machine learning approach to story generation is to use neural language models (Roemmele, 2016; Khalifa et al., 2017; Clark et al., 2018; Martin et al., 2018). These techniques have improved with the adoption of Transformer-based models, such as GPT-2 (Radford et al., 2019). While GPT-2 and similar neural language models are considered highly fluent from a grammatical standpoint.

In these systems, a neural language model learns to approximate the distribution $P_\theta(tok_n|tok_{<n})$ where θ is the parameters that approximate the pattern of an underlying dataset. Stories are produced by providing an initial context sequence, then iteratively generating additional tokens by sampling from the distribution. When the language model is trained on a corpus of stories, subsets of the generated text tend to also be a story.

One of the reasons why story generation is challenging is because of the strong requirement that stories be *coherent*. Coherence can refer to readability/fluency. However, stories also require *plot coherence*, which is how well the elements of a plot cohere with each other. Studies of human reading comprehension (Trabasso and Van Den Broek, 1985; Graesser et al., 1991, 1994) show that humans comprehend stories by tracking the relations between events. Reader comprehension studies suggest that readers rely on the tracking of at least four types of relations between events: (1) causal consequence, (2) goal hierarchies, (3) goal initiation, and (4) character intentions. The perceived coherence of a story is a function of the reader being able to comprehend how events correlate to each other causally or how they follow characters' pursuits of implicit goals.

To control the generation and achieve greater coherence, a high-level plot outline can either be generated or given as an input to a language model. (Fan et al., 2018; Peng et al., 2018; Rashkin et al., 2020; Brahman and Chaturvedi, 2020). These techniques can produce more coherent stories when their guidance forces different parts of the story to appear related or to follow a pattern acceptable to humans.

Tambwekar et al. (2018) attempt to train a neural language model to perform goal-based generation. They fine-tune a neural language model with a policy-gradient reinforcement learning technique that rewards the language model for generating events progressively closer to the goal event.

2.2 Story Generator Evaluation

Traditional automated measures of natural language quality such as perplexity or n-gram comparisons (e.g., BLEU) are generally considered insufficient for evaluating story generation systems. Perplexity is the measure of how well a model captures the patterns in an underlying dataset. Implicit in the notion of perplexity is the belief that the quality of a model is tied to its ability to reconstruct its own data. However, in automated story generation, stories that are very dissimilar to training and testing data can also be "good". Likewise, BLEU (and related techniques such as ROGUE and sentence mover techniques (Clark et al., 2019)) measure a language model's ability to produce n-grams in a specific target sentence, whereas a good story may not resemble a given target story and yet still be coherent.

The gold standard for evaluation of automated story generation systems is to use human participant studies. Many systems are evaluated with subjective questionnaires in which human partic-

[1] *Narratology* is the study of stories and storytelling.

ipants either rate generated stories on a scale, or rank pairs of stories. Often a single question is asked about overall quality. Other subjective questions focusing on different story attributes, such as coherence, may be asked as well. Asking questions about coherence is tricky as participants may have different notions of what coherence might mean, from grammatical notions of coherence to logical story structure.

Purdy et al. (2018) introduced a set of subjective questions for human participant studies about global coherence, local consistency, grammaticality, and overall story quality. Algorithms to predict how humans would answer these questions were also introduced. The goal of this work was to reduce reliance on expensive human-participant studies. One innovation is that they don't directly ask about coherence, which can be an ambiguous term, but instead ask questions such as "the story appears to be a single plot". This set of questions has been used by Tambwekar et al. (2019) and Ammanabrolu et al. (2020). The algorithms introduced by Purdy et al. (2018) were validated and proven to be reliable predictors but the measure of coherence was shown to be the weakest predictor.

The USER technique, introduced as part of Storium (Akoury et al., 2020), is a means of evaluating stories by giving human participants the means to edit a generated story. They measure the largest subsequence not edited by the author during a story continuation. They conclude that their measure is strongly correlated with human evaluation of coherency.

Li et al. (2013) evaluated their story generation system using an objective human participant study. They generated stories and then had humans add sentences, delete sentences, or swap sentence orderings. The number of edits is used to score the story generation system (lower is better).

Riedl and Young (2010) also evaluated their story generation system with an objective human participant study based on cognitive science. They conducted a question-answering protocol to elicit the cognitive model that humans had about the causal relations and goals of characters. Specifically they constructed a number of questions that the story generation system believed human readers should be able to answer. The measure of story quality was the degree to which humans answered the questions the way the algorithm predicted they would. This technique is the most similar in nature to our proposed measure of coherence; our technique is mathematically grounded and not tied to any particular way of generating stories.

3 Preliminaries

In this section we review narratological definitions that will be relevant to understanding how to measure the Fabula Entropy Indices.

Definition 3.1. A **narrative** is the recounting of a sequence of events that have a continuant subject and constitute a whole (Prince, 2003).

An event describes some change in the state of the world. A "continuant subject" means there is some relationship between the events—it is about something and not a random list of unrelated events. All stories are narratives, but also include some additional criteria that are universally agreed upon.

Structural narratologists suggest there are different layers at which narratives can be analyzed: *fabula* and *syuzhet* (Bal and Van Boheemen, 2009)

Definition 3.2. The **fabula** of a narrative is an enumeration of all the events that take place the story world.

Definition 3.3. The **syuzhet** of a narrative is a subset of the fabula that is presented via narration to the audience.

The events in the fabula are temporally sequenced in the order that they occur, which may be different than the order in which they are told. Most notably, the events and facts in the fabula might not all exist in the final telling of the narrative; some events and facts might need to be inferred from what is actually told. It is not required that the syuzhet to be told in chronological order, allowing for achronological tellings such as flash forward, flashback, ellipses (gaps in time), etc.

They key is that readers interact more closely with syuzhet and must infer the fabula through the text of the syuzhet. Because a fabula inferred, it may be occuring in one of many possible worlds in a modal logic sense (Ryan, 1991).

Definition 3.4. A **story world** is a set of possible worlds that are consistent with the facts and events presented to the reader in the syuzhet.

As events and facts are presented throughout the narrative, the probability cloud over story worlds collapses and a reader's beliefs become more certain.

Events in the fabula and story world have different degrees of importance:

Definition 3.5. A **kernel** is a narrative event such that after its completion, the beliefs a reader holds as they pertain to the story have drastically changed.

Definition 3.6. A **satellite** is a narrative event that supports a kernel. They are the minor plot points that lead up to major plot points. They do not result in massive shift in beliefs.

Satellites imply the existence of kernels, e.g. small plot points will explain and lead up to a large plot point, but kernels do not imply the existence of satellites—kernels do not require satellites to exist. A set of satellites, $s = \{s_1, \ldots, s_n\}$, is said to be relevant to a kernel k if, after the kernel's competition, the reader believes that the set of questions posed by k are relevant to their understanding of the story world given prior s.

An implication of kernels and satellites is that one can track a reader's understanding of a story over time by asking the reader questions relevant to the story before and after each major plot point. As kernels change the reader's beliefs about the story world and the fabula, then their answers to questions change as well.

4 Fabula Entropy Indexing

Fabula Entropy Indexing (FEI) measures story coherence based on human question-answering. Humans build cognitive structures to make sense of a story, which in turn can be used to answer simple true/false questions about the story. A coherent narrative results in readers having well-formed cognitive models of the fabula and story world(Graesser et al., 2003; Trabasso et al., 1982). Because the cognitive models formed during reading are predictable across readers one can infer that coherent stories result in readers being more likely to answer questions about a story similarly (Graesser et al., 1991). *Incoherent* stories thus result in readers making random guesses about the answers to questions. FEI looks at the entropy of the answers—how much readers disagree with each other—as a signal of coherence of the story.

We decompose FEI into two separate metrics. *Entropy of Transitional Coherence* (ETC) measures the necessity of transitional ordering: in time t, event or fact x is necessary to maintain a story's coherence. In other words, was this fact probable before t? This establishes whether a reader could reasonably anticipate the occurring between two events. *Entropy of World Coherence* (EWC) on the other hand is not time dependent. EWC measures the probability of an event or fact y occurring *at any time* in a story world.

The core idea of Fabula Entropy Indexing is that readers can be asked true/false questions and that the agreement in readers' answers indicates coherence. However, questions must take the form of implications $q : A \implies B$ (read "if A then B") and the two propositions A and B must have *relevance* to each other.

Definition 4.1. For a question about a story, q, of the form "if A then B" with possible values for $A = \{T, F\}$ and possible values for $B = \{T, F\}$. Identifying A with the set of possible answers to it, we say that the **relevance** of B to A given some prior γ is

$$H(A = a_i|\gamma) - H(B = b_j|A = a_i, \gamma) \quad (1)$$

where a_i and b_j are the true answers to A and B and H refers to binary entropy. (Knuth, 2004).

Note that the relevance of B to A *depends on the ground truth*. Consider the case where A is "is Harry Potter the prophesied Heir of Slytherin?" and B is "can Harry Potter speak Parseltongue because he is a descendent of Slytherin?". If Harry is a blood descendant of Slytherin and that is why he can speak Parseltongue, then B is highly relevant to A. However, the actual truth of the matter is that Harry's abilities are completely independent of his heritage. Therefore B does not have relevance to A even though *it could have had relevance* to A had the ground truth been different.

4.1 Entropy of Transitional Coherence

Certain facts or events in stories have temporal dependencies. For example, a protagonist may hammer a nail into the wall. If subsequent events reveal the fact that the protagonist never held a hammer this causes temporal or transitional incoherence.

If we force our question to be an implication, namely of the form "Given that A occurs within the story, then B", we are attempting to determine the relevance of a query B to a query $A = true$, specifically:

$$H(A = true|\gamma) - H(B = b_j|A = true, \gamma).$$

If A is given within the reader's inferred fabula, then A is always true and we simply want to query about B. However if A is undetermined within the reader's inferred fabula then we are as a whole querying about "If A then B," and forcing the reader to reconcile both A and B without any belief about A.

Entropy of Transitional Coherence therefore asks questions of readers in which A is a belief from before a kernel and B is a belief from after a kernel. Let question q be of the form "Given that A occurs within the story, then B." That is $q := A \implies B$. Let $P(q)$ refer to the proportion of story worlds where q is true. The stronger the reader's belief, the more possible worlds in which q is true, and the higher the probability. Across all readers answering the question:

$$\begin{aligned} H(P(q)) &= H(q|\gamma) \\ &= H(A = T|\gamma) - H(B = b_j|A = T, \gamma) \end{aligned} \tag{2}$$

By averaging across all questions Q that span kernels, we arrive at the definition of ETC:

$$E(Q) = \frac{1}{|Q|}\sum_{q \in Q} H\big(P(q)\big) \tag{3}$$

In the context of Entropy of Transitional Coherence, $ETC(Q) = E(Q)$.

Consider the following example for discussing the importance of ETC. A person needed a bath, so they went for a run. A possible query here would be "Given a person needed a bath, does this contradict that they went for a run?" In this particular example, we can assume going for a run is a kernel and as such this query measures if needing a bath is a plausible precondition to desiring to go on a run. Equivalently, does the reader believe "If the person needs a bath, then they go for a run." If the story makes less sense to the reader, the reader attempts to reconcile these two clauses and as such would be more likely to guess.(Trabasso et al., 1982; Mandler and Johnson, 1977)

4.2 Entropy of World Coherence

Whereas Entropy of Transitional Coherence measures coherence as events cause the story world to change, Entropy of World Coherence (EWC) measures the coherence of static fact about the story world. For example if a story contains a protagonist that is described as being short but is also described as hitting their head on the top of a doorframe, we might find readers have more varied responses to a question about the protagonist's height.

Entropy of World Coherence also uses Equation 3 (that is, $EWC(Q) = E(Q)$) but does not require that the questions reference before and after kernels. There need not be any temporal requirement to questions. Instead EWC relies on questions about descriptive elements in a story, as signified by adjective and adverbs. However, these descriptions of characters, objects, or places must be integral to at least one event in the narrative.

4.3 Measuring Coherence with Human Participant Studies

Having mathematically defined our two coherence metrics, ETC and EWC, as a function of readers responding to a set of questions about temporal or non-temporal aspects of a story, we now describe how we use ETC and EWC to measure coherence of stories, particularly those from by automated story generation systems. There are three key steps to Fabula Entropy Indexing as a methodology.

The first step is to use an automated story generation system to generate a number of stories that are representative of its capabilities. Typically this would be done by randomly seeding the generator.

The second step is to produce a number of questions. To produce questions for ETC, one identifies the kernels—the major plot points—and constructs questions such as:

- Does Entity A's sentiment/emotion change between line N-1 and N?
- Does Object A change possession in Line N+1?

To produce questions for EWC, one identifies adjectives and adverbs that could be changed, such as:

- Does [Adverb/Adjective] contradict an assertion on Line N?
- Could [Adverb/Adjective] be removed and the story world would remain unchanged?

One would want to produce as many questions as possible. Note that while the questions above do not read as implications immediately, they can be expressed as the required implications after a bit of work and thus still satisfy our constraint.

It doesn't matter what the questions are or what the answers are—we do not require a ground truth—as long as the questions reference aspects of the story that can impact readers' cognitive model formation. ETC and EWC guide us toward kernels and attributes, respectively. Fabula Entropy Indexing measures coherence by observing the agreement between human participants when answering these questions.

The third step is to recruit human study participants to read a story and then answer the associated questions. There is no ground-truth "correct" answers—we are not testing participants ability to answer in a certain way. Instead, we use Equation 3 to measure agreement between responses, under the assumption that more coherent stories prompt readers to construct more consistent mental models of the fabula and story world.

ETC and EWC can be compared between representative sets of stories between different automated story generation systems. Lower entropy values implies greater coherence.

5 Experiments

To validate Fabula Entropy Indexing in general, and ETC and EWC in particular, we need to verify that the methodology in Section 4.3 produces low entropy values for coherent stories and high entropy values for incoherent stories. Because automated story generation is still an open research question, we validate ETC and EWC on human-written stories that are known to be coherent. We assume that human-written stories are coherent. To compare entropy indices against incoherent stories, we devise a technique for corrupting human written stories in particular ways that are likely to result in incoherent stories. Exemplar corruptions include negating adjectives, swapping events from different stories or randomly changing key descriptors of characters.

5.1 Entropy of World Coherence Stories

For EWC, we source a number of short stories by authors such as Rumi, Tolstoy and Gibran. Specifically, this is a subset available in a public repository[2] unaffiliated with the authors of this paper. For each story we subdivide them into 10-line segments if the story was longer than 10 lines. We selected 9 stories for the experiment.[3]

To create a corrupted story baseline in which story coherence is less assured, we copied the 9 stories and made changes to them. We recruited 4 participants who are unaffiliated with the research team and asked them to independently select a subset of the adjectives and adverbs from a story and swap them for their antonyms. This produced stories that are, at a story world level, less coherent since due to the highly descriptive nature of the stories one swap was more likely to lead to a contradiction later on in the story. Participants were required to create the inconsistency and not to fix their incoherency with more swaps. Participants were compensated $20/hr to complete this task.

5.2 Entropy of Transitional Coherence Stories

For Transitional Coherence we require a direct correspondence between events and sentences. *Plotto* (Cook, 2011) is a compilation of plot points with annotations about which plot points can be followed by others. Plotto can thus be used to generate plot outlines assembled from human-written segments. The Plotto plot points contain few adjectives and plot outlines generated from the Plotto technique are unambiguous with respect to transitions in the story world. Since plotto consists of plot points, every vertex, and in our case line number, using the Plotto technique is a kernel. Within every kernel are a number of sentences, typically 2-3, that denote the satellites.

Since Plotto directly states plot points rather than having the reader infer them, this allows us to controllable corrupt the order of plot points by swapping lines- something that is rarely possible with human written short stories.

To construct stories for measuring ETC, we use the Plotto technique to generate 5-6 sentence short stories. For the experiment we generated 9 stories in this way.

To construct corrupted stories, we copied the 9 stories above and then swap the order of plot points, which results in incoherence (e.g. a burglar getting away with a crime before they're even born). We generate Plotto stories with 5 vertices, and randomly choose a span of 3 vertices. Within that span, we shuffle their order.

5.3 Question Generation

To measure ETC and EWC we require a set of true/false questions for each story. To ensure that we do not introduce experimental bias in questions for each story, we recruited 4 people to write questions for each story. Question writers were compensated $20/hr and produced 10-15 questions per

[2] https://github.com/pelagia/short-stories

[3] In both the ETC and EWC cases we had intended to evaluate over 10 stories but one story was rejected due to one of the stories inadvertently having a controversial interpretation when corrupted and which was only pointed out to us by one of the question-answering participants.

story.

For the corrupted sets of both Plotto and non-Plotto stories, we task a human participant to write questions guided by a set of templates which provide the best coverage over the more likely reader possible worlds. That is to say, if there were N reasonable interpretations of the story, we aimed to have our human subjects construct questions that could differentiate between N interpretations. Said another way, all templates probe the probability or plausibility of one plot point occurring or impacting the reader's comprehension of other plot points, in some way.

Participants were provided a packet which includes a description of the research, instructions for the task and a list of templates to follow when generating questions. Templates were also used to standardize the format of questions human participants in the subsequent experiment would receive. Question writing participants could freely choose the entities, properties and line numbers represented in each question.

A partial list of corruption prompts and a full list of question templates with some exemplar completions are provided in the Appendix.

5.4 Methodology

For each task, we recruit 180 participants on the Prolific platform, split evenly between ETC and EWC tasks. Demographic screening excluded any non-US individuals, individuals for whom English is not their first language, as well as those with linguistic impediments on the basis of the tasks' relative comprehension complexity. Each worker was either given corrupted stories or uncorrupted stories, but never both. This was done to prevent a worker from seeing both the uncorrupted and corrupted version of a story and as such biasing the results. Every worker received a randomized set of 3 stories. For each story, 10-15 yes or no questions were asked about interdependencies between sentences of the same story. Workers were compensated $20/hr for their time and given a screening question that was a handmade EWC and ETC example respectively. These examples were not used in computing the final result.

5.5 Results

The results are summarized in Figure 1 for Entropy of Transitional Coherence and Figure 2 for Entropy of World Coherence. The bars on the left are the results for uncorrupted, original stories and the bars

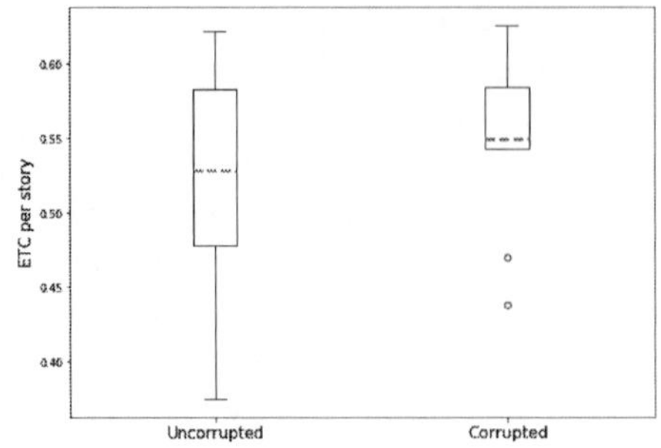

Figure 1: Entropic indices of transitional coherence derived from human participant evaluation of Plotto stories. Lower is better.

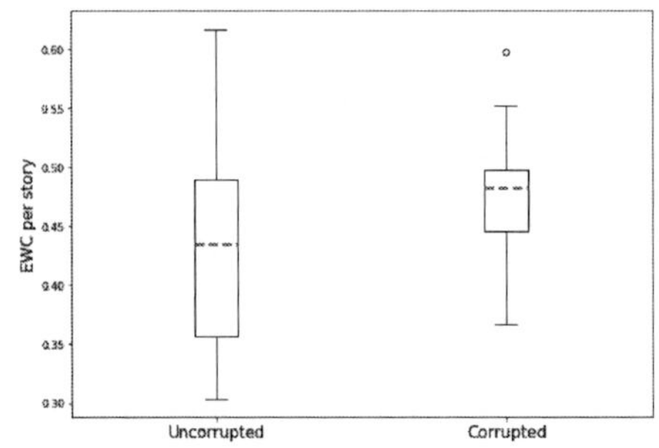

Figure 2: Entropic indicies of world coherence derived from human participant evaluation of the non-Plotto story dataset. Lower is better.

on the right are for the stories modified to corrupt coherence. The red line indicates the mean of each distribution. Median is not reported. The results suggest that original stories have lower entropy and are thus more coherent. This validates fabula entropy indexing because the corruptions we applied to the same set of stories are designed to interfere with readers' abilities to form a well-formed model of the fabula and story world.

We do not report statistical significance because statistical significance tests are undefined on entropy distributions, which are not probability distributions.

6 Discussion

From the results, we can make some observations. The first is that the corrupted stories are not a traditional experimental baseline. The corruptions were designed to show that intentionally introduced incoherencies do in fact result in an increase in entropy. Second, the corruptions are designed to introduce the smallest possible amount of incoherence to stories as possible. Therefore, we would not expect a large increase in entropy due to a single corruption per story. The fact that entropy increases with the introduction of minimalist corruptions indicates that Fabula Entropy Indexing is sensitive to such small changes. We would anticipate an automated story generator that routinely makes transitional or world coherence errors to result in much more significant differences in entropy values.

The entropies for corrupted stories have more dense distributions. Not only was there more disagreement about the answers to questions, but the disagreement was consistent across all stories. This is to be expected because the corruptions are synthetically designed to damage story coherence. The entropy distributions for real stories was spread over a wider range of entropy values per story.

ETC might not be as strong a metric as EWC. The average ETC of uncorrupted stories is higher than the EWC of uncorrupted stories. This may be due to (a) human tolerance for event ordering variations; (b) the Plotto technique may have produced plots in which plot points are only loosely connected; (c) our swap-based corruptions may not always produce incoherent stories.

The quality of the entropy indices are highly dependent on the extent to which the true/false questions target points in the story where potential incoherence can arise. It may theoretically be possible for some automated story generators to automatically generate good sets of questions, however this is currently an open research problem. The authors of this paper could have generated a better set of true/false questions targeting ETC and EWC than those unaffiliated with the research. However, doing so introduces the possibility of experimenter bias, which needs to be avoided by those who use this evaluation technique.

FEI has a couple of limitations. First, to measure ETC one must be able to identify kernels and make questions about elements before and after the kernels. Second, to measure EWC, the stories must be highly descriptive in nature and that there are plot points that are dependent on adjectives; many story generators do not produce descriptive texts.

FEI was validated on short stories, of 10 sentences or less. While there is no theoretical reason it will not work on longer stories, it will require substantially more questions to be produced and answered by human participant studies.

We have used the Fabula Entropy Indexing method described in this paper to evaluate an automated story generation system in (under review, 2021). The REDACTED system was designed explicitly to increase coherence of automatically generated stories over a large pretrained transformer language model baseline. The combined ETC and EWC for the experimental system were lower than the language model baseline. Moreover, we also compared the entropy indices of human-written baseline stories, showing that human stories result in lower entropy values than AI generated stories, which is to be expected at this time. This constitutes the first successful use of FEI for its intended purpose of evaluating automated story generation systems.

As part of the above real-world test case of FEI, we also performed a *subjective* human-participant study, showing that the entropy indices are low when humans report perceived coherence. We did not perform a subjective human participant study for this paper since we were working on stories that came from sources with reliable coherence.

7 Conclusions

Automated Story Generation research requires strong, reliable evaluation metrics, which have largely been absent, hampering research progress. We present the Fabula Entropy Indexing technique for objectively evaluating the coherence of stories. We demonstrate the effectiveness of this technique by showing how two FEI metrics, entropy world coherence and entropy transitional coherence, can be used to clearly discriminate between stories with and without coherence corruption. In contrast to subjective human participant studies, where it is challenging to get participants to answer questions about coherence, FEI provides a numerical rating of the coherence of stories that is grounded in theory.

References

Nader Akoury, Shufan Wang, Josh Whiting, Stephen Hood, Nanyun Peng, and Mohit Iyyer. 2020. Storium: A dataset and evaluation platform for machine-in-the-loop story generation.

Prithviraj Ammanabrolu, Wesley Cheung, William Broniec, and Mark O. Riedl. 2020. Automated storytelling via causal, commonsense plot ordering.

Mieke Bal and Christine Van Boheemen. 2009. *Narratology: Introduction to the theory of narrative*. University of Toronto Press.

Faeze Brahman and Snigdha Chaturvedi. 2020. Modeling protagonist emotions for emotion-aware storytelling. *arXiv preprint arXiv:2010.06822*.

Marc Cavazza, Olivier Martin, Fred Charles, Steven J Mead, and Xavier Marichal. 2003. Interacting with virtual agents in mixed reality interactive storytelling. In *International Workshop on Intelligent Virtual Agents*, pages 231–235. Springer.

Elizabeth Clark, Asli Celikyilmaz, and Noah A Smith. 2019. Sentence mover's similarity: Automatic evaluation for multi-sentence texts. In *Proceedings of the 57th Annual Meeting of the Association for Computational Linguistics*, pages 2748–2760.

Elizabeth Clark, Yangfeng Ji, and Noah A Smith. 2018. Neural text generation in stories using entity representations as context. In *Proceedings of the 2018 Conference of the North American Chapter of the Association for Computational Linguistics: Human Language Technologies, Volume 1 (Long Papers)*, pages 2250–2260.

William Cook. 2011. *PLOTTO: the master book of all plots*. Tin House Books.

Angela Fan, Mike Lewis, and Yann Dauphin. 2018. Hierarchical neural story generation. *arXiv preprint arXiv:1805.04833*.

Art Graesser, Kathy L. Lang, and Richard M. Roberts. 1991. Question answering in the context of stories. *Journal of Experimental Psychology: General*, 120(3):254–277.

Art Graesser, Murray Singer, and Tom Trabasso. 1994. Constructing inferences during narrative text comprehension. *Psychological Review*, 101(3):371–395.

Arthur C Graesser, Danielle S McNamara, and Max M Louwerse. 2003. What do readers need to learn in order to process coherence relations in narrative and expository text. *Rethinking reading comprehension*, 82:98.

Ahmed Khalifa, Gabriella AB Barros, and Julian Togelius. 2017. Deeptingle. *arXiv preprint arXiv:1705.03557*.

Kevin H. Knuth. 2004. Measuring questions: Relevance and its relation to entropy. *AIP Conference Proceedings*.

Michael Lebowitz. 1987. Planning stories. In *Proceedings of the 9th annual conference of the cognitive science society*, pages 234–242.

Boyang Li, Stephen Lee-Urban, George Johnston, and Mark Riedl. 2013. Story generation with crowdsourced plot graphs. In *Proceedings of the AAAI Conference on Artificial Intelligence*, volume 27.

Jean M Mandler and Nancy S Johnson. 1977. Remembrance of things parsed: Story structure and recall. *Cognitive psychology*, 9(1):111–151.

Lara Martin, Prithviraj Ammanabrolu, Xinyu Wang, William Hancock, Shruti Singh, Brent Harrison, and Mark Riedl. 2018. Event representations for automated story generation with deep neural nets. In *Proceedings of the AAAI Conference on Artificial Intelligence*, volume 32.

James Richard Meehan. 1976. The metanovel: writing stories by computer. Technical report, YALE UNIV NEW HAVEN CONN DEPT OF COMPUTER SCIENCE.

Kishore Papineni, Salim Roukos, Todd Ward, and Wei-Jing Zhu. 2002. Bleu: a method for automatic evaluation of machine translation. In *Proceedings of the 40th annual meeting of the Association for Computational Linguistics*, pages 311–318.

Federico Peinado and Pablo Gervás. 2005. Creativity issues in plot generation. In *Workshop on Computational Creativity, Working Notes, 19th International Joint Conference on AI*, pages 45–52.

Nanyun Peng, Marjan Ghazvininejad, Jonathan May, and Kevin Knight. 2018. Towards controllable story generation. In *Proceedings of the First Workshop on Storytelling*, pages 43–49.

Rafael Pérez y Pérez and Mike Sharples. 2001. Mexica: A computer model of a cognitive account of creative writing. *Journal of Experimental & Theoretical Artificial Intelligence*, 13(2):119–139.

Julie Porteous and Marc Cavazza. 2009. Controlling narrative generation with planning trajectories: the role of constraints. In *Joint International Conference on Interactive Digital Storytelling*, pages 234–245. Springer.

Gerald Prince. 2003. *A dictionary of narratology*. U of Nebraska Press.

Christopher Purdy, X. Wang, Larry He, and Mark O. Riedl. 2018. Predicting generated story quality with quantitative measures. In *AIIDE*.

Alec Radford, Jeffrey Wu, Rewon Child, David Luan, Dario Amodei, and Ilya Sutskever. 2019. Language models are unsupervised multitask learners. *OpenAI blog*, 1(8):9.

Hannah Rashkin, Asli Celikyilmaz, Yejin Choi, and Jianfeng Gao. 2020. Plotmachines: Outline-conditioned generation with dynamic plot state tracking. *arXiv preprint arXiv:2004.14967*.

Mark O Riedl and Robert Michael Young. 2010. Narrative planning: Balancing plot and character. *Journal of Artificial Intelligence Research*, 39:217–268.

Melissa Roemmele. 2016. Writing stories with help from recurrent neural networks. In *Proceedings of the AAAI Conference on Artificial Intelligence*.

Marie-Laure Ryan. 1991. *Possible worlds, artificial intelligence, and narrative theory*. Indiana University Press.

Pradyumna Tambwekar, Murtaza Dhuliawala, Lara J Martin, Animesh Mehta, Brent Harrison, and Mark O Riedl. 2018. Controllable neural story plot generation via reinforcement learning. *arXiv preprint arXiv:1809.10736*.

Pradyumna Tambwekar, Murtaza Dhuliawala, Lara J Martin, Animesh Mehta, Brent Harrison, and Mark O Riedl. 2019. Controllable neural story plot generation via reward shaping. In *IJCAI*, pages 5982–5988.

Tom Trabasso and Paul Van Den Broek. 1985. Causal thinking and the representation of narrative events. *Journal of memory and language*, 24(5):612–630.

Tom Trabasso et al. 1982. Causal cohesion and story coherence.

Scott R Turner. 2014. *The creative process: A computer model of storytelling and creativity*. Psychology Press.

Stephen Ware and R Young. 2011. Cpocl: A narrative planner supporting conflict. In *Proceedings of the AAAI Conference on Artificial Intelligence and Interactive Digital Entertainment*, volume 6.

A Appendices

A.1 Alteration Templates[4]

The [Adjective1] Object/Entity/Event -> The [Adjective2] Object/Entity/Event

The [Adjective1] Object/Entity/Event -> The not [Adjective1] Object/Entity/Event

Object/Entity/Event is [Adverb1] [Adjective1] -> Object/Entity/Event is [Adverb1] [Adjective2]

Object/Entity/Event is [Adverb1] [Adjective1] -> Object/Entity/Event is [Adverb2] [Adjective1]

Object/Entity/Event [Adverb1][Verb] -> Object/Entity/Event [Adverb2][Verb]

These are just a small sample of templates given the complex nature of certain sentences. You can make alterations beyond this but adhere to the rules above.

A.2 Question Templates: EWC

In the context of this narrative setting, is [Adverb/Adjective] plausible? (e.g. an "otherworldly" dog showing up in a short story about World War 2 where you might otherwise describe a "stray" dog. Note: This may not be a constraint for all readers - those answering questions will only assess based on *their* belief about the world.)

Prior to this line did you imagine [Adverb/Adjective] was a possible descriptor for Object/Entity/Event?

After this line containing [Adverb/Adjective] do you hold the belief this is a possible descriptor or do you reject it?

Because of [Adverb/Adjective] does Line N contradict information in another line?

Because of [Adverb/Adjective] does this indicate emotional valence (extreme sentiment) toward an Object/Entity/Event?

In the line with [Adverb/Adjective] does this alter Author or Entity sentiment toward Object/Event?
Because of [Adverb/Adjective] does this change your sentiment toward some Entity/Object/Event?

Does [Adverb/Adjective] contradict an assertion on Line N?

Could [Adverb/Adjective] be removed and the story world would remain unchanged?

Without [Adverb/Adjective] on Line N, Line N+1 would not have happened.

A.3 Question Templates: ETC

Does Entity A's perception of Entity B change?

Do all Entities in Line N observe or gain awareness of Events in Line N+1?

Do the Events in Line N+1 contradict Events in Line N?

Does Entity A's sentiment/emotion change between line N-1 and N?

Does Object A still retain State S?

Does Object A change possession in Line

[4]Additional clarifying examples were given to participants when they requested them during task completion.

N+1?

Is Object A in Line N+1 necessary for Events in line N to occur?

Is there a change in context or location between these lines?

Is knowledge of Object A necessary for understanding the following line?

Does Line N have causal dependencies established in Line N-1?

Could Line N-1 occur before Line N?

A.4 Selected Questions

Does "awful" contradict an assertion on line 1?

Could "shaped" in line 4 be removed and the story world would remain unchanged?

Because of "tall" does line 9 contradict information in another line?

Could line 1 and 5 both be removed and have no effect on the story?

Is there a change in context or location between line 2 and 5?

Do the events in line 3 contradict events in line 2?

Towards a Model-Theoretic View of Narratives

Louis Castricato* Georgia Tech EleutherAI lcastric@gatech.edu

Stella Biderman* Georgia Tech EleutherAI stella@eleuther.ai

Rogelio E. Cardona-Rivera University of Utah rogelio@cs.utah.edu

David Thue Carleton University david.thue@carleton.ca

Abstract

In this paper, we propose the beginnings of a formal framework for modeling narrative *qua* narrative. Our framework affords the ability to discuss key qualities of stories and their communication, including the flow of information from a Narrator to a Reader, the evolution of a Reader's story model over time, and Reader uncertainty. We demonstrate its applicability to computational narratology by giving explicit algorithms for measuring the accuracy with which information was conveyed to the Reader, along with two novel measurements of story coherence.

1 Introduction

Story understanding is both (1) the process through which a cognitive agent (human or artificial) mentally constructs a *plot* through the perception of a *narrated discourse*, and (2) the outcome of that process: i.e., the agent's mental representation of the plot. The best way to computationally model story understanding is contextual to the aims of a given research program, and today we enjoy a plethora of artificial intelligence (AI)-based capabilities.

Data-driven approaches—including statistical, neural, and neuro-symbolic ones—look to narrative as a benchmark task for demonstrating human-level competency on inferencing, question-answering, and storytelling. That is, they draw associations between event (Chambers and Jurafsky, 2008), causal (Li et al., 2012), and purposive (Jiang and Riloff, 2018) information extracted from textual or visual narrative corpora to answer questions or generate meaningful stories that depend on information implied and not necessarily expressed by stories (e.g. Roemmele et al., 2011; Mostafazadeh et al., 2016; Martin et al., 2018; Kim et al., 2019).

Symbolic approaches seek to understand narrative, its communication, and its effect by using AI techniques as computational modeling tools, including logic, constraint satisfaction, and automated planning. These include efforts to model creative storytelling as a search process (Riedl and Young, 2006; Thue et al., 2016), generating stories with predictable effects on their comprehension by audiences (Cardona-Rivera et al., 2016), and modeling story understanding through human-constrained techniques (Martens et al., 2020).

Despite recent advances, few works have offered a thorough conceptual account of narrative in a way that affords reconciling how different research programs might relate to each other. Without a foundation for shared progress, our community might strain to determine how individual results may build upon each other to make progress on story understanding AI that performs as robustly and flexibly as humans do (Cardona-Rivera and Young, 2019). In this paper, we take steps toward such a foundation.

We posit that such a foundation must acknowledge the diverse factors that contribute to an artifact being treated *as* a narrative. Key among these factors is a narrative's *communicative* status: unlike more-general natural language generation (cf. Gatt and Krahmer, 2018), an audience's *belief dynamics*—the trajectory of belief expansions, contractions, and revisions (Alchourrón et al., 1985)—is core to what gives a narrative experience its quality (Herman, 2013). Failure to engage with narratives on these grounds risks losing an essential aspect of what makes narrative storytelling a vibrant and unique form of literature.

To that end, we define a preliminary theoretical framework of narrative centered on information entropy. Our framework is built atop *model theory*, the set-theoretic study of language interpretation. Model theory is a field of formal logic that has been used extensively by epistomologists, linguists, and other theorists as a framework for building logical semantics.

Proceedings of the 3rd Workshop on Narrative Understanding, pages 95–104

Contributions. In this paper, we propose the beginnings of a formal framework for modeling narrative *qua* narrative. Our framework affords discussing the flow of information from a Narrator to a Reader, the evolution of a Reader's story model over time, and Reader uncertainty. Our work is grounded in the long history of narratology, drawing on the rich linguistic and philosophical history of the field to justify our notions.

We use our framework to make experimentally verifiable conjectures about how story readers respond to under-specification of the story world and how to use entropy to identify plot points. We additionally demonstrate its applicability to computational narratology by giving explicit algorithms for measuring the accuracy with which information was conveyed to the Reader. We also propose two novel measurements of story coherence.

2 Pre-Rigorous Notions of Narrative

Before we can begin defining narrative in a formal sense, we must examine the intuitive notions of what narrative *is supposed to mean*. While we cannot address all of the complexity of narratology in this work, we cover some key perspectives.

2.1 Narratives as Physical Artifacts

We begin with the structuralist account within narratology; it frames a *narrative* (*story*) as a communicative, designed artifact—the product of a *narration*, itself a realization (e.g. book, film) of a *discourse* (Hühn and Sommer, 2013). The discourse is the story's information layer (Genette, 1980): an author-structured, temporally-organized subset of the *fabula*; a discourse projects a fabula's information. The fabula is the story's world, which includes its *characters*, or intention-driven agents; *locations*, or spatial context; and *events*, the causally-, purposely-, and chronologically-related situation changes (Bal, 1997; Rimmon-Kenan, 2002).

As a designed artifact, a narrative reflects *authorial intent*. Authors design the stories they tell to affect audiences in specific ways; their designs ultimately target effecting change in the minds of audiences (Bordwell, 1989). This design stems from the authors' understanding of their fabula and of the narration that conveys its discourse. When audiences encounter the designed artifact, they perform story understanding: they attempt to mentally construct a fabula through their perception of the story's narration.

2.2 Narratives as Mental Artifacts

Story psychologists frame the narration as instructions that guide story understanding (Gernsbacher et al., 1990). The fabula in the audience's mind is termed the *situation model*—a mental representation of the virtual world and the events that have transpired within it, formed from information both explicitly-narrated and inferable-from a narration (Zwaan and Radvansky, 1998). The situation model itself *is* the audience's understanding; it reflects a tacit belief about the fabula, and is manipulated via three (fabula-belief) update operations. These work across memory retrieval, inferencing, and question-answering cognition: (1) *expansion*, when the audience begins to believe something, (2) *contraction*, when the audience ceases to believe something, and (3) *revision*, when the audience expands their belief and contracts newly inconsistent beliefs.

2.3 Narratives as Received Artifacts

To the post-structuralist, the emphasis that the psychological account puts on the author is fundamentally misplaced (Barthes, 1967). From this point of view, books are meant to be *read*, not written, and how they influence and are interpreted by their readers is as essential to their essence as the intention of the author. In "Death of the Author" Barthes (Barthes, 1967) reinforces this concept by persistently referring to the writer of a narrative not as its creator or its author, but as its sculptor - one who shapes and guides the work but does not dictate to their audience its meaning.

3 A Model-Theoretic View of Narrative

The core of our framework for modeling narrative come from a field of mathematical logic known as model theory. Model theory is a powerful yet flexible framework that has heavily influenced computer scientists, literary theorists, linguists, and philosophers (Sider, 2010). Despite the centrality of model theory in our framework, a deep understanding of the topic is not necessary to work with it on an applied level. Our goal in this section is thus to give an intuitive picture of model theory that is sufficient to understand how we will use it to talk about narratives. We refer an interested reader to Sider (2010); Chang and Keisler (1990) for a more complete presentation of the subject.

3.1 An Outline of Model Theory

The central object of study in model theory is a "model." Loosely speaking, a model is a world in which particular propositions are true. A model has two components: a domain, which is the set of objects the model makes claims about, and a theory, which is a set of consistent sentences that make claims about elements of the domain. Models in many ways resemble fabulas, in that they describe the relational properties of objects. Model theory, however, requires that the theory of a model be *complete* – every expressible proposition must be either true or false in a particular model.

Meanwhile, our notion of a fabula can be *incomplete* - it can leave the truth of some propositions undefined. This means that the descriptions we are interested in do not correspond to only *one* model, but rather that there is an infinite set of models that are consistent with the description. This may seem like a limitation, but we will show in Section 6 that it is actually amenable to analysis.

As an example, consider a simple world in which people can play cards with one another and wear clothes of various colours. The description *"Jay wears blue. Ali plays cards with Jay."* is incomplete because it does not say what colours Ali wears nor what other colours Jay wears. This description is consistent with a world in which there are characters other than Jay and Ali or colours other than blue (varying the domain), as well as one where additional propositions such as *"Ali wears blue."* hold (varying the theory).

Although we learn more about the domain and the theory of the narrator's model as the story goes on, we will never learn every single detail. Some of these details may not even be known to the narrator! For this reason, our framework puts a strong emphasis on consistency between models, and on the set of all models that are consistent with a particular set of statements.

Another very important aspect of model theory is that it is highly modular. Much of model theory is independent of the underlying logical semantics, which allows us to paint a very general picture. If a particular application requires augmenting the storytelling semantics with additional logical operators or relations, that is entirely non-problematic. For example, it is common for fabulas to contain Cause(X, Y) := "X causes Y" and Aft(X, Y) := "Y occurs after X." Although we don't specifically define either of these relations, they can be included in a particular application by simply adding them to the underlying logic.

3.2 Story-World Models and the Fabula

As detailed in section 2, the fabula and story-world (i.e., situation) model are two central components of how people talk about storytelling. In this section, we introduce formal definitions of these concepts as well as some of their properties.

Definition 3.1. A language, $\mathcal{L}$, is a set of rules for forming syntactically valid propositions. In this work we will make very light assumptions about $\mathcal{L}$ and leave its design largely up to the application.

A language describes *syntactic* validity, but it doesn't contain a notion of truth. For that, we need a model.

Definition 3.2. A story world model, S, over a language $\mathcal{L}$ is comprised of two parts: a domain, which is the set of things that exist in the story, and an interpretation function, which takes logical formulae and maps them to corresponding objects in the domain. In other words, the interpretation function is what connects the *logical expression* "A causes B" to the signified *fact in the world* that the thing we refer to as A causes the thing we refer to as B.

Definition 3.3. The theory of a story world model, S, is the set of all propositions that are true in S. It is denoted $\tilde{S}$. When we say "P is true in the model S" we mean that $P \in \tilde{S}$.

Formalizing the concept of a fabula is a bit trickier. Traditionally, fabulas are represented diagrammatically as directed graphs, but this representation gives little insight into their core attributes. We posit that, at their core, fabulas are relational objects. Specifically, they are a collection of elements of the domain of the story-world model together with claims about the relationships between those objects. Additionally, there is a sense in which the fabula is a "scratch pad" for the story-world model. While a reader may not even be able to hold an entire infinite story-world model in their head, they can more easily grasp the distillation of that story-world model into a fabula.

Definition 3.4. A reasoner's fabula for a story world model S, denoted F, is a set of propositions that makes claims about S. A proposition P is a member of F if it is an explicit belief of the reasoner about the narrative that the reasoner deems important to constructing an accurate story-world model.

4 Conveying Story Information

An important aspect of stories is that they are a way to convey information. In this section, we will discuss how to formalize this process and what we can learn about it. Although stories can be constructed and conveyed in many different ways, we will speak of a Narrator who tells the story and a Reader who receives it for simplicity.

The core of how we model storytelling as an act of communication can be seen in Figure 1.

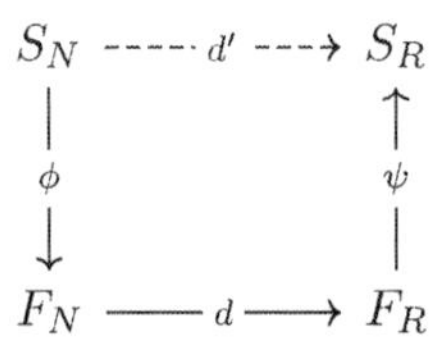

Figure 1: A commutative diagram outlining storytelling.

This diagram represents the transmission of information from the Narrator's story-world (S_N) to the Reader's (S_R), with each arrow representing the transmission from one representation to another. In an idealized world, stories would be conveyed by d': straight from the story world of the narrator (S_N) to the story world of the reader (S_R). In actuality, narrators must convey their ideas through media[1]. To do this, the narrator compresses their mental story world (via ϕ) into a fabula (F_N) which is then conveyed to the reader via speech, writing, etc. The conveyance of the fabula *as understood by the Narrator* (F_N) to the fabula *as understood by the Reader* (F_R) is denoted in our diagram by d. d is in many ways the real-world replacement for the function d' the Narrator is unable to carry out. Once the discourse has been consumed by the Reader, the Reader then takes their reconstructed fabula (F_R) and uses the received information to update their story world model (S_R, via ψ).

4.1 Accurately Conveying Information

Often times, information conveyed from the Narrator to the Reader is "conveyed correctly." By this, we mean that the essential character of the story was conveyed from the Narrator to the Reader in such a way that the Reader forms accurate beliefs about the story-world. While accuracy is not always a primary consideration - some stories feature unreliable narrators or deliberately mislead the Reader to induce experiences such as suspense, fear, and anticipation - the ability to discuss the accuracy and consistency of the telling of the story is an essential part of analyzing a narrative.

The d' arrow in our diagram suggests a reasonable criteria for accurate conveyance: a story is accurately conveyed if the path $S_N \to F_N \to F_R \to S_R$ and the path $S_N \dashrightarrow S_R$ compute the same (or, in practice, similar) functions. In mathematics, this property of path-independence is known as commutativity and the diagram is called a "commutative diagram" when it holds. For the purposes of narrative work, the essential aspect is that the arrows "map corresponding objects correspondingly." That is, if a story is accurately conveyed from N to R then for each proposition $P \in S_N$ there should be a corresponding $P' \in S_R$ such that the interpretations of P and P' (with respect to their respective models) have the same truth value and $(\phi \circ d \circ \psi)(P) = P'$. In other words, P and P' make the same claims about the same things.

4.2 Time-Evolution of Story-World Models

The transference of information depicted in fig. 1 gives rise to a straightforward way to understand how the Reader gains knowledge during the course of the story and incorporates new information into their existing story-world model. One pass through the diagram from S_N to S_R represents "one time step" of the evolution of the Reader's world model[2].

Iterating this process over the the entire work gives a time series of story-world models, $S_R(t)$, with $S_R(i)$ representing the Reader's story-world model at time $t = i$. We are also typically interested in how the story-world model changes over time, as the Reader revises their understanding of the story-world through consuming the discourse. This will be the subject of the next section.

5 A Detailed Look at Temporal Evolution, with Applications to Plot

A commonly accepted notion in narratology is that at any given moment, a reader contains a potentially infinite set of possible worlds. Determining which of these worlds agree with each other is a required attribute for consuming discourse. How do we discuss the notion of collapsing possible worlds upon acquiring new knowledge?

[1]Nevertheless, having a conception of d' is very important on a formal level as we will see later.

[2]For simplicity we will speak of this as a discrete time series, though for some media such as film it may make sense to model it as a continuous phenomenon.

Assume that we have a narrator, N, and reader R with fabulas F_N and F_R respectively. Given our definition of a story world model, S, we define $\mathbf{S}(t)$ as the set of all world models that satisfy $F_R(t)$. Let ρ_{t+1} refer to the set of formulae that are contained in $F_R(t+1) \backslash F_R(t)$. Let

$$S'_R(t+1) = \mathbf{S}_R(t+1) \cap \mathbf{S}_R(t)$$

and similarly

$$\tilde{S}'_R(t+1) = \tilde{\mathbf{S}}_R(t+1) \cap \tilde{\mathbf{S}}_R(t)$$

refer to the shared world models between the two adjacent time steps. Note that it must follow $\forall \rho \in \mathcal{P}_{t+1}$, $\forall s \in \tilde{\mathbf{S}}'_R(t+1)$, $\rho \in s$. That is to say, the story worlds that remain between the two time steps are the ones that agree on the propositions added by consuming $F_N(t+1)$. Since this can be repeated inductively, we can assume that for any such t we have that all such models agree on all such provided propositions.

Something to note that for $\rho \in \mathcal{P}_{t+1}$, ρ will always be either true or false in $\tilde{S}_R(t)$- regardless if it is expressed in the fabula or not since $\tilde{S}_R(t)$ is the logical closure of $S_R(t)$.

5.1 Collapse of Worlds over Time

Note that a set of story worlds $\tilde{\mathbf{S}}_R(t)$ does not provide us a transition function to discuss how the world evolves over time. Furthermore, there is no reasonable way to infer $\tilde{S}_R(t) \mapsto \tilde{S}_R(t+1)$, as $\tilde{S}_R(t)$ provides no information about the actions that could inhibit or allow for this transition- it simply provides us information about whether a proposition is true within our story world. To rectify this, we need to expand our commutative diagram to act across time. The full diagram can be found in the appendix.

Let ζ_N denote the transition function from $F_N(t)$ to $F_N(t+1)$. Define ζ_R likewise. See Figure 2 on page 10. Note that there is no inherent general form of ζ_N or ζ_R as they are significantly context dependent. One can think of them as performing graph edits on F_N and F_R respectively, to add the new information expressed in $S_N(t+1)$ for ζ_N and $(d \circ \phi)(S_N(t+1))$ for ζ_R.

The objective of ζ_R in turn is to guide the fabula to reach goals. This imposes a duality of ψ and ζ_R. ψ attempts to generate the best candidate story worlds for the reader's current understanding, where as ζ_R eliminates them by the direction the author wants to go.

This in turn brings us to the notion of compression and expansion. If ψ is left unchecked, it will continuously expand the fabula. In turn ζ_R is given the goal of compressing the story worlds that ψ produces by looking at the resulting transition functions that best match the author's intent.[3]

5.2 Plot Relevance

Stories contain many different threads and facts, and it would be nice to be able to identify the ones that are relevant to the plot. We begin with the idea of the relevance of one question to another.

Definition 5.1. Consider a question q about a story, where q has the form "if A then B" and possible values for $A = \{T, F\}$ and possible values for $B = \{T, F\}$. We say that the **relevance** of B to A given some prior γ is

$$H(A = a_i|\gamma) - H(B = b_j|A = a_i, \gamma) \quad (1)$$

where a_i and b_j are the true answers to A and B and H refers to binary entropy.

Note that the relevance of B to A *depends on the true answers*. This is perhaps surprising, but after some consideration it should be clear that this has to be true. After all, the causal relationship between A and B could depend on the true answers! Consider the case where A is "is Harry Potter the prophesied Heir of Slytherin?" and B is "can Harry Potter speak Parseltongue because he is a descendent of Slytherin?" If Harry is a blood descendant of Slytherin and that's why he can speak Parseltongue, then B is highly relevant to A. However, the actual truth of the matter is that Harry's abilities are completely independent of his heritage and arose due to a childhood experience. Therefore B does not in fact have relevance to A even though *it could have had relevance* to A.

Having defined a notion of the relevance of Question A to Question B, our next step is to connect our work to existing narratological analysis. Consider Barthes' notion of kernels and satellites.(Barthes and Duisit, 1975)

Definition 5.2. A **kernel** is a narrative event such that after its completion, the beliefs a reader holds as they pertain to the story have drastically

[3]There is no single best way to define an author's intent. For instance, we could have easily said that ψ denotes author intent while ζ_R determines which intents are best grounded in reality. The choice, however, needs to be made.

changed.[4]

Definition 5.3. A **satellite** is a narrative event that supports a kernel. They are the minor plot points that lead up to major plot points. They do not result in massive shift in beliefs.

Of importance to note is that satellites imply the existence of kernels, e.g. small plot points will explain and lead up to a large plot point, but kernels do not imply the existence of satellites- kernels do not require satellites to exist. One can think of this as when satellites exist kernels must always exist on their boundary whether they are referred to in the text or not.

A set of satellites, $s = \{s_1, \ldots, s_n\}$, is said to be relevant to a kernel, k, if after the kernel's competition, the reader believes that the set of questions posed by k are relevant to their understanding of the story world given prior s.

Note the definition of relevance. Simply put, A denotes the questions that define some notion of story world level coherency while B denotes the set of questions that define some notion of transitional coherency.

6 Possible Worlds and Reader Uncertainty

So far we have spoken about the Reader's story-world model as if there is only one, but in light of the discussion in section 3 it is unclear it truly makes sense to do so. In actuality, the Reader never learns to "true story-world model" (insofar as one can even be said to exist). Rather, the Reader has an evolving set of "plausible story-world models" that are extrapolated based on the incomplete information conveyed in the story. The purpose of this section is to detail how these "plausibilities" interact with each other and with plausibilities at other time steps.

It likely seems natural to model the Reader's uncertainty with a probabilistic model. Unfortunately, the topological structure of first-order logic makes that impossible as there is no way to define a probability distribution over the set of models that are consistent with a set of sentences. Instead, we are forced to appeal to *filters*, a weaker notion of size that captures the difference between "large" and "small" sets. Again we develop the theory of ultrafilters only to the extent that we require, and refer an interested reader to a graduate text in mathematical logic for a thorough discussion.

Definition 6.1. Let Q be a set of sentences that make claims about a narrative. A non-empty collection $\mathcal{F}_w \subseteq \mathcal{P}(Q)$ is a weak filter iff

1. $\forall X, Y \in \mathcal{P}(Q),\ X \in \mathcal{F}_w$ and $X \subseteq Y \subseteq \mathcal{P}(Q)$ implies $Y \in \mathcal{F}_w$
2. $\forall X \in \mathcal{P}(Q),\ X \notin \mathcal{F}_w$ or $\mathcal{P}(Q) \backslash X \notin \mathcal{F}_w$

We say that $\mathcal{F}_w$ is a weak ultrafilter and denote it $\mathcal{UF}_w$ if the second requirement is replaced by $\forall X \in \mathcal{P}(Q),\ X \in \mathcal{F}_w \iff \mathcal{P}(Q) \backslash X \notin \mathcal{F}_w$ (Askounis et al., 2016).

A reader's beliefs at time t defines a weak filter over the set of possible story-world models $\{S_R^i\}$. Call this filter $\mathcal{F}_w$, dropping the t when it is clear from context. Each element $U \in \mathcal{F}_w$ is a set of story world models that define a *plausibility*. This plausibility describes a set of propositions about the story that the reader thinks paints a coherent and plausible picture. Formally, a plausibility identified with the largest set of sentences that is true for every model in U, or $\cap_{S \in U} T(S)$ where $T(S)$ denotes the set of true statements in S. That is, the set of plausible facts.

The intuition for the formal definition of a weak filter is that 1. means that adding worlds to an element of the filter (which decreases the number of elements in $\cap_{S \in U} T(S)$) doesn't stop it from describing a plausibility since it is specifying fewer facts; and that 2. means that it is not the case that both P and $\neg P$ are plausible. It's important to remember that membership in $\mathcal{F}_w$ is a binary property, and so a statement is either plausible or is not plausible. We do not have shades of plausibility due to the aforementioned lack of a probability distribution.

As a framework for modeling the Reader's uncertainty, weak filters underspecify the space of plausible story world as a whole in favor of capturing what the reader "has actively in mind" when reading. This is precisely because the ultrafilter axiom is not required, and so for some propositions neither P nor $\neg P$ are judged to be plausible. When asked to stop and consider the truth of a specific proposition, the reader is confronted with the fact that there are many ways that they can precisify their world models. How a Reader responds to this confrontation is an experimental question that we leave to future work, but we conjecture that with

[4] The notion of "drastic" is equivalent to "majority." To rigoriously define Barthes' Kernel, and hence Barthes' Cardinal, we would require ultraproducts- which is outside of the scope of this paper.

sufficient time and motivation a Reader will build a weak ultrafilter $\mathcal{UF}_w$ that extends $\mathcal{F}_w$ and takes a position on the plausibility of all statements in the logical closure of their knowledge.

Once the Reader has fleshed out the space of plausibilities, we can use $\mathcal{UF}_w$ to build the *ultraproduct* of the Reader's story-world models. An ultraproduct (Chang and Keisler, 1990) is a way of using an ultrafilter to engage in *reconciliation* and build a single consistent story world-model out of a space of plausibilities. Intuitively, an ultraproduct can be thought of as a vote between the various models about the truth of individual propositions. A proposition is considered to be true in the ultraproduct if and only if the set of models in which it is true is an element of the ultrafilter. We conjecture that real-world rational agents with uncertain beliefs find the ultraproduct of their world models to be a reasonable reconciliation of their beliefs and that idealized perfectly rational agents will provably gravitate towards the ultraproduct as the correct reconciliation.

7 Applications to Computational Narratology

Finally, we demonstrate that our highly abstract framework is of practical use by using it to derive explicit computational tools that can benefit computational narratology.

7.1 Entropy of World Coherence

It is important to acknowledge that a reader can never reason over an infinite set of worlds. Therefore, it is often best to consider a finite sample of worlds. Given the (non-finite) set of story worlds, $\mathbf{S}(t)$, there must exist a set $s' \subset \mathcal{UF}_w(t)$ such that every element in s' is one of the "more likely" interpretations of the story world. This notion of more likely is out of scope of this paper; however, in practice, "more likely" simply denotes probability conditioned from $\tilde{\mathbf{S}}(t-1)$.

It is equally important to note that every element of s', by definition, can be represented in the reader's mind by the same fabula, say $F(t)$. Let Q be some set of implications that we would like to determine the truth assignment of. Let $P_{s'}(q)$ refer to the proportion of story worlds in s' such that q is true.[5] Clearly, $P_{s'}(q)$ is conditioned on s'. We can express the entropy of this as

$$\begin{aligned} H(P_{s'}(q)) &= H(q|s') \\ &= H(A=T|s') - H(B=b_j|A=T,s') \end{aligned}$$

Therefore averaging over $H(P_{s'}(q))$ for all $q \in Q$ is equivalent to determining the relevance of our implication to our hypothesis. This now brings us to EWC, or entropy of world coherence. These implications are of the form "Given something in the ground truth that all story worlds believe, then X" where X is a proposition held by the majority of story worlds but not all. We define EWC as

$$\text{EWC}(s', Q) = \frac{1}{|Q|} \sum_{q \in Q} P_{s'}(q)$$

7.2 Entropy of Transitional Coherence

Note our definition of plot relevance. It is particularly of value to not only measure the coherency of the rules that govern our story world but also to measure the coherency of the transitions that govern it over time. We can define a similar notion to EWC, called Entropy of Transitional Coherence, which aims to measure the agreement of how beliefs change over time. In doing so, we can accurately measure the reader's understanding of the laws that govern the dynamics of the story world rather than just the relationships that exist in a static frame.

To understand ETC we must first delve into the dynamics of modal logic. Note that for a proposition to be "necessary" in one frame of a narrative, it must have been plausible in a prior frame. (Sider, 2010) Things that are necessary, the reader knows; hence, the set of necessary propositions is a subset of a prior frame's possible propositions.

We must define a boolean lattice to continue

Definition 7.1. A **boolean lattice** of a set of propositions, Q, is a graph whose vertices are elements of Q and for any two $a, b \in Q$ if $a \implies b$ then there exists an edge (a, b) unless $a = b$

Note that a boolean lattice is a directed acyclic graph (DAG) and as such has source vertices with no parents. In the case of boolean lattices, a source vertex refers to an axiom, as sources are not provable by other sources.

We define one reader at two times, denoted $\mathcal{UF}_w(t)$ and $\mathcal{UF}_w(t')$ where $t' < t$. We define

[5] An equivalent form of $P(q)$ exists for when we do not have a form of measure. Particularly, define $P(q) = 1$ when q is true in the majority of story worlds, as defined by our ultrafilter. Similarly, let $P(q) = 0$ otherwise. For those with prior model theory experience, $P(q) = 1$ if q holds in an ultraproduct of story world models.

a filtration of possible worlds $s'(t')$ similar to how we did in the previous section.

Given $W(t) \in \mathcal{UF}_w(t)$, a ground truth at time t, we restrict our view of $W(t)$ to the maximal PW of time t'. This can be done by looking at

$$W' = \text{argmax}_{W(t) \cap s'_i} |B(W(t)) \cap (\cap_{s \in s'_i} B(s))|$$

Reason being is that it does not make sense to query about propositions that are undefined in prior frames. This effectively can be viewed as a pullback through the commutative diagram outlined previously. See Figure 2 on page 10. Something to note however is that this pullback is not necessary for ETC in the theoretical setting, as all world models would agree on any proposition not contained in their respective Boolean lattices- this is not the case when testing on human subjects. Human subjects would be more likely to guess if they are presented with a query that has no relevance to their current understanding. (Trabasso et al., 1982; Mandler and Johnson, 1977)

We can however similarly define ETC by utilizing W' as our ground truth with EWC. Since W' is not the minimal ground truth for a particular frame, it encodes information about the ground truth where the narrative will be going by frame t. Therefore, define Q similarly over time t' relative to W'. We can also use this to define $P_{s'(t')}(q)$ $\forall q \in Q$. We denote ETC as

$$\text{ETC}(s'(t'), Q) = \frac{1}{|Q|} \sum_{q \in Q} P_{s'(t')}(q)$$

ETC differs from EWC in the form of implications that reside in Q. Particularly since ETC wants to measure the coherency of a reader's internal transition model, $\forall q \in Q$ where $q := A \implies B$ we have that A is the belief a reader holds before a kernel and that B is a belief the reader holds after a kernel. Since the kernel is defined as a plot point which changes the majority of a reader's beliefs, we are in turn measuring some notion of faithfulness of ζ_R.

Conclusions and Future Work

In this paper, we defined a preliminary theoretical framework of narrative that affords new precision to common narratological concepts, including fabulas, story worlds, the conveyance of information from Narrator to Reader, and the way that the Reader's active beliefs about the story can update as they receive that information.

Thanks to this precision, we were able to define a rigorous and measurable notion of plot relevance, which we used to formalize Barthes' notions of kernels and satellites. We also give a novel formulation and analysis of Reader uncertainty, and form experimentally verifiable conjectures on the basis of our theories. We further demonstrated the value of our framework by formalizing two new narrative-focused measures: Entropy of World Coherence and Entropy of Transitional Coherence, which measure the agreement of story world models frames and faithfulness of ζ_R respectively.

Our framework also opens up new avenues for future research in narratology and related fields. While we were unable to explore their consequences within the scope of this paper, the formulation of narratives via model theory opens the door to leveraging the extensive theoretical work that has been done on models and applying it to narratology. The analysis of the temporal evolution of models in section 5 suggests connections with reinforcement learning for natural language understanding. In section 6 we make testable conjectures about the behavior of Reader agents and in section 7 we describe how to convert our theoretical musings into practical metrics for measuring the consistency and coherency of stories.

References

C. E. Alchourrón, P. Gärdenfors, and D. Makinson. 1985. On the Logic of Theory Change: Partial Meet Contraction and Revision Functions. *Journal of Symbolic Logic*, pages 510–530.

Dimitris Askounis, Costas D. Koutras, and Yorgos Zikos. 2016. Knowledge means all, belief means most. *Journal of Applied Non-Classical Logics*, 26(3):173–192.

Mieke Bal. 1997. *Narratology: Introduction to the theory of narrative*. University of Toronto Press.

Roland Barthes. 1967. *The death of the author*. Fontana.

Roland Barthes and Lionel Duisit. 1975. An introduction to the structural analysis of narrative. *New literary history*, 6(2):237–272.

David Bordwell. 1989. *Making Meaning: Inference and Rhetoric in the Interpretation of Cinema*. Cambridge: Harvard University Press.

Rogelio E. Cardona-Rivera, Thomas W. Price, David R. Winer, and R. Michael Young. 2016. Question Answering in the Context of Stories Generated by Computers. *Advances in Cognitive Systems*, 4:227–246.

Rogelio E. Cardona-Rivera and R. Michael Young. 2019. Desiderata for a Computational Model of Human Online Narrative Sensemaking. In *AAAI Spring Symposium on Story-enabled Intelligence.*

Nathanael Chambers and Dan Jurafsky. 2008. Unsupervised learning of narrative event chains. In *Proceedings of Annual Meeting of the Association for Computational Linguistics*, pages 789–797.

Chen Chung Chang and H Jerome Keisler. 1990. *Model theory*. Elsevier.

A. Gatt and E. Krahmer. 2018. Survey of the state of the art in natural language generation: Core tasks, applications and evaluation. *Journal of Artificial Intelligence Research*, 61:65–170.

Gérard Genette. 1980. *Narrative Discourse: An Essay in Method.* Cornell University Press.

Morton A. Gernsbacher, Kathleen R. Verner, and Mark E. Faust. 1990. Investigating differences in general comprehension skill. *Journal of Experimental Psychology: Learning, Memory, and Cognition*, 16(3):430–445.

David Herman. 2013. *Storytelling and the Sciences of Mind.* MIT Press.

Peter Hühn and Roy Sommer. 2013. Narration in poetry and drama. In Peter Hühn, John Pier, Wolf Schmid, and Jörg Schönert, editors, *the living handbook of narratology*. Hamburg U., Hamburg, Germany.

Tianyu Jiang and Ellen Riloff. 2018. Learning prototypical goal activities for locations. In *Proceedings of the 56th Annual Meeting of the Association for Computational Linguistics*, pages 1297–1307.

Junyeong Kim, Minuk Ma, Kyungsu Kim, Sungjin Kim, and Chang D. Yoo. 2019. Progressive attention memory network for movie story question answering. In *Proceedings of the IEEE Conference on Computer Vision and Pattern Recognition*, pages 8337–8346.

Boyang Li, Stephen Lee-Urban, Darren Scott Appling, and Mark O. Riedl. 2012. Crowdsourcing narrative intelligence. *Advances in Cognitive Systems*, 1:1–18.

Jean M Mandler and Nancy S Johnson. 1977. Remembrance of things parsed: Story structure and recall. *Cognitive psychology*, 9(1):111–151.

Chris Martens, Rogelio E. Cardona-Rivera, and Neil Cohn. 2020. The visual narrative engine: A computational model of the visual narrative parallel architecture. In *Proceedings of the 8th Annual Conference on Advances in Cognitive Systems.*

Lara J. Martin, Prithviraj Ammanabrolu, Xinyu Wang, William Hancock, Shruti Singh, Brent Harrison, and Mark O. Riedl. 2018. Event representations for automated story generation with deep neural nets. In *Proceedings of the 32nd AAAI Conference on Artificial Intelligence.*

Nasrin Mostafazadeh, Nathanael Chambers, Xiaodong He, Devi Parikh, Dhruv Batra, Lucy Vanderwende, Pushmeet Kohli, and James Allen. 2016. A corpus and cloze evaluation for deeper understanding of commonsense stories. In *Proceedings of the 2016 Conference of the North American Chapter of the Association for Computational Linguistics: Human Language Technologies*, pages 839–849.

Mark O. Riedl and R. Michael Young. 2006. Story planning as exploratory creativity: Techniques for expanding the narrative search space. *New Generation Computing*, 24(3):303–323.

Shlomith Rimmon-Kenan. 2002. *Narrative Fiction: Contemporary Poetics*. Routledge.

Melissa Roemmele, Cosmin Adrian Bejan, and Andrew S. Gordon. 2011. Choice of plausible alternatives: An evaluation of commonsense causal reasoning. In *2011 AAAI Spring Symposium Series.*

Theodore Sider. 2010. *Logic for philosophy*. Oxford University Press, USA.

David Thue, Stephan Schiffel, Ragnar Adolf Árnason, Ingibergur Sindri Stefnisson, and Birgir Steinarsson. 2016. Delayed roles with authorable continuity in plan-based interactive storytelling. In *Interactive Storytelling*, pages 258–269, Cham. Springer International Publishing.

Tom Trabasso et al. 1982. *Causal cohesion and story coherence.* ERIC.

Rolf A. Zwaan and Gabriel A. Radvansky. 1998. Situation models in language comprehension and memory. *Psychological Bulletin*, 123(2):162–85.

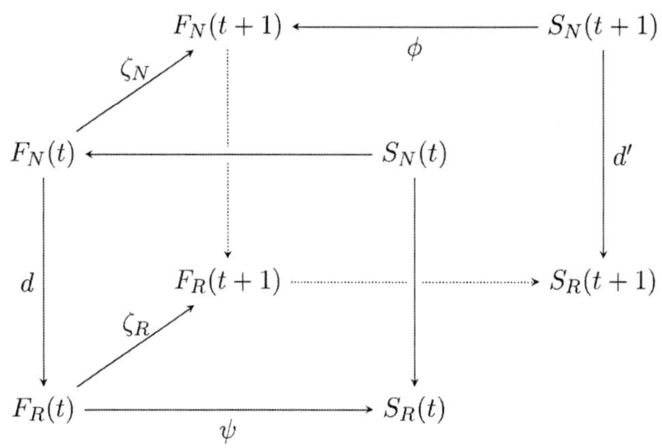

Figure 2: Commutative diagram expressing ζ_R and ζ_N. Some edge labels were removed for clarity. Refer to figure 1 on page 4.

Author Index

Association for Computational Linguistics
209 N. Eighth Street
Stroudsburg, Pennsylvania 18360

ISBN 978-1-7138-3033-7

CURRAN ASSOCIATES INC.
proceedings.com